SISTAH VEGAN

green
press
INITIATIVE

SISTAH VEGAN

BLACK FEMALE VEGANS SPEAK ON FOOD, IDENTITY, HEALTH, AND SOCIETY

A. BREEZE HARPER
EDITOR

Lantern Books • New York

A Division of Booklight, Inc.

2010
Lantern Books
128 Second Place
Brooklyn, NY 11231
www.lanternbooks.com

Cover artwork: "Yum!" by Janine Jackson, 2006. Jackson says about the piece: "Delicious. Nourishing. Life. Various recipes swirl about her reminding her of the multiple delights she experiences while consuming natural foods. Yum!"

Notice: This book is intended as a reference volume only, not as a medical manual. The information given here is designed to help you make informed decisions about your health. It's not intended as a substitute for any treatment that may have been prescribed or recommendations given by your health care provider. If you suspect that you have a medical problem, we urge you to seek competent medical help.

Printed in the United States of America

LIBRARY OF CONGRESS CATALOGING-IN-PUBLICATION DATA

Sistah vegan : food, identity, health, and society : black female vegans speak / A. Breeze Harper.
    p. cm.
    Includes bibliographical references.
    ISBN-13: 978-1-59056-145-4 (alk. paper)
    ISBN-10: 1-59056-145-7 (alk. paper)
    1. Vegetarianism—United States. 2. Veganism—United States. 3. African American women. I. Harper, A. Breeze.
    TX392.S56 2009
    641.5'636—dc22
                                                        2009015277

CONTENTS

APPRECIATIONS

There are so many people to thank and acknowledge who supported me through this project and through life in general!

Thanks Dad for first introducing me to the world of herbalism and holistic health while I was growing up. Thanks Mom and Talmadge for always encouraging me to write and to approach whatever I am passionate about with confidence.

Much love, gratitude, and appreciation to Oliver, for being a wonderful soul mate and introducing me to compassionate consumption and mindful living.

Dick Gregory and Queen Afua: Although I have never met you in real life, your philosophies took my activism—in terms of empowering Black people—to a holistic level. I hope to one day meet you lovely spirits.

Thich Nhat Hanh: Your translation of the fourteen precepts in your book *Inter-Being* is a blessing. I meditate on it every week to remember that my health and food activism should continue to be grounded in compassion, love, and nonviolence.

Bryant, your brilliance as a food-justice chef and author continue to inspire me. Thank you for being a positive force for people of color and food-justice activism.

Emily, our food, health, and feminist brainstorming "chit chats" have helped encourage me to develop this anthology in creative and thought-provoking ways. Thanks!

Raquel, my twin sis! So glad you came into my life and I appreciate your wisdom at such a young age.

Jason, your dedication to your activism with your Oakland Food Connection constantly inspires me and keeps me on the path of doing the work that I do. Thank you for being part of my life!

Tulaine, thank you for teaching me about leadership as well as compassion, when addressing the emotional subject of health and food with my peers.

Noah, I am glad my initial email to you did not scare you away! I am forever grateful for your support and courage to fight against the status quo and inequality for nonhuman animals and us human animals. Thanks for being an ally, despite the challenges you faced in your animal-rights work.

Kevin, thank you for "getting it" and constantly sending me news about local and global injustices about food, environment, and health, around the world.

Frances Ufkes, thank you for introducing me to the wonderful world of Food and Geography, freshman year at Dartmouth College. Since then, I have never looked at food quite the same way.

Zoe E. Masongsong, thank you so much for volunteering to help Sistah Vegans edit their anthology pieces. This was a truly a selfless act and I know some sistahs may not have had the confidence to submit their creative-genius pieces had you not been there to let them know they could do it.

Derrick, you always said I could do it. Thank you for your support and believing in my potential to publish this project.

Pandora, my beautiful sistah: our intense dialogues about healing, love, food, institutionalized racism, and life in general have helped me to never forget that "we are what we've been waiting for." Thank you for such a tremendous gift.

Sister Jayne, I love you big sister! Thank you for your love and support. Your enthusiasm for my health and food activism has helped me stay on my spiritual path to help humanity understand that we have the power of the divine within ourselves to be our own healers.

To the staff at Lantern Books, thank you for believing in the importance of this book, and for giving it such care and attention through the process.

Lastly, thank you Holly and Uriel, my best buds since freshman year in college. Your trust in me to help heal your ailments through the years made me realize that I can be a leader and teacher of holistic healing through literary activism, and share my wisdom with all who are willing to embrace it.

A. Breeze Harper

PREFACE

In 2006, Dr. Ian Smith partnered with State Farm Insurance to issue a clarion call in promoting healthier lives and more nutritious diets, primarily among African-Americans. As the latest data illustrate, obesity is the number one health crisis facing all Americans—children and adults alike. The statistics on African-Americans are almost at an extreme, with the majority of adult women and men being categorically defined as overweight. As more and more young people of color contract Type 2 diabetes, high blood pressure, and even heart disease, the combination of poor diet, lack of exercise, and inadequate medical guidance and care is all the more lethal.

At least one solution is being provided by Smith's "50 Million Pound Challenge." Other solutions, however, can be found in taking control over one's life by engaging in a more conscious effort to consume foods that are deemed whole—fresh (organic even) fruits and vegetables, whole grains, and so on. To be sure, making healthier lifestyle decisions is key to living longer and stronger.

But how is this option possible when one has little or no control over one's environment? How is making healthy lifestyle choices directly tied to issues of racism—environmental and medical—and even genocide? These and other questions are at the heart of the *Sistah Vegan* anthology.

This book brings to the fore an awareness that adopting a lifestyle of vegetarianism and veganism is not limited to one racial or age group. Rather, there are many people of color who adhere to this way of thinking, consuming, and engaging the earth and its bounty. In the instance of this powerful anthology, voices come from far and wide to represent women of color who speak not only to food and choice, but also to food and its intersections with numerous forms of injustice that are insidiously destructive to their lives.

As one of few, if any, major works to address such intersections, this anthology is poised to reveal several realities about the ways that Black and other bodies of color ingest and digest the glaring racial disparities of our nation's health system. From medical misdiagnoses to the lack of adequate health care and on, many people of color suffer needlessly. When you combine this reality with the fact that the majority of neighborhoods of color promote junk foods—from triple-layer cheeseburgers to forty ounces of malt liquor, to the latest and greatest sugary cereal—and that these locations are wholly deficient in offering grocery stores that provide fresh and affordable produce, then living healthier is not simply about choice. It is also about choices that get made to grant and deny access to a better way of life. Consequently, a lifestyle of health is also about inherent race and class discrimination. This anthology gives voice to these disparities and highlights their consequences.

What the sistah vegans tell us is that we, as people of color, can no longer live by mainstream definitions. For example, we cannot all drink milk and eat foods from the bread and cereal group, especially when these foods do not represent our ethnic heritage. Moreover, it is not ethical and it is certainly not culturally appropriate to insist that we do so. Society could, however, provide nutritional advice on how to eat the foods that *are* culturally specific in ways that will promote optimum health. Women of color need to reclaim their voice on the cafeteria lines and insist that their children be given foods that not only are nutritious but reflect their cultural space—sweet potatoes, okra, collard greens, brown rice, corn tortillas, and so on. This anthology begins to enlighten us on this process; we must pass the word and follow suit.

I am not a vegan. My own contributions to this anthology are through food studies and Black women's studies. As a woman of color who was introduced to the dangers of a diet high in sugar, salt, fat, and refined carbohydrates early in my life, I long ago decided to eat whole. Not trim and thin by any means, I perhaps fall into the category of being a full-figured sistah living in a society that defines healthy as the antithesis of my appearance. I am blessed, however, to have the knowledge and understanding of what refined foods and meat products can and will ultimately do to our bodies. I am also clear about what it means to eat healthily in order to live longer. But I make informed choices. I have access to healthy foods of every variety and I pay handsomely for them. This is all to say that knowledge is power, and that knowledge also provides a certain amount of access.

A. Breeze Harper has assembled a fascinating variety of writings to heighten our awareness and consciousness of what it means to "decolonize our bodies, minds, and spirits." We would do well to read and to take individual and collective action, to combat the injustices and disparities—including those of the culinary nature—that continue to pervade our society!

Dr. Psyche Williams-Forson
University of Maryland, College Park

INTRODUCTION

THE BIRTH OF THE SISTAH VEGAN PROJECT

A. Breeze Harper

During one evening in the summer of 2005, I strolled through the latest discussion boards on BlackPlanet.com and found a discussion forum that centered on a controversial ad, "The Animal Liberation Project," which PETA (People for the Ethical Treatment of Animals) had created. As I read the content of the forum, I learned that the NAACP had been pushing to censor a PETA ad because of the "offensive" content the organization felt it contained. Within seconds, I found the PETA site and began to watch the campaign video advertisement. In my opinion, it appeared that PETA was trying to capture viewers and induce "critical consciousness" in them to question their own normative practices with respect to human-to-nonhuman animal relationships.

My eyes stayed glued to the images of human suffering juxtaposed with nonhuman animal suffering: a painting of Native Americans on the Trail of Tears positioned next to a photo of herds of nonhuman animals being led to their demise; the atrocity of a Black man's lynched and torched body next to a picture of an animal that had been burned; a black-and-white Jewish Holocaust photo next to animals in confined, crammed structures on a meat-production farm. As I watched, I realized that most images were of Black Americans drawn from America's cruel past of slavery and Jim Crow segregation.

I navigated my web browser back to the BlackPlanet.com forum and read all the contributions from the PETA forum discussion. Twenty-eight Black-identified people had voiced their opinion about the ad; only one participant agreed with the anti-speciesism message that PETA was trying to promote with the ad.[1] Everyone else agreed that PETA was an organization filled with "white racists" who think that Black-identified people are "on the same level as animals."

As I attempted to understand the PETA campaign and the BlackPlanet.com participants' anger, I drew upon the books I had recently read by Marjorie Spiegel and Charles Patterson.[2] With those titles as a foundation, I could assume that PETA's campaign was implying that the exploitation and torture of nonhuman animals come from the same master/oppressor ideology that created atrocities such as African slavery, Native American genocide, and the Jewish Holocaust. In *The Dreaded Comparison*, Spiegel notes:

> Comparing the suffering of animals to that of Blacks (or any other oppressed group) is offensive only to the speciesist: one who has embraced the false notions of what animals are like. Those who are offended by comparison to a fellow sufferer have unquestioningly accepted the biased worldview presented by the masters. To deny our similarities to animals is to deny and undermine our own power. It is to continue actively struggling to prove to our masters, past or present, that we are similar to those who have abused us, rather than to our fellow victims, those whom our masters have also victimized.
>
> This is not intended to oversimplify matters and to imply that the oppressions experienced by Blacks and animals have taken identical forms—but, as divergent as the cruelties and the supporting systems of oppression may be, there are commonalities between them. They share the same basic relationship—that between oppressor and oppressed.[3]

Even though I am an animal-rights supporter, I feel that PETA's campaign strategies often fail to give a historical context for why they use certain images that are connected to a painful history of racially motivated violence against particular nonwhite, racialized humans. In the years prior to PETA's debacle, Spiegel and Patterson provided sensitive, scholarly explorations of these topics, whereas the PETA exhibit, and the ensuing controversy, were handled insensitively. The lack of sociohistorical context by PETA is perhaps what is upsetting to many racial minorities, for whom such images and textual references trigger trauma and deep emotional pain.

Now, this doesn't mean that *all* those in the United States who were offended by PETA absolutely don't care about the suffering of animals; it's much more complex than a simple binary of "we care" versus "we don't care" about animal suffering. But I do believe it means that the wounds and scars of United States's sordid history of violent racism, in which Black

Americans were *derogatorily* categorized *as* animals within a racist colonial context (I understand that outside of this context being called an "animal" isn't derogatory), need to be addressed and reconciled at a national level that I have yet to see. In addition, PETA campaign strategists could be more cognizant of the consequences of not offering a sociohistorical context to many of their outreach campaigns that contain emotionally sensitive materials.

It has been over four years since I first viewed "The Animal Liberation Project." I have been thinking more in depth, and I have begun to reexamine veganism as an alternative, food ways movement, as well as a personal health choice from a Black feminist, antiracist, and decolonizing perspective. I hope that the *Sistah Vegan* anthology can help start formulating answers to the following questions:

1. How are Black female vegans using veganism and other holistic health practices to decolonize their bodies and engage in health activism that resists institutionalized racism and neocolonialism?

2. Bodies in vegetarian/vegan, organic, and alternative-living advertisements are depicted as mostly white and thin, showing an underlying theme of "veganism equals thin white body." How does this affect Black females' willingness to explore vegetarianism/veganism when the full-sized body is typically accepted as healthy and beautiful in the North American Black community?

3. As indicated in the BlackPlanet.com forum, is it that some Black Americans do not want to embrace an ethical eating philosophy because they do not care, or is it that they perceive it as only being part of a legacy of white racism and an elitist view of culinary ideologies?[4]

4. If a majority of Black people have had negative experiences with "whiteness as the norm" (because of collective experiences of racism/classism), and they have come to believe that veganism or an ethical eating philosophy is a "white thing" and in no way connected to deconstructing institutionalized racism/classism, how can sistah vegans and allies present a model that presents veganism and vegetarianism as a tool that simultaneously resists (a) institutionalized racism/classism, (b) environmental degradation, and (c) high rates of health dis-eases plaguing the Black community?

Alka Chandna, a woman of color from Canada and a research associate with PETA, wrote a commentary about the NAACP reaction to the advertisement. In her recollection, she writes about how acts of racism were directed toward her family's house. One of her memories is of eggs being thrown because her brown family was not welcomed in the community. However, she is perplexed by the NAACP attacks on the PETA campaign:

> Although the photos of poor immigrants, children used in forced labor, Native Americans, and African slaves are extremely upsetting, why is it so shocking to suggest that the mindset that condoned exploitation of people in the past is the same as the mindset that permits today's abuse of animals in laboratories, in factory farms, and on fur farms? And why is it assumed that this display—and indeed the entire animal-rights movement—was generated by insensitive white people? As a person of color, I am hurt and perplexed that my two decades of work in the animal-rights movement, as well as the efforts of my many colleagues who are people of color, are discounted. . . .
>
> Here in the United States, the NAACP and others are now painting animal-rights activists as white racists in order to marginalize and dismiss us. I can't help but think that this sort of "analysis" that persists in painting our movement with a broad brush is the same disparagement that people engage in when the truth makes them uncomfortable. Racists dismissed Martin Luther King as a womanizer. Colonists dismissed Gandhi as a short brown man in a loincloth. Sexists dismiss feminists as ugly, angry women.
>
> Yet many people of color work every day to change attitudes toward animals. My own beliefs, and those of many of my colleagues, sprang from an understanding of right versus wrong. It is not racism that inspires us, but justice. *I ask other people of color who have had eggs thrown at their windows or experienced other forms of racism to stop condemning for a moment and to consider that what they are now saying about animals—that animals are lesser beings whose suffering can be dismissed—was once said about them and was used as an excuse to keep them in bondage.*[5]

It is Dr. Chandna's last sentence that intrigued and motivated me to find Black-identified females who practice veganism, as well as support anti-speciesism and/or see the connections speciesism has to all the "isms." Furthermore, the goal of *Sistah Vegan* is to function as an effective literary model for teaching about alternative health and decolonizing strategies that benefit personal health and the environment, while simultaneously resisting institutionalized racism, environmental pollution, and other legacies of Western colonialism.

Why I Chose to Practice Ahimsa-based Veganism

I can honestly say that my transition into veganism was not a sudden overnight decision. It initially evolved from my childhood experiences with institutionalized racism, heterosexism, and sexism. Many people who have transitioned into veganism reference animal rights as the most important reason for their initial transition. Experiencing life as a working-class, Black-identified female led me eventually to practice *ahimsa*-based veganism from a different point of entry that didn't initially involve animal rights as the catalyst to my "awakening."

When I was twelve years old, I entered the halls of Lyman Memorial Junior High School for my first day of seventh grade. The first greeting I heard was, "Look at that skinny little nigger. Run, skinny little nigger, run." From this point on in my consciousness, I became very aware of my historically and socially constructed position in the United States through the unique fusion of Black/girl. Racially socialized and gendered through Eurocentric heteropatriarchal and capitalism-based society, my experiences differed drastically in comparison with my peers in our over-97-percent-white, rural town. Although whiteness was the "invisible" and comforting norm for this majority, it was the neverending and constantly visible, "in-your-face" foreign, and suffocating "norm" for me. It was expected that being teased for being "the Black girl" was what I'd have to accept, simply because none of my peers ever seemed to be reprimanded or chastised for being racist. Similarly, speciesism was the acceptable norm in my town; folk engaged in the sport of deer hunting, turkey derbies, and using animals in the annual Lebanon Town Fair every August. Racism and speciesism simply *were* the norm, and the suffering and misery they caused were largely invisible to most.

Several years later, I began reading books that uncovered the roots of the types of oppressive acts I encountered in high school and college. I read Black feminist writers like bell hooks, Audre Lorde, and Patricia Hill Collins and then expanded into *ahimsa*-based philosophy by authors such as Jiddu Krishnamurti.

What truly moved me into practicing veganism was reading about Dick Gregory and seeing the connections he made to institutionalized racism/classism/sexism, Black liberation, the Black community's "health crisis," and dietary beliefs/practices. Dick Gregory, cited in Doris Witt's *Black Hunger*, notes:

> I have experienced personally over the past few years how a purity of diet and thought are interrelated. And when Americans become truly concerned with the purity of the food that enters their own personal systems, when they learn to eat properly, we can expect to see profound changes effected in the social and political system of this nation. The two systems are inseparable.[6]

While being introduced to Dick Gregory's philosophies, I also began reading Queen Afua's *Sacred Woman*. She is a raw foodist who advocates womb health and harmony through veganism. It was with the help of these two critical thinkers that I finally saw the interconnectedness to my own "out of harmony" reproductive health (I had been diagnosed with a uterine fibroid and was seeking an alternative to allopathic medicine to address it) as a symptom of systematic racism, sexism, nonhuman animal exploitation (which I would later learn is called "speciesism"). Immediately, I made the transition to *ahimsa*-based veganism. *Ahimsa* means a life of practicing noninjury or harmlessness to *all* living beings.[7]

After my introduction to Queen Afua and Dick Gregory, Spiegel's *The Dreaded Comparison* and Patterson's *Eternal Treblinka* further expanded my understanding of the interconnectedness of institutionalized racism, nationalism, and sexism; the mistreatment of nonhuman animals; and the abuse of the planet's natural resources. Eventually, years after I started down my path on that first day of seventh grade, I made the connections between institutionalized oppression and unmindful consumption and what it *means* to be socialized as a Black female in a society in which I must navigate through racist legacies of slavery, while simultaneously being part of an economically "privileged" global northern nation in which overconsumption is the "norm." It is this type of unique experience—the social implications and historical context of being both Black and female in a neocolonial global society—that has led me to request voices from females of the African diaspora living in the U.S.

The Ladies in the Sistah Vegan Project

When I conducted research about Black health on my university's online library, I was inundated with articles that depicted how horrible the state of health is among the Black female population: that we continue to eat too much junk food and not enough fruits and vegetables; that we are addicted to junk food and postindustrialized Soul Food practices to the point of killing ourselves. Articles and essays painted a grim picture: Black females do not know how to combat these health disparities.

However, after receiving a plethora of imaginative and thought-provoking contributions, I saw that there are many of us who know how to fight back. This book holds a collection of narratives, poetry, critical essays, and reflections from a diverse North American community of Black-identified females/females of the African Diaspora. Collectively, these ladies are actively decolonizing their bodies and minds via whole-foods veganism and/or raw food-ism, resisting becoming a "health disparities" statistic by kicking the junk food habit, questioning the soulfulness of postindustrial Soul Food, raising children who have never tasted a McDonald's (not so) Happy Meal, and making the connections that compassionate consumption has to creating a compassionate and eco-sustainable society.

Sistah Vegan is not about preaching veganism or vegan fundamentalism. It is about looking at how a specific group of Black-identified female vegans perceive nutrition, food, ecological sustainability, health and healing, animal rights, parenting, social justice, spirituality, hair care, race, sexuality, womanism, freedom, and identity that goes against the (refined and bleached) grain. Not all contributors necessarily agree with each other, and that is the beauty of this edited volume: even though we do identify as Black and female, we are not a monolithic group. I hope that *Sistah Vegan* will be an inspirational and thought-provoking read for all who are interested in how dietary habits and food production connect to either the dismantling or maintenance of environmental racism, speciesism, ecological devastation, health disparities, institutional racism, overconsumption, and other social injustices.

I welcome your readership of the first book ever written by and about Black female vegans in North America. It's nice to finally be at the table with some food for thought.

THINKING AND EATING AT THE SAME TIME

REFLECTIONS OF A SISTAH VEGAN

Michelle R. Loyd-Paige

It was the Saturday after Thanksgiving in 2005. I was out shopping at the local mall when my husband called and asked me if I would pick up a six-piece chicken-wing snack for him on my way home because he was tired of the turkey leftovers. Soon after his call, I found myself at a fast-food chicken restaurant. I was standing in line trying to remember what type of sauce he said he wanted—*Was it the hot barbeque, the honey mustard, or the teriyaki? Was that with or without ranch dressing?*—when, from out of nowhere, I began wondering what happened to the rest of the bodies of the three chickens it took to create this snack for my husband that I was about to so casually order. Almost immediately, other questions popped into my head: *Just how many other people would stand in this same line in this restaurant to order chicken wings today? And how many other fast-food chicken restaurants are experiencing an increase in business today because people are out shopping and they are tired of leftover turkey from Thanksgiving? Just how many chickens were being grown so my husband, and three hundred million other Americans, could have chicken wings anytime they wanted—not to mention in the world?*

Little did I know that my questions about chicken wings on that day would lead to a radical change in the way I eat. Believe me, it's not that I have some great love for chickens as a part of God's creation and think that they should have the same sacred status as cows in India or humans in every part of the world. My thinking and eating habits changed as a result of what I call a *kairos* moment. *Kairos* is an ancient Greek word meaning the "right or opportune moment."[1] In my faith tradition it also means "the appointed time in the purpose of God." At this appointed time, four previously unassociated thoughts—the content of a lecture I had just presented four days prior on the global inequities in food distribution; a vague recollection of a statement from PETA about the cruelties associated with chicken production; the remembrance of how surprisingly good I felt physically while on a forty-day spiritually motivated fast from meat and dairy at the beginning of the year; and my own desire to live an authentic life—yanked me into an uncomfortable realization that, when it came to food consumption, I was not living according to my beliefs.

I did purchase the chicken-wing snack for my husband, but with that sales transaction I began earnestly thinking about what I ate. I became conscious that what I ate was not merely a combination of taste preference, convenience, and cultural heritage. Before that moment in the chicken restaurant, I had given very little thought to how the food I enjoyed got to my table, and I certainly didn't think I was hurting anything or anyone. I am a socially aware college professor who challenges her students to think about how their social (and predominantly white) privilege supports the inequities that position people of color on the fault lines of life AND how their privilege allows them to be unconcerned about issues they do not think pertain to them. *How could I be guilty of the offense with which I indicted my students?*

As a middle-class citizen of the United States, I had been exercising status privilege every time I went to the grocery store or picked up a takeout dinner on my way home from work or shopping. It's a privilege to be able to eat what I want without ever having to think about how the food gets to my table. As I exercise this privilege, I am unconsciously participating in patterns of indifference and oppression. *I was guilty of the offense with which I indicted my students!* And here was truth in a Styrofoam box, which held six whole chicken wings covered in hot barbeque sauce with a side of ranch dressing. The truth is that no matter how good a person I was, my eating habits were contrary to what I believed. All of my actions either contribute to patterns of social inequities or to the solutions to the ills of our society. All social inequities are linked. Comprehensive systemic change will happen only if we are aware of these connections and work to bring an end to all inequalities—not just our favorites or the ones that most directly affect our part of the universe. No one is on the sidelines; by our actions or inactions, by our caring or our indifference, we are either part of the problem or part of the solution. I was beginning to see my lifestyle as it really was: a part of the problem and not part of the solution.

Not liking what I saw, I made a conscious decision to change my eating habits so that they would more closely represent my thinking on issues of social justice, the equitable use and distribution of global resources, and the health-diet-survival connection for African-Americans. Since my *kairos* moment in a chicken fast-food restaurant, I have chosen to eat like a vegan and have changed my shopping habits. I now buy fair trade tea and chocolate, and when possible, I purchase fresh and organic produce from local farmers. I do have a few nonvegan-friendly clothing items hanging in my closet from before my transformation, but none of my post-transformation clothing purchases contain animal skins or animal products.

My initiation into veganism actually occurred eleven months before that *kairos* moment in the fast-food chicken restaurant. I usually spend the first weekend of a new year on a personal spiritual retreat. In January 2005, I also participated in a month of fasting from meat, dairy, and sugar, facilitated by my church. The fast was voluntary and was supposed to *detoxify* the mind, body, and spirit. My church called it a "Daniel Fast." With the exception of the sugar restriction, the diet fit the vegan way of eating—soybean products became the mainstay of family and church dinners. (I'm sure the local health-food store was wondering what was going on with *all* these Black people buying up everything soy during that month.)

Twenty of us stuck with the fast for the entire month without slipping back into old eating habits. We all saw improvements in our health. Not unexpectedly, we lost weight; I lost ten pounds. But to my surprise, by the end of the month I was also experiencing fewer hot flashes (associated with approaching menopause) and was sleeping better at night. However, as soon as the fast was over, I added poultry, dairy, and sugar products back into my diet. Red meat was no longer on the menu in my home because it was giving my daughter headaches and my husband had been told to change his diet in order to lower his cholesterol levels. A month after reintroducing these foods to my diet, the hot flashes began to return. Several months after the reintroduction of meat and dairy, right around the time of the chicken-restaurant moment, the hot flashes were becoming so bothersome that I actually began to think seriously about hormone replacement therapy. I spoke to my doctor, and he suggested that I first consider adding the soy back into my diet.

I now credit the end of my hot flashes to the elimination of all meat and dairy from my diet, the eating of organic produce (when possible), and the daily consumption of soy. January 2005 marked the beginning of my understanding of how food affects the functioning of my body. It was November 2005 that marked the beginning of my understanding of how the food I ate contributed to social inequalities, and it marked my transformation to eating like a vegan; in late November I began thinking and eating at the same time.

Thinking about what I was eating led me on a search for the answer to the question I had raised to myself about chicken consumption in the U.S. I discovered that in 2005 the total number of broilers—chickens raised for their meat—produced in the U.S. for the year was 8.87 billion.[2] "Each week, Pilgrim's Pride (the number-two poultry producer) turns about 30 million chickens into nuggets, wings, drumsticks, and sundry other parts." According to the National Chicken Council, "American consumers are eating an unprecedented 81 pounds of chicken per person this year…and plan to purchase more in the months to come."[3] The U.S. appetite for chicken has grown steadily since 1970 when the per-person average was 37 pounds.[4] Americans eat more chicken than beef (69 pounds) and pork (52 pounds). The amount of meat in a typical American diet far exceeds the daily allowances suggested by the U.S. Department of Agriculture's food pyramid.[5]

The sheer number of feed animals necessary to satisfy the American diet is staggering. In order to keep costs low and production high, animals and chickens are routinely crowded in to small pens or cages, mutilated, and drugged with antibiotics and growth hormones. Crowded and stressful conditions have been associated with feed animals and chickens becoming ill. Because chickens in such conditions will turn on each other, chickens are de-beaked so they will not kill each other. Feed animals that do not grow fast enough or are too old or sick are sometimes killed and ground into animal feed. Cows, who are by nature herbivores, are routinely fed a protein mixture prepared from ground cows.[6] Laying chicks who are the wrong sex are discarded in garbage bags—sometimes still living.[7] The conditions under which many feed animals are raised are inhumane. While humankind may have been granted dominion over animals,[8] I don't believe we were also given the right to be cruel, brutal, and heartless in our treatment of them. Animals are a part of creation, just as humans. Treating them so callously is symptomatic of a general disregard for anything our culture defines as inferior and expendable.

In the U.S., how we treat food animals is reminiscent of how people of color were treated. Andrea Smith made such a connection with Native women and children and animals in her book *Conquest*:

Native people often view their identities as inseparable from the rest of creation, and hence, creation requires care and respect, but colonizers viewed Indian identity as inseparably linked to animal and plant life, and deserving of destruction and mutilation. This equation between animals and Native people continues.[9]

Smith's statement was in the context of discussing the U.S. government's practices of medical experimentation on Native inhabitants in reservations. African-Americans have also been used as human guinea pigs for some of our government's medical experiments: The Tuskegee syphilis studies are a well-known example. Africans were brought to this country in mass numbers as slaves. They were chained together and kept in the cramped holds of ships as they crossed the Atlantic. In order to justify the brutality of slavery, the oppressors deemed Africans as less-than-human and undeserving of decent housing, education, food, health care, justice, or respect. African women who were enslaved were often used as breeders for a new crop of slaves. It was not uncommon for Africans who were too sick, too old, or too rebellious to be killed if it was thought cheaper to replace them than to keep them. Prized animals were often treated better than slaves.

Seeing a connection between the treatment of feed animals, laying chickens, and people of color is a rather recent phenomenon for me. Two years ago, I wouldn't have believed there was such a connection. Today, I know better. The connection becomes clear with a careful reading of our history and an understanding of the true nature of food production in the United States. The connection, however, is also observable by a thorough analysis of today's headlines and an informed critique of social policy and community life. Understanding the connection strengthens my resolve to continue eating like a vegan. Choosing to eat this way is a reminder to myself and a demonstration to those around me that all of creation is worthy of respect and humane treatment, even chickens.

At the time I raised my questions about chicken consumption, I was simply curious about how many chickens Americans ate. As I searched to satisfy my curiosity of that day, I have changed from wondering about numbers of chickens to the costs of the American diet. *What are the health-related costs to the lives of people eating a typical American diet? Why does it cost more to eat healthy? Why is it "unusual" to have a meal without meat? Why do feed animals need so many growth hormones and antibiotics in their feed? What do these animal growth hormones and antibiotics do in our human bodies? Why do we commit so much of our land and water resources to growing feed for animals when we could grow grain that is a healthier source of protein? Can we really afford to not know where our food comes from and how it is produced?* I am convinced that eating a meat-based diet—not to mention dairy products, eggs, and fish— is not only hazardous to food animals and harmful to the land, but, more important to me, perilous to the health of my people.

The top five leading causes of death among African-Americans are: heart disease, cancer, cerebrovascular disease, accidents, and diabetes.[10] Currently, 27 percent of deaths in the Black U.S. population are from heart disease, and the death rate from diabetes for Blacks is twice that of whites.[11] According to the American Heart Association, women of color are particularly vulnerable:

> African-American and Hispanic women have higher prevalence rates of high blood pressure, obesity, physical inactivity, diabetes and metabolic syndrome than white women. Yet they are less likely than white women to know that being overweight, smoking, physical inactivity, high cholesterol and a family history of heart disease increase their heart disease risk.[12]

The prevalence of being overweight (including obesity) in African-American women is 77 percent; the prevalence of obesity is 49 percent.[13] Obesity has a strong correlation to diabetes. The traditional African-American diet is loaded with deep-fried chicken; meats are smothered in cream-based gravies; vegetables are slow-cooked with pork and pork fat until the color of the vegetables is no longer bright; and desserts are loaded with butter and cream. Soul Food (a.k.a. Southern home-cooking or comfort food) is often jokingly referred to as a "heart-attack on plate."

For African-Americans, however, it's no laughing matter. We are literally killing ourselves and decreasing our quality of life by the way we eat. Of the leading causes of death for African-Americans, all but one, accidents, have a connection to diet and lifestyle. Heart disease, obesity, and diabetes do not have to be such a prominent part of the African-American experience. Switching to an all-plant or nearly all-plant diet is one of the most effective ways to stop the progress of heart disease,[14] reversing the tendency to obesity, and controlling the onset of diabetes.

Every now and then my husband will ask me, "How long are you going to eat like this?" He used to ask because he and the rest of my immediate family thought that I wasn't going to get enough protein in my diet. Through my sharing of nutrition facts with them, they no longer think that eating like a vegan is unhealthy—strange for a Black person, perhaps, but not unhealthy. In fact, my husband has switched to soy butter and eats several meatless meals a week with me. My mother has also declared that a vegan restaurant I introduced her to is now one of her favorites and has dined there several times without me. Now when my husband asks, "How long are you going to eat like this?" it's because he has noticed that I no longer have hot flashes and he wants me to stay hot-flash-free, because "if momma is happy, everybody is happy." Although he appreciates the improvement in my comfort level and disposition, he and I are reminded of just how challenging it can be to maintain this lifestyle every time we try to go out for dinner, attend a birthday party, or go to a church potluck.

I'm the only vegan in my household. I think I'm the only Black female in all of western Michigan who eats like a vegan; if I'm not, it sure seems like it. There are no true vegan restaurants within ninety miles of our home. The closest vegetarian restaurant is forty-eight miles away, in a trendy, white, college-student side of town. When we do go out to eat (which is not very often) I usually opt for a salad without meat or cheese. Family holiday dinners, church potlucks, and birthday parties call for several different strategies. There's the "I'll be happy to bring something" so I can be sure that there's at least one item I can eat; there's the "Really, I am full. I just ate, all I want is a glass of water" so I don't have to explain to sistah sistah why I'm not eating her prized chicken salad; and then there are the times when I feel up to being an educator and I share with people why I no longer eat meat.

How long will I continue to eat like this? I can't see returning to eating meat, eggs, or dairy products, even with the inconveniences associated with eating out, dinner parties, church potlucks, family holiday dinners, and birthday parties. I am healthier now. I know too much now. I am committed to living an authentic life and to working for the elimination of all forms of injustice. I am now thinking and eating at the same time. There is no turning back.

2

VEGANISM AND ECOWOMANISM

Layli Phillips

I want to talk about veganism as an expression of ecowomanist practice and philosophy. Ecowomanism is a social change perspective based on a holistic perception of creation encompassing humans and all living organisms plus the nonliving environment and the spirit world. The focus of ecowomanism is healing and honoring this collective human-environmental-spiritual superorganism through intentional social and environmental rebalancing as well as the spiritualization of human practices. Ecowomanism assumes that this superorganism has been wounded by careless human endeavor and that this damage hurts humans, animals, plants, and the nonliving environment—and offends the spirit(s).

Veganism is an expression of ecowomanism because it is a practice rooted in conscious harmlessness, which is a major tenet of ecowomanism's healing praxis.[1] Conscious harmlessness is closely aligned with the principles of *ahimsa* as expounded in Hindu, Jain, and Buddhist scriptures. *Ahimsa* means nonviolence and respect for all life. While individuals vary in the degree to which they practice various aspects of veganism (or even whether they practice veganism at all), the assumption of ecowomanism, being a gentle philosophy, is that all movement toward greater harmlessness is of value, regardless of an individual's starting point. Veganism is a strong expression of conscious harmlessness toward animals and plants and the earth's other resources. It is aligned with a variety of spiritual belief systems that suggest a relationship between biological self-purification and spiritual growth. Thus, from an ecowomanist perspective, veganism supports both physical and spiritual well-being at both collective and individual levels. Last but not least, veganism is an expression of love, and love is a central social change modality within both womanism and ecowomanism.[2] Love, broadly conceived, is an expansive and enlivening force that counteracts the restrictive and deadening forces of fear and anger. Thus, love is a social change modality while veganism is a healing tool for people and the earth.

The story of my own gradual transition into veganism is closely intertwined with the story of my transition into womanist philsophy. Before I tell that story, however, I will explain my perspectives on both veganism and womanism, particularly for readers who may be unfamiliar with either.

Veganism

Veganism, as I define it now, can be described at its simplest as the practice of refusing animal-based foods and products. Most vegans, however, espouse a more complex set of beliefs and practices, including an interest in environmental sustainability and social justice in the production of food; a preference for organic and minimally processed foods that have not been genetically modified (non-GMOs); adherence to principles of food combining and healing through plant-based foodstuffs; support for products that have not been subjected to animal testing; interest in alternative, naturalistic, or integral health/medicinal practices; and an overall concern for mind–body wellness. Thus, veganism is not just a way of eating; it is a way of life.

People choosing veganism offer a number of distinct rationales, from practical to ethical: disliking meat; love of animals; health concerns; politico-economic commitments; and philosophical or spiritual beliefs. Many people who are vegans endorse several of these rationales simultaneously.

People who advocate for or practice veganism based on a love for animals often argue that animals, like humans, have rights. Being sentient creatures, animals have feelings and experience pain and pleasure. They become stressed by the farming practices (such as overcrowding, confinement, injection of hormones and antibiotics, bodily mutilation or medical neglect, and consumption of unnatural feedstuffs) and the life-terminating procedures used in meat production.[3] Animal experimentation is considered cruel and unnecessary; it is assumed that not only are alternative means of product testing available that can ensure human safety, but also that products that cannot be safely tested without harming humans or animals shouldn't be offered for human use.[4] People who choose veganism based on a love for animals are most likely to reject not only animal-based foods but also other animal-based products, such as leather, various cosmetics (for example, lipstick, which often contains bat dung, or shampoo, which often contains placental byproducts), and medicines derived from animal sources. For these individuals, alternative shoes and clothes, cosmetics, and remedies are available.

People who choose veganism based on health concerns are often worried about the effect of stressed, diseased, and/or drugged animal flesh on the human body. These individuals are also aware of the length of time that meat takes to digest in the human intestinal system and the likelihood of putrefaction during that process, which leads to a variety of human ailments, from flatulence and constipation, to halitosis, skin problems, parasites, and even, potentially, colon cancer.[5] Hormones injected into animals to stimulate milk production or to affect the quality of meat contribute to the over-estrogenization of humans, disrupting the hormonal balance in children and adults, resulting in everything from early puberty and premenstrual syndrome (PMS) to infertility.[6] Antibiotics administered to animals contribute to the development of drug-resistant bacterial strains, thus increasing the risk of bacteria-based illnesses in both animals and humans. In addition, vegans with health concerns often wonder whether animals fed unnatural foodstuffs (for example, fat-soaked newspaper, the offal of their farm-mates, or GMO grain) can actually yield healthful food for humans. Factory-farmed animals drink pesticide- and hormone-laced water, indirectly transferring these chemicals to the human system. For people with health concerns, meat eating is just plain risky. Vegans whose primary rationale is health-related are also those most likely to insist that their plant-based foodstuffs meet the highest standards of purity and safety.

Vegans whose chief concern is the relationship between the consumption of animal products and other politico-economic considerations may focus on a variety of problems. For instance, vegan ecofeminists focus on the symbolic connection between meat production, the oppression of women, and pornography (the dissection, objectification, sale, and consumption of women and animals).[7] Other vegans are concerned with the relation between factory farming and the destruction of the world's rainforests, particularly for cattle production. This links to a concern with global warming, which is exaerbated by removal of carbon repositories such as trees.[8] Some vegans are concerned about economic justice and fair trade practices, particularly how large-scale meat production can interfere with local, diversified economies and family farms, and divert needed natural resources, such as water and land, away from people who already live at subsistence levels, particularly in countries outside the U.S. Some people are morally opposed to large corporations, hyperconsumption, and the excesses of capitalism generally and express this sentiment through veganism. They may pay particular attention to who makes or sells the products they consume.

People whose veganism is rooted in philosophical or spiritual beliefs are often aligned with, or students of, religions and faiths that advocate nonviolence or restrict the consumption of animal foods. Religions, including but not limited to Buddhism, Hinduism, Islam, Christianity, Judaism, Zoroastrianism, and the Baha'i Faith, all advocate a plant-based diet somewhere within their writings or traditions.[9] In some instances, veganism is considered a form of mercy or respect for animals; in other cases, veganism is a way to protect the body as a temple for the spirit and thus to prepare a physical substrate for enlightenment. In *The Essene Gospels of Peace: Book 1*, for example, one discovers that Jesus advocated a vegan, raw-foods diet (and even colonic irrigations!).[10] Some ecospiritual, nature-based, and pagan traditions also endorse veganism. In addition to these religious and spiritual perspectives, there have historically also been particular philosophical traditions that advocate veganism. At this point in time, veganism itself is considered a philosophical tradition, even a religion, by some.

While veganism may sound rigid and ideological, I would argue that this is a misconception. While some vegans, for instance members of the Straight Edge community, demand unswerving commitment to vegan ideals and practices, many people practice some form of partial veganism. For instance, many vegans refrain from eating meat, dairy, and eggs, yet eat honey or wear leather. Other vegans shop vegan and eat vegan at home but look the other way at a vegetarian restaurant for dishes that use a small amount of butter, cream, or cheese. Some vegans may take a bite of cake that contains eggs at the party of a really good friend who isn't vegan. Some vegans are vegan everywhere except at their grandmother's house! You get the idea: for many people, veganism is a principle, not a law. Some hardcore vegans reject these "sloppier" vegans as profligates, but an ecowomanist perspective, as I mentioned above, would be gentler, respecting nonjudgmentally an individual's right to decide when and where they will engage in veganism (or any other dietary practice). Having said that, let me now turn my attention to womanism.

Womanism

As I have defined it in my article, "Womanism on Its Own," in *The Womanist Reader*, *Womanism* "is a social change perspective rooted in Black women's and other women of color's everyday experiences and everyday methods of problem solving in everyday spaces, extended to the problem of ending all forms of oppression for all people, restoring the balance between people and the environment/nature, and reconciling human life with the spiritual dimension."[11] Thus, womanism is a tripartite theory, philosophy, praxis—whatever you want to call it—that rests upon three intertwined relationships: humans to humans, humans to environment, and humans to the spirit world. The assumption is that imbalance and the need for healing or rectification exist in all these relationships; the agency of the womanist is to promote and advance healing in any or all of these areas. Social change is thus equated with healing. Ecowomanism, in particular, is most concerned with the humans-to-environment relationship, but not without regard for the way human group dynamics and the spirit world are fundamentally interconnected with it. Stated differently, all of these entities—humans, the environment, and the spirit world—interpenetrate and co-constitute each other; they are not really separate, even though we talk as though they are. This axiom underlies and animates womanism.

Stated succinctly, womanism exhibits five overarching characteristics: 1) It is antioppressionist; 2) it is vernacular; 3) it is nonideological; 4) it is communitarian; and 5) it is spiritualized. That is, it is concerned nonpreferentially with all forms of oppression, named and unnamed; it is identified with and gains its soul from everyday people; it neither advocates nor enforces a party line and instead recognizes only the quest for the betterment of humankind in its relationship to nature and the spirit world; it rests on the principle of commonwealth, which requires the harmonization and coordination of the interests of individuals and diverse collectivities; and it takes spirit—however defined—as a given, allowing spirit to infuse all politics and progress. Given its breadth, its overt spirituality, and its operationalization of social change as healing rather than protest, integration rather than disruption, I argue that womanism is not a form of feminism, but rather is a distinct and independent (albeit mutually reinforcing) perspective.[12]

Ecowomanism is most evident in the life work of Alice Walker, who coined the term "womanist" in 1979 and whose subsequent writing, activism, and spiritual pursuits have given meaning and illustration to the womanist idea.[13] At a time when nonracial, nongender, and non–class-based political concerns were not on the forefront of Black feminist discourse, Walker confronted and contested militarism, nuclear proliferation, environmental destruction, and other issues.[14] At the same time, she followed a nontraditional spiritual course that empowered and spiritualized her politics and art.[15]

Other womanist authors and activists also evidence an ecowomanist perspective. Notably, Chikwenye Okonjo Ogunyemi brings two important issues to bear: first, she notes that womanist praxis concerns itself with environmentalism as part of an overall strategy for healing human society, and reconciling humans with nature and humans with the spirit world (which resides in, infuses, or speaks through nature).[16] Using Osun of the Yoruba Orisha pantheon as a prototype of womanist praxis, Ogunyemi demonstrates that a certain degree of harmony and cooperation with nature is essential for the optimal functioning of society. Osun's roles as mother, mediator, independent businesswoman, and water deity illustrate the womanist penchant for working for social change and community well-being through diverse means simultaneously.

Second, Ogunyemi shows that food itself can be used as a means of social integration, diplomacy, and conflict resolution. In particular, she focuses on the role of palava sauce—a complex and tantalizing condiment comprised of numerous ingredients for which each person has her own "secret" recipe—in Nigerian social exchange. Quite literally, food can be used as a means of bringing people together who otherwise would not interact, for smoothing tensions when people disagree, and for facilitating celebration when victories of reconciliation have been achieved. Food is also known as a form of medicine among traditional healers, and the art of healing with food can be considered a lost art in industrialized society. In a society that requires healing on individual and collective levels, food itself can be considered a method for social change. This very accessible, ground-level, folk-oriented approach highlights the uniqueness of both womanism and ecowomanism. Furthermore, it intimates how veganism can serve as an expression of ecowomanist praxis.

My Story

I began toying with the idea of vegetarianism in 1980 when a beloved adult mentor gave me *Kripalu Kitchen: A Natural Foods Cookbook & Nutritional Guide* for my fifteenth birthday. The Kripalu Center is a well-known center for yoga practice and holistic living located in the Berkshires of Massachusetts. My friend, a Baha'i, yoga enthusiast, and vegetarian, visited Kripalu and saw fit to share the spirit of her experience with me, in whom I'm sure she detected a kindred spirit, even at such a young age.

Coincidentally (as if there are any coincidences), around this same time my father had instructed me to begin learning how to cook. Rather than being a dictate of gender-role enforcement, my father's injunction reflected his desire for me to become a fully autonomous and self-sufficient person with many life skills. Being a bookish girl, my response was to go to the public library and start checking out cookbooks. To this day, I still remember the Dewey decimal number for cookbooks: 641. I noticed immediately, when left to my own devices, that I was drawn to "international" cookbooks, particularly cookbooks of the global South and East, where recipes were rich with spices and vegetables, and included, more often than not, rice (which had always been one of my favorite foods). At the time, I did not make the connection that the preponderance of vegetables, fruits, and grains in the global South diet was partially a function of global class dynamics and the legacy of colonialism as well as the retention of a closer relationship to the earth and healthful eating practices in many of the societies in question. I simply liked the food. As I tried different vegetarian recipes and presented them to my family of seven (of which I was the eldest child), I found myself drawn deeper and deeper into vegetarianism. I was the first to spring stir-fry on my family (complete with my own made-up honey-mustard sauce), as well as tofu (usually in the form of tofu-spinach quiche, given the quiche craze of the early 1980s). These were greeted with great applause, as interesting departures from my mother's customary, albeit delicious way of cooking.

In 1982, as I headed off to Spelman College, where my mother and aunt had gone before me, I was presented with a gift from my mother. Somehow she'd found an institutional vegetarian cookbook that even had photos of Black cafeteria workers on the dust jacket. Proudly, I presented it to the chefs of the Alma Upshaw Dining Hall, who listened with at least feigned interest to my zealous spiel about vegetarianism. Unfortunately, I never witnessed the appearance of any of the book's offerings on the cafeteria line, and I began to wonder on what dimly lit shelf it might be gathering dust. My first attempt at vegetarian activism had come and gone, generating not even a ripple.

It wasn't much more than a year later when I was exposed to Alice Walker and womanism. Not only had my mother obtained a copy of *In Search of Our Mothers' Gardens: Womanist Prose* through one of her many book clubs, but my human sexuality teacher at Spelman had us read and analyze Walker's *The Color Purple* for our final project. I was captivated by the womanist idea—indeed, these, along with Barbara Smith's *Home Girls: A Black Feminist Anthology*, were my entrée into feminism—as well as the diverse ideas about, and expressions of, sexuality and activism that I encountered in these texts. But these seeds lay dormant a long time before sprouting.

It is perhaps ironic (or not) that a few years into my college career I myself fell off the vegetarian bandwagon for a while. In the spring of my sophomore year, as a young nineteen-year-old, I became pregnant and got married in short order. The man in my life, a Morehouse brother from a squarely upper-middle-class family, was not a vegetarian. To make matters worse, his mother was a really good cook. Wanting to fulfill my good wife fantasies, I expanded my cooking repertoire to include all manner of meats, fowl, and fish, often learning to prepare these dishes using "famous" recipes that my family had never consumed: stuffed teriyaki steak, chicken divan, chicken kiev, broiled salmon with lemon and dill, and grouper tempura were among my specialties. I even served lamb with mint sauce more than once, not thinking twice about, or even being aware of, the conditions in which lambs are raised for consumption. This was well before I'd ever heard of veganism or animal rights, although I did purchase organic meats as soon as our local grocery store—Big Star, at the time—began to offer them.

Two years into this situation, aged twenty-one, I had a second child. It was my senior year when I got pregnant, the fall of my first year of grad school when I gave birth. I'd considered raising my children as vegetarians but didn't do so initially. It took a divorce after five years of marriage and my welcomed entry into single-parenthood to return to my preferred vegetarian diet. At this time, I usually cooked vegetarian food for myself and my kids, only occasionally caving into their desires for meat-based foods. But we were all big dairy eaters!

I loved cheese (perhaps because my father is a Wisconsinite and his sister sent us big cheese baskets filled with cheddar and gouda every Christmas) and eggs (perhaps because my family ate scrambled eggs, often with ham and peppers, almost every Saturday morning, right along with oil-recipe biscuits). Also, for that lean period when I was a graduate student and single mom, WIC (the federal Special Supplemental Nutrition Program for Women, Infants, and Children) provided us with lots of milk and eggs! When money was short, eggs or cereal and milk were a meal. Of course, now I realize the relationship between WIC and farming subsidies, but at the time it was a survival mechanism.

Nevertheless, I became radicalized around environmental issues during that single-parent, graduate-school period. I read books such as Jeremy Rifkin's *The Green Lifestyle Handbook* and Anita Roddick's *Body and Soul: Profits with Principles*. I subscribed to magazines like the *Utne Reader*, hearkening back to when I used to read *Mother Earth News* religiously at the public library when I was a teenager. I joined a health-food co-op in Philadelphia, where I was living, and I started buying recycled and green products like Seventh Generation, not to mention recycling my family's waste to the greatest extent possible. In the circles where I ran, I frequently came across animal rights and vegetarian tracts, and I shared this information with my kids. Occasionally, they grew weary of all the gory animal-cruelty tales, toxic-food rhetoric, and mom-based proselytizing, insisting that they weren't going to give up their McDonald's Happy Meals and frozen KidCuisines no matter what I said. I swore to them that they would both be vegetarians by the time they were twenty-five. That remains to be seen!

Strangely enough, I never really processed what veganism was until my very first job interview at Antioch College. Considered one of America's "radical" colleges, Antioch offered a vegan food option at all events at which food was served. I was intrigued and asked a few students about veganism. Even though, at that time, I had no plan to give up cheese, I listened with great interest as another seed was planted in my mind.

I eventually took my first job in Georgia and entered a ten-year phase during which I cycled in and out of vegetarianism. To begin with, the lure of southern food (which I had missed up north), announced by the omnipresent and wafting scent of barbecue, tempted me back into meat-eating. Barbecue chicken was standard, macaroni and cheese was gold, collard greens were the stuff of life (and rarely did they come without pork). Various cakes and pies, from red velvet to sweet potato, were like dying and going to heaven. So, I confess, I did inhale. Then I'd find my way back to vegetarianism after a period of self-reproach, feel sancti-fied, and slip again. Jokingly, I used to refer to myself as "the Jimmy Swaggart of vegetarians."

Eventually, I partnered with another nonvegetarian, and even though she was able to countenance my vegetarianism for a while, after a period of time she and the kids collectively clamored for the traditional meat-and-three diet. As chief shopper and cook, I half-heartedly complied, having neither the time nor energy to prepare separate meals for myself. Because at the time I still found the taste of meat foods appealing—particularly if they were slathered in some sort of sauce like barbecue, tandoori, or curry—my own palate served as no deterrent to a carnivorous practice. Also, since I love the creativity of cooking, I was able to enjoy the preparation of meat as much as the preparation of vegetables and fruits. I can no longer claim this to be true.

I markedly remember one conversation my partner and I had over dinner with two of our friends who were hardcore vegetarians. We were arguing the merits of vegetarianism and one of the friends said, "To tell the truth, I'm even tempted to become a vegan, but I just don't know if I could hack it." Because, on the inside, I still very much wanted to engage in a con-sistent vegetarian practice, her statement tugged at my heart. I remember thinking, *If I ever go back to vegetarianism, I'm going to check into veganism.*

Long story short, I departed from that relationship and breathed a sigh of relief that I could now construct the dietary lifestyle of my choice without impediments. An interesting period ensued during which I craved fish (because my former partner detested it and wouldn't allow it in the house) and onions (for the same reason). Although I had given up beef long before, I gradually parted ways with pork and chicken, finally giving up fish right around the time I joined forces with my current partner. A vegetarian when we met, he became vegan shortly thereafter, ultimately incorporating raw-food practices, and inspired and fortified me to do the same. In his library was a wealth of information about nutrition and the body, with which I found myself fascinated if not periodically overwhelmed by.

What is interesting is that, in many respects, I discovered that turning vegan was what I'd really wanted to do all along but for whatever reason couldn't manage. Social pressure, care-taking responsibilities, and even the advertising industry had all played a role in my self-denial around veganism. It felt good and right now to be aligned with someone whose food-related beliefs and desires were similar to my own and whose practices more closely reflected those beliefs and desires, instigating me to self-actualize.

My veganism, and now raw foodism, are also closely aligned with my womanism and, in particular, womanism as an expression of social-change praxis. Womanism is, for me, an articulation of everyday-women-folklove-and-social-change expressed in political and academic terms. As a discourse, it's a bridge between what everyday people feel, think, and do and what academic folk feel the need to codify and philosophize about. As a womanist, I exist in both worlds—the everyday and the academic (as if any kind of split is really possible)—and what I like about womanism is that it "doesn't mind." I don't feel split in womanism, and thus I can put my energy on the real problem at hand, namely, making the world a better place for folk, which includes healing people and the earth as well as realizing the spirituality of everything and spiritualizing human experience. The ungrammatical folksiness with which I speak here—the shift in voice—is intentional; it's meant to reflect the creativity of the human heart when it's faced with terrible problems, unwell people, frustrated spirits, and limited or unreliable resources. Ultimately, the best resource in these situations is one's self, a.k.a inner resources. Joining with like-minded and like-hearted others—not just women, but everybody, from all walks of life—is what makes womanism what it is.

As I once uttered in a dream, "Womanism is like a neighborhood, with everybody coming together for a common purpose." In this neighborhood, some people, like myself, are vegans because they want to interrupt certain processes perceived to be destructive—human harming, animal hurting, earth disrupting, and spirit negating—such as factory farming and animal cruelty, gross disparities in access to food and food distribution around the world, exploitation of people living on subsistence incomes, risks in the medical-care industry, and, in general, creating artificial distance between humans and the earth in their symbiotic and spiritual relationship. Veganism is a way of keeping the interior of the body clean so that it doesn't waste valuable energy on coping with toxicity—energy that can be applied to other, non–self-oriented pursuits. It is an embodiment of the axiom "Live simply so that others may simply live." Veganism is also a way of living and a way of eating that can make good nutrition and plentiful food available to all people on earth, even as the planet's population grows exponentially. Veganism, especially raw foodism, is also a mode of eating that works well when extremely simple living is desired or required. Thus, a vegan practice is both symbolic and practical, and it is an embodiment of activist loving.

I have been a vegan now for three years (it will be longer by the time this chapter is published). My vegan and raw-food practices have caused me to appreciate the elegance of nature, the splendor of creation, and the pure pleasure inherent in the earth. They have also relieved me of the illusion that processing by humans is always necessary for "a better life." Veganism—and I'm no extremist, being gentle with myself and others—has filtered into and supported my appreciation for "living simply" more generally, compelling me to reduce my material possessions significantly, downsize to a more compact living space, and take on other intentional practices that prepare me for living in a more balanced and sustainable way with a more populated and interconnected global human society. Contrary to what others looking in might perceive, all this actually feels really good. I don't miss my former way of eating or living, and while I respect where everyone is on their own journey, I now revel wholeheartedly in my own.

3

SOCIAL JUSTICE BELIEFS AND ADDICTION TO UNCOMPASSIONATE CONSUMPTION

FOOD FOR THOUGHT

A. Breeze Harper

I grew up working class in a blue-collar town. Since my teenage years, I have been a fervent literary activist when it comes to antiracism, anticlassism, and antisexism. However, I was never able to understand how eco-sustainability, animal rights, and plant-based diets could be integral to my work. I honestly thought that these issues were the domain of the privileged, white, middle- and upper-class people of America. *Sure, it was easy for them*, I had thought with ignorance and prejudice. *Race and class struggle is not a reality for them, so they can "waste" their time on saving dolphins, whining about recycling cans, and preserving Redwood trees while my Black and brown brothas continue to be denied "human rights" because of the color of our skin.*

It has been only in the past several years that I realized that eco-sustainability, nonhuman animal rights, plant-based diets, and human rights *are* inextricably linked. Unfortunately, in my opinion, it has been the *tone and delivery* of the message—via the white, class-privileged perspective—that has been offensive to a majority of people of color and working-class people in America. Though there are many factors that prevent people of color and working-class people from practicing plant-based diets, eco-sustainability, and more (such as environmental racism, financial stability, connections food has to ethnic solidarity, and so on), this chapter focuses largely on why people of color engaged in antiracism and antipoverty social justice work can strengthen their understanding of social justice by taking a critical and often difficult look at how our consumption choices—dietary and nondietary—may actually be hindering our social justice activism.

20

I know that health problems due to improper nutrition and knowledge about food are not specific to "ethnic diets," such as postindustrialist Soul Food among Black people. A significant number of people in the U.S. are suffering from improper nutrition and inadequate health care. My research interests are specific to the intersections of health disparities, and perceptions of social justice, animal rights, environmental racism, and critical race theory as it pertains to Black- and brown-identified people in North America.

> I have experienced personally over the past few years how a purity of diet and thought are interrelated. And when Americans become truly concerned with the purity of the food that enters their own personal systems, when they learn to eat properly, we can expect to see profound changes effected in the social and political system of this nation. The two systems are inseparable.[1]

The above quote is by Dick Gregory, civil rights activist, comedian, and nutritional liberationist, who has spent much of his adult life advocating that people in America—particularly African-Americans—cannot obtain *true* social justice until we begin to question our postindustrial, unhealthy dietary practices and food beliefs.[2] Gregory believes that the sugar-laden, meaty-dairy, high-fat-saturated, junk-food diet of Black America is at the root of many of our social justice problems.[3] Gregory's concerns, voiced decades ago, ring especially true for today's Black population in the U.S., whose health has been compromised due to our diets and inadequate health care.[4] Gregory states:

> I personally would say that the quickest way to wipe out a group of people is to put them on a Soul Food diet. One of the tragedies is that the very folks in the Black community who are most sophisticated in terms of the political realities in this country are nonetheless advocates of "Soul Food." They will lay down a heavy rap on genocide in America with regard to Black folks, then walk into a Soul Food restaurant and help the genocide along.[5]

The implications of this brotha's words are profound and unsettling—especially since Soul Food has been rooted in how many Black-identified people embrace or define their "Blackness."[6] However, it is with Gregory's words that I feel I must scrutinize how collectively our health and consumption practices (food as well as nondietary) are frequently contradictory to our social justice beliefs, in the Black community as well as other communities engaged in antiracist and antipoverty social justice work in the U.S.

Let me start with our overconsumption of sugar products. The Dunkin Donuts slogan "America runs on Dunkin" scares the hell out of me. The suggestion that a country prides itself on being "nourished" on donuts and lattés is rather curious. Since entering the workforce in 1994, I've witnessed my friends and colleagues become depressed, restless, and irritable when they don't get their coffee and pastry in the morning. Wait a minute! Aren't these the same traits shown by a heroin or cocaine addict in need of a fix? I'm mesmerized by the American work culture. These sugar- and caffeine-induced mood swings are deemed normal. What would a colleague do if their officemate displayed these characteristics, then excused himself with "I'll be fine once I snort some cocaine"? He or she would most likely be reported, fired, or arrested. Isn't it hypocritical to respond differently to illegal drugs or alcohol as opposed to our addictions to legal drugs and health-decaying junk food on the job?

I used to eat at least three donuts per work day. When I first moved to Boston in 2000, twenty-three years old, thin, and exercising religiously, I naively thought that as long as I exercised four times a week I could load up on as many sweets as I wanted. Simultaneously, I'd wonder why I was *mysteriously* experiencing highs and lows, apathy, paranoia, depression, and insomnia. I was a sugar addict! I was going nuts and didn't even realize it was my addiction to sugar-drenched foods that was causing severe disharmony within my brain chemistry.[7]

William Dufty, author of *Sugar Blues*, is convinced that yearly increases in sucrose (refined cane sugar) and beet sugar consumption are the reason why emotional disharmony—such as depression—has drastically risen within the United States.[8] Likewise, from historical times to the present, the First World initiated civil unrest and legalized slavery—starting in the 1700s—to get our fix of sugar products.[9] In addition, we've taken fertile land and used it to grow a plant of which the end product for a majority of people in the United States is a nutritionally deficient substance. Sugar consumption in the U.S. has gone from ten pounds per year per person in 1821[10] to 150 pounds per person.[11] In addition, an estimated one hundred million people in the United States drink coffee in the morning, "a total of two *billion* cups of java every single day."[12] What happens to an entire nation if a majority of the population goes from taking crack or heroin a few days per year to every day and in high quantities? Dufty argues that sugar might as well be "dope":

> On summer vacation, I hitchhiked thousands of miles and lived on Pepsi Cola in those large, economy-sized nickel bottles. It was not until I visited the South for the first time that a girl turned me onto something called "dope." They served it at soda fountains with lots of crushed ice, vanilla flavoring, syrup, and soda. Up North it was called Coca-Cola.[13]

So, how does this tie into social injustices such as exploitation, classism, and racism? Well, authors such as William Dufty and Sidney Mintz both theorize that the African slave trade started because of sugar.[14] I argue that slavery manifested itself in multifaceted ways, too: the obvious one is the enslavement of Africans and other indigenous populations. However, addiction is another form of slavery. As Derrick Jensen notes, "to be addicted is to be a slave. To be a slave is to be addicted."[15] What happens if a significant number of people in the world's "most powerful" nation are sugar-addicted slaves? Are sugar and caffeine addictions truly the reason why the British Empire fell?

A majority of Americans are dependent on sucrose, bleached flour, high fructose corn syrup, flesh food, and caffeine. Therefore, what does it mean that "America runs on Dunkin"? Who and what are we hurting, deceiving, and stealing from to bring us our powdered-sugar donut, that Coolatta, or that ham, egg, and cheese English muffin? Recent research shows that we're hurting ourselves and exploiting and enslaving others—nonhuman animals and humans—in a way that is similar to colonialism; similar to when many of our African ancestors were torn from their communities and shipped to the Caribbean and Americas to chop cane for the production of sucrose and rum for addicted Europeans: an entire nation whose civilization rested on the shoulders of the savage African and indigenous American slaves to harvest their drug.[16]

It is 2009, and sugar consumption continues to increase globally. Sucrose is a toxin and has no nutritional value to the human body.[17] *Isn't that a little strange?* Particularly, since sugar cane is grown upon thousands of acres of land to produce sucrose. Eight hundred and thirty million people in the world are undernourished, and 791 million of them live in so-called developing countries.[18] Hence, what nourishing foods could these acres potentially grow if (a) sugar cane were no longer in high demand from the U.S. (as well as the rest of the top consumers—Brazil, Australia, and the EU) and (b) the land was used specifically to grow nourishing foods for the population in the global South?

Back to breakfast in the United States…a Dunkin Donuts meaty dairy breakfast meal, such as the Supreme Omelet on a Croissant, not only has 38g of fat, 590 calories, hydrogenated oils, sugar, and bleached flour, but the production of this food encompasses multiple layers of suffering. Production of addictive "civilized" substances such as refined sugar, processed flesh foods, chocolate, and coffee take away and often pollute land that could be used to grow whole foods that can feed the malnourished and starving human beings of this planet. Even more important, human beings *and* nonhuman animals and the ecosystem suffer greatly because of our First World addiction to unmindful human, egocentric consumption.

Many people do not know this (I include myself, when I used to eat meat), but the pig that had been enslaved and eventually killed, mutilated, and processed to become part of America's Dunkin Donuts breakfast sandwich (or any other pig-filled meal) required a lot of water to be raised and eventually slaughtered. Pig farming—along with all nonorganic meat and dairy farming production—is overconsuming and contaminating the world's water supply.[19] "Farm animals directly consume about 2.3 billion gallons of water per day, or over 800 billion gallons per year. Another 200 billion gallons are used to cool the animals and wash down their facilities, bringing the total to about 1 trillion gallons."[20]

This cannot be taken lightly. You like clean drinking water, right? Every single being on this planet requires water for survival. Yes, this includes *you*, your grandbaby, your family cat, your best friend, the turnips in your garden, and the physician that you may seek medical services from. I recently learned that the World Resources Institute predicts that at least 3.5 billion people—that's more than half of us—will be struggling with water shortages by 2025. Water is likely to join oil as a primary cause of armed conflicts. Already, multinational corporations have used their power within donor nations to force indebted nations to privatize some water resources. This is just one example of how, yet again, those who are already oppressed will be hurt the most by environmental crises. Around the world, women and girls are those mostly responsible for obtaining household water.[21]

Yes, my brothas and sistahs in the United States, even if you're one of the many human beings on the planet who aren't concerned with nonhuman animals rights at this point in your antiracism and antipoverty praxis and spiritual path, your consumption of unsustainably produced animal products may not only be increasing your chances for cancer, obesity, and heart disease,[22] you may be (in)directly oppressing and causing suffering to people who *look just like you*. I was astounded to learn that the poor and people of color have a much higher chance and likelihood of suffering and dying simply because they don't have rightful access to clean water, water that has been polluted and/or misused for our American addiction to flesh foods. To give you some more perspective on how much water is used in animal farming, here are some statistics:

- Five times as much water is used for irrigation to grow animal feed grains compared to fruits and vegetables.
- 4,500 gallons of water are needed to produce a quarter pound of raw beef.
- 8,500 square miles is the size of the dead zone created in the Gulf of Mexico by fertilizer runoff carried by the Mississippi River from the upper Midwest.
- 17 trillion gallons is the amount of irrigation water used annually to produce feed for U.S. livestock.[23]

I must elaborate once again that those who will potentially suffer and/or die from lack of clean water access will be the poor and people of color. My brothas and sistahs in the struggle, that could be *you*.

There was a time when I didn't realize how much is at stake if we continue to overconsume animal products, which have been proven to be not only unnecessary in the diets of most people,[24] but a threat to our personal health because of our overconsumption of them. This is no small matter; a majority of Americans—especially Black, brown, and indigenous people—suffer from obesity, diabetes, heart disease, reproductive ailments, and colon cancer at rates higher than the white population.[25] Health is suffering in the United States:

- *50 percent*: how much less dietary fiber Americans consume than recommended (note: animal products contain no fiber, which is necessary for prevention of diabetes and colon cancer).

- *$37 billion*: the annual cost of drugs to treat high blood pressure, heart disease, and diabetes.

- *$50 billion*: the annual cost of coronary bypass operations and angioplasties (just imagine what we could do with that money if it hadn't been spent on diseases that stem significantly from unhealthy meat, dairy, and junk-food diets).

- *24 percent*: how much lower the rate of fatal heart attacks is in vegetarians compared to nonvegetarians.[26]

If nonorganic and nonsustainable animal farming is causing this much pollution and jeopardizing the water supply to the point that 3.5 billion people will be struggling to find clean water, why should we stand for such environmental racism, degradation, and pollution in communities of color and working-class communities in the U.S. and abroad? We all know too well what happens to the economically poor and people of color during environmental disasters…we get the sh*t end of the sh*t stick first.

When Hurricane Katrina ravaged New Orleans in 2005, the consensus among Black Americans was that the Bush administration's less-than-stellar response indicated just how pervasive institutional as well as overt racism and classism still are in the United States. Black America and our antiracist allies cheered when hip-hop artist Kanye West bravely said on live television, "George Bush doesn't care about Black people."[27] However, if the Bush administration's lack of quick and effective rescue actions indicate that he "doesn't care about Black people," what do the consequences of our own unmindful, uncompassionate, and/or overconsumptive dietary practices say about how we care about ourselves? About the plethora of people in the global South who are starving and dehydrating, enslaved for our American addictions? About our own Black and brown communities here?

Let's reflect on how our own overconsumption, unhealthy, and environmentally unsustainable patterns—indoctrinated as normal—are collectively contributing to the suffering of ourselves, nonhuman animals, and the ecosystem. We speak of how addictions to illegal drugs and alcohol can ruin entire families and neighborhoods within households and communities in the U.S. However, let's look deeper into ourselves and ask how flesh food products, cane sugar, caffeine addiction, and overconsumption in general are not only destroying our beautiful bodies, but Black and brown families, neighborhoods, and communities, locally and globally, along with the global ecosystem.

Interestingly, such consumption may be linked to how many of us, from the past to the present, have dealt with institutionalized racism. bell hooks writes:

> We deal with White supremacist assault by buying something to compensate for feelings of wounded pride and self-esteem.... We also don't talk enough about food addiction alone or as a prelude to drug and alcohol addiction. Yet, many of us are growing up daily in homes where food is another way in which we comfort ourselves.
>
> Think about the proliferation of junk food in Black communities. You can go to any Black community and see Black folks of all ages gobbling up junk food morning, noon, and night. I would like to suggest that the feeling those kids are getting when they're stuffing Big Macs, Pepsi, and barbecue potato chips down their throats is similar to the ecstatic, blissful moment of the narcotics addict.[28]

Why is she bashing Big Macs? Well, in addition to contributing to our collective health ailments, American fast-food, flesh-based meals actually mean that land must be deforested for grazing cattle that are slaughtered primarily for fast-food hamburgers in the United States.[29] Forests also recycle and purify our water. Tropical forests actually produce a substantial amount of the earth's oxygen supply:

> An ever-increasing amount of beef eaten in the United States is imported from Central and South America. To provide pasture for cattle, these countries have been clearing their priceless tropical rainforests. It stretches the imagination to conceive how fast the timeless rainforests of Central America are being destroyed so Americans can have seemingly cheap hamburgers. In 1960, when the U.S. first began to import beef, Central America was blessed with 130,000 square miles of virgin rainforest. But now, only 25 years later, less than 80,000 square miles remain. At this rate, the entire tropical rainforests of Central America will be gone in another forty years.[30]

Many human communities indigenous to tropical forests are starving to death; native rainforest tribes are being wiped out.[31] I was startled and saddened to realize that America's addictions and overconsumption are in collusion with environmental racism and cultural genocide of our own brown and Black indigenous brothas and sistahs as well as the working poor, locally and globally. Once I learned these truths about the fast-food industries, I felt betrayed by restaurants such as McDonald's and Burger King. McDonald's was always promoting its food through this "happy-go-lucky-I-care-about-kids" clown (a.k.a. Ronald McDonald). However, it seems they only cared (in terms of profit) about the kids whose parents supported this "death foods" industry by treating their children to Happy Meals—foods not only produced without eco-sustainability in mind, but also contributing to today's diabetes and obesity crisis among children. Brain nutrition specialist Carol Simontacchi wrote in 2000, "according to the McDonald's Nutrition Facts, the child's soft-drink portion is twelve ounces, and the small size is sixteen ounces. The child's serving of Coca-Cola Classic contains nearly ten teaspoons of sugar."[32]

Our unmindful consumption is not only harming our own health in the U.S.; we are supporting the pain, suffering, and cultural genocide of those whose land and people we have enslaved and/or exploited for meat as well as sucrose, coffee, black tea, and chocolate, too. Unless your addictive substances are labeled "fair trade" and "certified organic," they are most likely supporting a company that pays people less than they need to live off, to work on plantations that use toxic pesticides and/or prohibit the right to organize for their own human rights.

Take a look at your diet and the ingredients of everything you put in your mouth. Is your health suffering because of your addiction to sugar? Is your addiction causing suffering and exploitation thousands of miles away on a sugar-cane plantation, near a town that suffers from high rates of poverty and undernourishment simply because that land grows our "dope" instead of local grains and produce for them? I wonder, has America confused our addictive consumption habits with being "civilized"? The British who sipped their sugary teas considered themselves civilized, despite the torture and slavery it took to get that white sugar into their tea cups, along with the cotton and tobacco they used.

Collectively, maybe we in the U.S are too addicted to see clearly, to see past the next fix. This addictive behavior has occurred for centuries. Sadly, those who were originally enslaved to harvest sugar cane (Africans and indigenous Americans) are now enslaved in multiple ways: as consumers of sucrose, hormone-injected processed meat and dairy products, and junk food. This enslaved palate—along with other nutritionally dead foods such as bleached white flour and partially hydrogenated oil—has helped to foster an astronomical rise in health disparities (obesity, heart disease, diabetes) in African-American communities that far exceed the health statistics of white America.[33]

Statistically, Black folk are far sicker than white Americans. Unfortunately, institutionalized racism and the slave health-deficit, which are manifestations of the inequities of Black slavery in America, are key reasons why so many Black people struggle daily to get access to proper health information, food, and resources to maintain optimal wellness.[34] Health disparities between Black and white Americans are one of the worst legacies of slavery and colonialism.

This is why compassionate and environmentally sustainable health and nutritional practices *must* be part of our antiracist and antipoverty praxis in our own fight against the continued colonization of our Black and brown bodies and the ecosystem. If in Black America, health and nutrition are still suffering because of institutional racism and colonialism, we should be the first people to want to prevent this from happening to anyone else who is now on the receiving end of American addiction and materialism-induced neocolonialism, neo-slavery, and neo-imperialism in the developing world. This means supporting our indigenous cousins in the tropical forest, Coca-Cola factory workers in Latin America, and exploited and abused cane sugar harvesters in the Dominican Republic, because, yes, we Black, brown, and working poor American folk were in similar positions when we were enslaved for European sugar, spice, and cotton addictions, as they are now.

I ask you to envision that you are a slave in the 1700s, on an American plantation. How would you feel, after your wife or son had just been sold and you're suffering from emotional and physical trauma, when those who benefit from your slave labor tell you that they don't care about your pain and agony because their addiction to sugar, cheap cotton, and tobacco is worth more than you? This is a serious question, because the same can be applied today, except now *you* would be asked the same question by a plantation worker in the global South harvesting sugar, cocoa, coffee, or cotton for *you*.

The time is now. We must extend our antiracist and antipoverty beliefs to all people, nonhuman animals, and Mother Gaia. Yes, unless the cane sugar you are consuming is labeled "organic" (as well as "fair trade"), our collective overconsumption of and addiction to cane sugar also helps destroy—not nurture—Mother Gaia's ecosystem. Phosphorus-laden fertilizers that run off the sugar fields destroy the land and water.[35]

Let's talk about soda. In the U.S., addiction to sodas such as Coca-Cola not only loads the body with empty calories and nutritionally dead substances, such as refined sugars and caffeine, but consumers who support Coca-Cola may unknowingly encourage a corporation that supports torture, kidnapping, and murder of the workers to ensure that people in the U.S. will never be without their effervescent drug. Murder? Torture? Kidnapping? Weren't these the same methods used in European imperialism to create an African and indigenous-based slave economy?

> The SINALTRAINAL, the Colombian food and beverage workers unions, have attempted to organize the [Coca-Cola] bottling plants. But the bottling companies, in response, have contracted Colombian paramilitaries to do their dirty work—meaning the murder, kidnapping and torture of hundreds of union organizers, forcing many to live under 24-hour death threat…. [T]echnically, neither Coca-Cola USA nor Coca-Cola Inc. own the bottling plants. They intentionally maintain less than 49 percent of ownership for the purpose of distancing themselves from these activities. That said, they maintain control of the board in terms of voting rights and membership. And more importantly, the bottling plants exist only because of Coca-Cola.[36]

Also, in terms of clean water rights, how much water in soda production, such as Coca-Cola, is being used, just for the taste of it? It's striking to me that racially and socioeconomically oppressed minorities in America, who continue to experience institutionalized and overt classism and racism, are collectively complicit—and usually unknowingly—in being oppressors to our brothas and sistahs of color and the poor from afar because we buy without knowing how it got to the store. I ask you to envision this: You are an employee at your local plant. You have fought long and hard to finally have the opportunity to organize. This is incredibly important to you, because you firmly believe that everyone at your plant has the right to organize. Now that I have familiarized you with Coca-Cola's practices, how would you feel about drinking a can of Coke like you usually do? Is it okay to support Coca-Cola now? Another scenario: If you're an activist in the eco-sustainability movement, ask yourself how many times you and/or your peers have had a meeting about environmentalism while drinking Coca-Cola. Crazy, no? This isn't judgment on my part. I'm simply asking you to rethink your perceptions of activism by reflecting on how and what we consume in America connects to suffering and lack of human rights far away.

Coca-Cola is one example; our addictive dependence on sugar from the Dominican Republic is another:

> Each year, approximately 20,000 Haitians cross the border into the Dominican Republic to work on sugar cane plantations, whereupon they are subject to forced labor, restrictions of freedom, inadequate living environments and dangerous working conditions. The U.S. is the largest consumer of Dominican Republic sugar.[37]

Now, let's take a deep, calm breath. Perhaps this is your first exposure to how potentially devastating your consumption habits have been. It's okay if you start feeling angry because you've been lied to for so many years about where your food comes from. It's all right if you start feeling shame or guilt because of how many people and nonhuman animals have suffered, due to the standard American diet and nonfood consumption patterns; these feelings are normal. Maybe you are like how I was, years ago, unmindfully indulging in refined sugar and flour pastries, Dr. Pepper soda, Hershey's chocolate bars, grilled ham and cheese sandwiches, and Hostess cupcakes, while simultaneously being dedicated to obliterating sexism, heterosexism, classism, and racism in my home country of America. I don't know why it took the first twenty-seven years of my existence to begin to understand that I was living a half-truth as a social justice activist. Perhaps it's because many of us who were born and raised in the U.S. are immediately indoctrinated to believe that addiction, ecocide, and overconsumption are a normal part of our lives.[38]

Granted, the words *addiction*, *ecocide*, and *overconsumption* were not explicitly used during my K–12 education. However, the school texts I read, the movies my friends and I watched, the food (and nonfood) advertisements my twin and I consumed, never told us how many human and nonhuman animals have been maimed, tortured, killed and/or enslaved for our individual freedom to choose a ham croissant in the morning, non–fair trade Dunkin

Donuts iced coffee to cool us down in the summer, or a T-shirt made of cotton harvested by an Uzbek child laborer. Damn, at that time I thought that, now that I'd gained the right to consume these products, *this* was racial equality, not neocolonialism. Little did I know that American society is a continuum of colonialism and imperialism driven by the collective addiction of material acquisition. These materials are usually stolen then extracted from the land as a natural resource, then drastically altered into a controlled, artificial, and addictive product perpetuating a life-killing imperial ideology we call *civilization*.[39] This [American] empire dictates that the corporations

> enslave those whose labor is necessary for this theft [of natural resources from the land].... [T]hey force the remaining humans to live under the laws and moral code of the occupiers. They inculcate future generations to forget their non-occupied past and to aspire to join the ranks of their occupiers, to actually join the degradation of [their bodies] and of the landbase that was once theirs.[40]

It was within this perspective that I initially built my social justice beliefs. Never did I fully look at how my perception of antiracism and anticlassism was clouded by this.

Ultimately, we must deeply consider, do our addictions and other forms of consumption contradict our antiracist and antipoverty social justice beliefs? For twenty-seven years, my practices did, simply because I did not see the reason why I should even question whether my consumption contradicted my activism or understanding of equality.

> We live in a crazy time, when people who make food choices that are healthy and compassionate are often considered weird, while people are considered normal whose eating habits promote disease and are dependent on enormous suffering.—John Robbins, *Diet for a New America*

When I was diagnosed with a tumor in my uterus in 2004, aged twenty-seven, I actively began engaging in research to learn how it was possible I could have a tumor in my uterus at such a young age. Afrikan holistic health practitioners, such as Queen Afua, opened my eyes to a world of lies, pointing to how the hormones and antibiotics in meat and dairy, refined sugar and wheat flour, nonorganic produce consumption, and environmental pollution were at the source of my reproductive ailments. Furthermore, Afua suggests that the womb of the African-descended woman in the U.S. suffers from disease not just from the toxicity of the standard American diet, but also from four hundred years of trauma induced by slavery. She implores women of African descent to understand that much of our pain has come from our ancestor's wombs being raped and forced to breed slaves and breastfeed the slave master's children; we have silenced that aspect of our spirits that needs to be healed.[41]

Queen Afua's wisdom and my learning about American food (that eventually manifested as disease in my womb), health disparities, and environmental racism in the Black community were the impetus for my transition into practicing social justice for Mother Gaia and all of her inhabitants. Discovering this led me to uncover an American system of lies founded for the sole purpose of maintaining production and profit based on an entire nation's addictions. Such a system, I believe, is at the root of the health-disparities crisis affecting low-income people and people of color in the U.S.

European colonizers and imperialists argued that it was their right to enslave, maim, rape, and/or kill many of our great-great-great-great-great grandmothers to support their addiction to cotton, sugar cane, and caffeine. Is our perception and practice of freedom and liberation defined through support of materials and foods produced through the *massa*'s system of domination, exploitation, and genocide? If you honestly feel that obtaining access to prime rib steak (rather than the parts of the animal *massa* didn't want), buying Starbucks non–fair trade coffee, or using expensive bath and beauty products containing animal byproducts that have probably been sprayed in animals eyes and/or forcibly injected into test animals who have only known a life of hell, is your right, I implore you to think again. How can this creation of suffering—because we believe we deserve to engage in materialism and overconsumption to show we're "no longer shackled"—be anybody's right?

In *Eternal Treblinka*, Charles Patterson argues that humanity's capacity to enslave, torture, and maim animals led certain groups of humans to accept a natural hierarchy of animal species and the inferiority of certain human beings; and that they themselves were the "superior" race/gender—that is white, class-privileged males—and had the right to do with all other human beings, nonhuman animals, plants, minerals, etc., as they pleased.[42] This attitude led to the Nazi Holocaust, Native American genocide, African slavery, and the medical experimentation and abuse of people of color and the working poor in America, such as the Tuskegee syphilis experiment and the forced sterilization of poor women in America. Patterson's research conveys an example of how we in the West constitute a society based on violence, oppression, misery, and domination that has led to an ongoing societal trauma from the microscale to the macroscale for all of us—whether we are the oppressors, the oppressed, or both.[43] I see this clearly in how we collectively consume and how we rationalize why it is okay if our products come from a place of suffering, violence, and inequality.

Contrary to what we've been taught, many of us in the U.S. do not need meat with every meal in order to be healthy or get enough protein. This is one of the first myths of nutrition we must acknowledge: that protein can only come from an animal-based diet. Just as most whites during antebellum America believed they couldn't live without the benefits of African slavery, so it's a misconception that all human beings cannot live without meat protein derived from enslaved nonhuman animals. If you think a cow is the only way you can get protein, then how does the cow itself get protein? This big, beautiful animal is an herbivore. Some of the most powerful and strongest animals, such as elephants and horses, are herbivores. Like elephants and horses, the human digestive system is suited for a plant-based diet.[44] The current medical research on proper whole-foods, plant-based diets makes it clear that we're not designed to be healthy by consuming the standard American diet of junk food and meaty, dairy-saturated meals, but rather by eating diets high in whole grains, greens, and fiber (remember animal products *do not* contain fiber).[45]

Though it may not feel like it at the moment, you're not being asked to give up anything; you're being asked to reflect on your possible addictions to unhealthy materials, acknowledge this, and discover how life-giving alternatives can strengthen your body and community's social-justice goals. If you're one of the many people in America who support fighting racism and poverty, what good is this effort if the planet's water and land are so toxic in fifty years that no living thing can live on them, due to our collective addictions and poisonous lifestyles? A human being cannot live without water for more than a week, and oxygen for more than a few minutes.

What I'm asking you to consider deeply may seem like a lot. I know I felt I was being asked to give up everything at first, too. When I met those "crazy, tree-hugging" environmentalists and vegetarians (and the occasional vegan) for the first time, while attending Dartmouth College from 1994 to 1998, I couldn't believe they thought they had the right to tell me I shouldn't be eating Kentucky Fried Chicken or taking thirty-minute showers or buying GAP clothing. *Who the hell were they to tell me this?* I naively thought with prejudice. *They're just bored overprivileged rich white kids who do not have real problems.* I realized nearly a decade later that they simply weren't trained or well read enough in antiracist and antipoverty praxis to deliver their message to me in a way that connected to my social justice work as a Black working-class female trying to deal with sexism, classism, and racism at Dartmouth. Though I would have appreciated a much more culturally sensitive delivery in their message—and cultural sensitivity is something I think the largely white, middle-class, eco-sustainable, and alternative-health movements in the U.S. need to work on—these kids' concerns were not only real, but substantial; it was their white, middle- and upper-class, privileged perception of health and eco-sustainability that made most of them unable to connect to working-class people and to Black and brown people like myself.

My experience with this is not singular. Researchers such as Rachel Slocum, Saskia Poldervaart, Arnold Farr, Narina Nagra, Chithra Karunakaran, and Liz Appel have argued that predominantly white, liberal, social-justice initiatives—from community food organizing and antiglobalization protests, to veganism, to dismantling the prison-industrial complex—are often entrenched in covert whiteness and white privilege that are collectively unacknowledged by white-identified people engaged in them. This has blunted the effectiveness of these movements' outreach and intent to people of color like myself, who perceive the tone and delivery of their message as elitist and colonizing.[46] I believe this is one of the key reasons why so many people of color in the U.S. feel that ethical consumption is a "white thing" only and don't delve into how it will help our antiracism and antipoverty praxis.

Until I made the connections on my own, I too felt this way. However, I realized that the message made sense but was usually lost in an oppressive tone that reminded me of another form of trying to colonize people of color to live in a way the white class-privileged people deemed as civilized and healthy. I was also weary of the message of Euro-Anglocentric "healthy consumption," because I remembered that cow's milk has been constructed in America as "healthy for everyone"—despite that myself as well as most Native Americans, Asians, and African-Americans are more lactose intolerant than white people. I thought these kids at Dartmouth were preaching yet another ethnocentric message about health and food that assumed everyone was from a Euro-Anglocentric ancestry, could digest the same things as them, and had monetary stability to make it happen.

As you read this, maybe you're asking yourself the same thing: *What right does she have to ask me to strongly consider how my current consumption pattern impacts my goal of abolishing race and class oppression? To ask the ways in which our own American consumption practices are frequently diametrically opposed to our antiracist and antipoverty practices?* Let's go back to the 1700s antebellum South. How many whites angrily asked abolitionists: *What right do they have to take away my freedom to have access to cheap cotton and labor?* Most of us know that the answer was, *No damn right at all.*

Now, are we going to emulate the European colonizers and American slave masters from centuries ago who thought they had the right to kill or enslave people and damage the land to fulfill their addiction to material goods? Or will we start transitioning into antiracist and anticlassist lifestyle, philosophy, and practice that will cause the least amount of suffering for our bodies, our friends, family, and all life on this planet?

I'm not asking you to consider waking up tomorrow morning and becoming a raw foods vegan who only buys local organic produce and has access to your own land to grow your own food. Such a suggestion would imply that everyone on this planet no longer has to battle the poverty, environmental racism, and sexism that make this transition incredibly challenging—a reality that the white, class-privileged, eco-sustainable, and alternative foods movements in the United States tend to ignore. What I'm asking, instead, is for you to perhaps reflect on how you can start consuming with compassion within your own economic, health, and geographical situation. Veganism works for my particular situation because I'm able to buy most of my food, unpackaged, from local, organic, and eco-sustainable resources. However, you may be one of many folk who must reflect on whether it's more ethical and environmentally friendly to get protein and essential fatty acids from tofu shipped across the world in plastic and an avocado trucked all the way from Mexico, or from free-range chickens' eggs that come from a town forty-five miles away? In an ideal world, people who want to practice whole-foods veganism would have access to local and eco-sustainably–grown plant-based foods that would give them all the nutrients they need—without the use of animal products or the waste of fuel and resources to package, process, and ship produce around the globe.

Our antiracist and antipoverty praxis must promote a break from addictive, ecocidal, uncompassionate consumption. Our praxis for social justice must center on ending our addictions and ecocidal habits. Addiction is the opposite of fully living. We must choose to live fully—not simply survive—and understand that we're not sacrificing anything by ridding ourselves of old addictive and unmindful habits that are largely based on the colonizer's imperialistic and uncompassionate consumption practices and value system.

I understand that many of us have our ethnic and racial identities embedded in the foods that we and our families have been eating since colonial times. We are scared to lose these. However, there are many ways to be Black without eating the traditional Soul Food diet. There are thriving communities of color throughout America that are rooted in holistic healing and have adapted their ethnic identity to more plant-based diets from their people's indigenous philosophy *before* colonization, while simultaneously practicing eco-sustainability, decolonization, and respect for nonhuman animals. These communities wholeheartedly know that "the master's tools will not dismantle the master's house," nor will his concept of food production or abuse of natural resources and nonhuman animals. They have chosen to live and thrive in ways that the postindustrial Soul Food and junk-food diets could not holistically support.

I emphasize this because I've met many people of color who are misinformed that eco-sustainability and plant-based diets are a "white thing"; that it goes against what makes them Black, Asian, Chicano, Native American, and so on. However, this is simply not true. I believe that much of the confusion stems once again from lack of cultural sensitivity from the mainstream ethical-consumption movements, whose tone and delivery make it seem like it's part of white, class-privileged identity. However, I do ask you, How did our ancestors eat *before* colonization? For example, was our concept of Soul Food destroying our body temples? Was our concept of consumption polluting our water? Was our concept of equality similar to that of the colonizer's model of consumption? Many people of color in African communities practiced plant-based holistic nutrition and herbalism and didn't aspire to join the ranks of their occupiers and degrade their own bodies and the land that was once theirs. Today, many of these communities exist in America and quite a few are rooted in Blackness (many from an Afrikan holistic philosophy).

For example, many African Hebrew Israelite communities throughout the U.S.[47] practice holistic health and nutrition. The Queen Afua network throughout America teaches sistahs how to reclaim our reproductive gifts by decolonizing our wombs from the colonial diet and recentering our bodies and spirits through Afrikan/Egyptian-centered, plant-based diets and eco-sustainability.[48] And though I may not agree with these communities' entire philosophies (they appear to be quite heterosexist, while I am LGBTQ supportive), these communities have chosen to live and thrive, and break the addictions we learned from colonialism.

But what does "live" mean?

Choosing to live means that we no longer support the system as it is. Choosing to live means that we cannot eat much of the food in our supermarkets, breathe the air in many of our cities, allow our groundwater to be polluted by toxic wastes, or sit back and wait for the nuclear holocaust. The Addictive System asks us to accept these things—and more—as inherent to being because they are inherent to the addictive, nonliving system in which we live and hence, "reality . . .". The Addictive System asks us to become comfortable with actively participating in our own non-aliveness. Addictions take the edge off, block awareness that could threaten our seeming equilibrium, and allow us to grow, and keep us too busy to challenge the system. [Addictions] are essential to the system. . . . It is caring to confront the disease in the individual, and it is caring to confront the disease of the system. By definition, addiction *has control* of the individual. By definition, addiction *has control* of society.[49]

Confronting unmindful consumption and addiction is a challenge, but it is not impossible. Looking back, I feel blessed that I was able to confront my addictions, learn moderation with shopping, and question where my goods come from. My health is much better and my understanding of how my own antiracist activism must be directly linked to all social and environmental justice issues is now clearer and indisputable. Most important, I learned how to heal my womb from the ravages of colonialism and slavery that have greatly impacted the reproductive health of us women of color, who have lost the wisdom of our ancestral mid-wives due to colonialism and/or slavery.

Even as I write this, I continue to challenge myself and question my own habits and per-ceptions of social and environmental sustainability every single day. Compassion and aware-ness of the suffering we potentially cause to ourselves, those we love, nonhuman animals, and the environment constitute an ongoing journey. For me, whole foods veganism—inspired by Queen Afua—was a logical starting point because it simultaneously alleviated my own bodily suffering, the suffering of nonhuman animals, and the ecosystem. However, it isn't surpris-ing to me that nearly four years after being diagnosed with a fibroid tumor and questioning the lies I had been taught about food, health, and American social justice, I am still learning. Hell no, I'm not perfect! Yes, I know that the transition to mindful consumption is challeng-ing and often frustrating, isolating, confusing, and alienating at first, particularly if you are not part of class-privileged communities in which access to healthier lifestyles is easier, or if you have family members of color who feel you are "trying to be white" by rejecting your mama's southern fried chicken in favor of hummus or quinoa.

However, we must come to terms with the fact that the foods we've grown accustomed to—that have even helped to create the concept of our ethnic identity—may actually be feeding the machine of neocolonialism; that we remain enslaved to a system that thrives on our addictions and mental, physical, and emotional illnesses. Access to locally grown fresh fruits and vegetables, proper nutritional information, and community gardens is currently very difficult in most low-income communities and communities of colors.[50] This may prove challenging for many whose food choices are limited to Jack in the Box, White Castle, conve-nience stores, or grocers that do not sell fresh produce. In addition, TV food advertisements aimed toward people of color convey unhealthier items than those aimed toward whites,[51] which potentially makes unlearning current concepts of food and nutrition difficult.

However, we must challenge the norm. We must no longer accept the lack of healthy food resources, community gardens, and nutritional information in our neighborhoods. People of color have organized at the grassroots level to bring necessary social justice changes to our communities that many found inconceivable, such as abolishing slavery and getting the Civil Rights Act enacted. We boycotted the bus line to desegregate the buses and it worked. I know this is not going to happen overnight, but maybe if we start now, we will be able to get what we need to have access to local and eco-sustainable goods for harmoniously balanced plant-based lifestyles for our children. Let's start now.

Here are some of the things we can do:

1. Organize and petition to get natural foods co-operative grocers or natural chains (like Whole Foods) to consider coming to your neighborhood but charging people fifty percent less for the food.

2. You don't have to be from Georgia to benefit from the resources on the Black Vegetarian Society of Georgia's home page (bvsga.org).

3. Look at Queen Afua's site (queenafuaonline.com) to learn about healing our wombs and overall health, mind, body, and soul through whole foods veganism.

4. Contact organizations such as Oakland Food Connection (foodcommunityculture. org), or The People's Grocery (peoplesgrocery.org/content) in Oakland, California. Ask them how you can get started in bringing healthy but low-cost human rights–oriented foods to your community.

5. Try to bring eco-sustainable and food education workshops that connect to your communities' antiracism and antipoverty agendas to your school, community center, or church. Go online to www.Blackbrowngreen.com to get some good ideas.

6. Because there's a tendency for people of color to think only white people do this, share with your friends and family the literature that has been written by people of color that connects antiracism, decolonization, and freedom to plant-based diets, respect for animals, and eco-sustainability. These sites will be helpful as well: www. Blackbrowngreen.com, vegansofcolor.wordpress.com, and www.soulvegfolk.com.

7. The Food Project (thefoodproject.org) helps to teach young people from diverse backgrounds about food activism and eco-sustainable living.

8. Check out Solidarity, Sustainability, and Nonviolence at www.pelicanweb.org, an e-newsletter.

9. The Eagle Eye Institute (eagleeyeinstitute.org) teaches urban youth about the power of nature and eco-sustainable philosophy.

10. Greenaction.org is a site about health and environmental justice.

11. KillerCoke.org is a site that references the human rights abuses of Coca-Cola.

12. Check out United Poultry Concerns (upc-online.org) to learn ways to teach yourself and your community about how and why chickens suffer.

13. Check out The Compassionate Living Project (compassionatelivingproject.org).

14. To learn about current slavery, read Kevin Bales's *Disposable People: New Slavery in the Global Economy*. If your local library doesn't stock it, have them request it from another library.

15. Check out Bryant Terry's recipe and food justice book, *Vegan Soul Kitchen: Fresh, Healthy, and Creative African-American Cuisine* (www.bryant-terry.com/site/books).

16. Check out Althea's Raw Mocha Angel blog. She has great recipes and ideas for raw, vegan, and gluten-free living: therawmochaangel.blogspot.com.

17. California Food and Justice Coalition: www.foodsecurity.org/california.

4

ON BEING BLACK AND VEGAN

Delicia Dunham

It's lonely being vegan in a world where ninety-nine percent aren't.[1] Most people neither know nor care what vegan means, and even those who claim they do more frequently do not. Still, for many of us, there is no other option. We're in it for the revolution, for the liberation of animals.

The world can be even lonelier for a vegan when you're Black and female. Imagine the small numbers of us there must be. We're unique beings for sure, so we're isolated. And our culture, if not culture*s*, are typically far from supportive of the life we have been called to lead. So we find our vegan selves existing in states of duality, conflicted and torn, wearing masks over our faces as we try to fit in, even as we do not. This, in addition to the dual states we already exist in as regards our race, our gender, and our sexualities.

Involvement in animal-rights issues as a Black woman for me means injecting myself into a subculture where Black women are rare. It means going to protests and holding signs decrying abuse of animals and wondering why no other Black people are there, also raising their voices. It means going against the grain of my own cultural norms to participate in the bigger social issue of eradicating animal torture. It means using my one Black voice to try to sway an entire Black Nation, in one fell swoop.

The duality exists in that my own Black popular culture, as fed to me through hip-hop and the media, tells me that I am neither good enough nor Black enough unless I am exploiting animals (women included). I must be ever-rocking the chinchilla coats (i.e., chinchilla animals as fabric products rather than as living, breathing beings), ever-sporting the finest leathers (i.e., killed cow carcasses as outerwear), and ever-welcoming of Black women shaking their ass for cash or to have a credit card swiped down its crack (as in Nelly's "Tip Drill"

42

video). Further, I should go onstage pulling Black women bound in chains and call myself a Dogg (i.e., Snoop). And I should be dissing, if not totally ignoring, anyone who dares to call me out about my choices (e.g., Beyoncé when confronted by PETA). I must do these things or I am less than Black. I must do these things to maintain my rep, my swagger. I must support Black sneaker manufacturers (like Russell Simmons) by buying the leather wares that he peddles, and I must do this while ignoring the fact that he refers to himself as a "vegan."[2] Because, after all, Russell is Black. And to be Black in the greater hip-hop culture is to be notoriously nonvegan.[3]

Before we delve deeper into these and other examples of what is nonvegan, let's clarify and define its opposite: vegan. Vegan is a word that was invented in the United Kingdom in 1944 by Donald Watson and Elsie Shrigley, founders of the Vegan Society.[4] This couple defined veganism in a memorandum:

> [T]he word "veganism" denotes a philosophy and way of living which seeks to exclude—as far as is possible and practical—all forms of exploitation of, and cruelty to, animals for food, clothing or any other purpose; and by extension, promotes the development and use of animal-free alternatives for the benefit of humans, animals and the environment. In dietary terms it denotes the practice of dispensing with all products derived wholly or partly from animals."[5]

The goal of the Vegan Society is to provide advice on living free of animal products for the benefit of people, animals, and the environment.[6] To vegans, anything that does not meet this definition of vegan is not vegan.

Thus, we get back to nonvegan Black culture and the co-opting of the *vegan* label by those with their own agendas, with disregard to the true meaning of the word and what it entails. The problem with many Black women who label themselves as vegan, in my experience, is that they aren't. They may claim to be vegan but they are merely concerned about avoiding certain animal products for superficial health or so-called spiritual reasons, paying little to no attention whatsoever to the detrimental impacts of their consumption decisions on nonhuman animals and on environment. For example, many of these so-called vegans eat honey, saying it's good for them and listing ways in which it benefits their health. Never do they mention, or express any concern over, the fact that honey is derived from an animal (the bee) and from the raping and exploitation of bees and their hives. Many Black so-called vegan women will also wear wool and leather. But you're not a vegan if you embrace wearing wool and leather, no matter how many tofu dinners and steamed vegetables you eat.

In addition, it is common to find a desire by people in the Black community to avoid what they call "swine," meaning the flesh of pigs. While many Black people come from a slave culture that gorged itself on things like ham hocks and chitlins, it's very common these days to find Blacks who will eat anything under the sun, *except* "swine." If *vegan* was the name given Blacks who ate anything *but* swine, the percentage of Black vegans in the world would be astounding.

In the movie *Mandingo*, a Black enslaved field hand is cooked alive in a cauldron at the end of the film. The film is about slavery and how Black men and women are bred on a Southern plantation. Modern viewers of this time period would be appalled at the behaviors portrayed in the film. Beings are given no choice of mate; they are forced to engage in sexual activity with one another while their "master" watches, to live in separate quarters from loved ones, and to give birth to beings who are promptly taken away and sold to other plantations. They are forced to suckle beings not their own for the benefit of others. Yet when situations like this occur each day to farm animals, where is the outrage? When birds are de-beaked and scalded alive so that brothas and sistahs on the south side of Chicago can eat them some fried chickens in KFC, where is the outrage? What makes a chicken's life any less valuable than a Black human life?

The word to describe the difference and displacement in value is speciesism. The term *speciesism* was coined by Richard D. Ryder in 1970 to denote prejudice against animals that is similar in kind to sexism and racism.[7] As Black people, we need to struggle to eradicate speciesism in society as fervently as we work to overcome racism. We have our NAACP, but why not a NAANA? (National Association for the Advancement of Nonhuman Animals). Along with PUSH, how about a PUSS (People United to Stop Speciesism)? When we as a people learn that "isms" are interrelated and that oppression of any being of any kind is tied to our own oppression, then we can begin to overcome those oppressions for the benefit of all. Racism, sexism, heterosexism, and homosexism are all interconnected.

One thing that prevents Black people from being considerate of the plight of animals and how they are tortured, beaten, abused, raped, and exploited, is the way that animals are portrayed in the media—particularly in media by Black producers of popular culture. You can't turn on the radio or watch a music video these days without either hearing or seeing animal abuse and exploitation. Black women especially are complicit in this degrading behavior. We like to make a big deal about women shaking their asses in music videos and how damaging that is to Black culture, but where is the outrage when Beyoncé Knowles sings adoringly about murdered chinchillas ("She goin' be rockin' chinchilla coats if I let you go"),[8] or when her boyfriend, Jay-Z, raps longingly with her about it ("My texture is the best fur, of chinchilla"),[9] or when Mary J. Blige preemptively lashes out at PETA, an organization committed to the end of animal exploitation, regarding any attempts on their part to educate her about how animals are brutalized and exploited to manufacture the coats that she wears?

> Those PETA people don't want to mess with me, they don't want to throw paint on my coat because it's not just going to be throwing paint. It's going to be Mary in the news the next day, you know what I mean? What gives them the right to destroy someone's coat because their opinion is that you shouldn't wear animals? Understand what I'm saying?[10]

Beyoncé has also been confronted by PETA about her penchant for fur wearing and promotion, to which pleas she was nonresponsive.[11]

Part of the fear that Black women have in caring about the plight of animals that causes them to distance themselves from nonhuman animals is that for so long, Black women have been likened to these beings and thus subjugated as such by speciesist racists. So there is frequently a gut reaction against being referred to in any way that recalls that subjugation. Saartjie Baartman, commonly referred to as the Hottentot Venus, was one historical Black woman taken from her African home and put on display in Europe for the size of her buttocks.[12] She was essentially treated as a modern-day zoo animal or sideshow freak, for voyeurs. According to Patricia Hill Collins:

> Animals can be economically exploited, worked, sold, killed, and consumed. As "mules," African-American women become susceptible to such treatment.... It is no accident that racist biology, religious justifications for slavery and women's subordination, and other explanations for nineteenth-century racism and sexism arose during a period of profound political and economic change. Symbolic means of domination become particularly important in mediating contradictions in changing political economies.

The exhibition of Sarah Bartmann [sic] and Black women on the auction block were not benign intellectual exercises—these practices defended real material and political interests. Current transformations in international capitalism require similar ideological justifications.... Publicly exhibiting Black women may have been central to objectifying Black women as animals and to creating the icon of Black women as animals.[13]

Mass numbers of Black women will not become vegan unless other enlightened Black women lead by example. This leadership entails enticing those who are vegetarian to make the transition to veganism as well as inducing those completely outside of the veggie box to convert to veganism outright. One key Black female role model is Alice Walker, author of *The Color Purple* and other acclaimed literary works. Walker is well known within the vegan community for her foreword to the book *The Dreaded Comparison* by Marjorie Spiegel, in which she writes:

The animals of the world exist for their own reasons. They were not made for humans any more than Black people were made for whites or women for men. This is the essence of Ms. Spiegel's cogent, humane, and astute argument, and it is sound.[14]

Media are key to how vegans are perceived in the world. The lack of images available to compete against the likes of the Beyoncés and Mary J. Bliges of the world is problematic. We need to see more vegan-identified Black women in the spotlight. Alice Walker spoke openly about her past romantic relationship with singer Tracy Chapman in an interview with the UK *Guardian* newspaper.[15] But Tracy is not vegan; she has been noted to have given up on veganism and started to eat fish due to a so-called challenging spell of eating on the road while on tour.[16] One might ask, do Black women vegans have a responsibility to partner with other vegans as a way to strengthen the vegan movement?

The challenge in being a Black female vegan is in standing tall about what we believe in and being a guiding light for others, being somebody else's impact. It is a difficult position to be in but one that we must embrace and claim proudly. We must use every pedestal given to us to advance the cause of veganism and increase societal awareness of the issue. We have to let the world know that pro-animal advocacy is not a "white thing" but a RIGHT thing of which people of all colors and backgrounds need to be a part.

5

NUTRITION LIBRATION

PLANT-BASED DIETS AS A TOOL FOR
HEALING, RESISTANCE, AND SELF-RELIANCE

Melissa Danielle

"[How] and what we eat determines to a greater extent the use we make of the world—and what is to become of it. To eat with a fuller consciousness of all that is at stake might sound like a burden, but in practice few things in life can afford quite as much satisfaction."
—MICHAEL POLLAN, *The Omnivore's Dilemma*

"I am sick and tired of being sick and tired."
—FANNIE LOU HAMER (quoted in Susan L. Smith,
Sick and Tired of Being Sick and Tired)

Some Black people I encounter are surprised when they find out I don't consume animal products. Some are offended, and many proceed to "educate" me on the traditional Black diet. I am reminded that I am not a true member of the race for not eating pork. When I suggest that traditional West African diets are plant-based, and that most of what Black Americans understand to be traditional is a blend of European and African food traditions, I am surprised that they have nothing more to say, and often walk away.

A well-planned, plant-based diet that is varied, and low in fat, sugar, refined flours, and junk food has the power to reduce, if not eliminate, many of the diseases that affect Black communities.[1] A plant-based diet can improve mental clarity, gastrointestinal issues, asthma, energy levels, and can help maintain a healthy weight. It is also a conscious, sustainable diet.

Collectively, we can embrace it as more than just a change in our way of eating. It is a political statement, another weapon in our fight for economic, social, and political empowerment.

If you are what you eat, then what do your food choices say about you? If you eat fast food, does it imply that you are quick, cheap, and easy? If you buy nonorganic produce, meat and dairy products from industrial agriculture sources (factory farms), coffee, sugar, and chocolate from major corporations, does it mean that you advocate air, water, and soil pollution, inhumane treatment of animals and workers, unfair wages, little or no employee training, unsafe labor conditions, child slavery, loss of open spaces, farmers mandated to monocropping solely for profit when a diversity of crops means the ability to feed their families and community, and lastly, the loss of small family farm (which increases poverty, foreclosure, and unemployment rates) due to unnecessary subsidies for corporate agriculture?

I am always amazed at how some people, specifically Black people, can justify the purchase of a $200 pair of sneakers, a $1,500 flat-panel television, or a $60,000 SUV (which then requires another $80 to $100 weekly for a full tank of gas) but take offense at the mere mention of adding natural, unprocessed foods, especially plant foods, to their diet. I am in no way referring to the hundreds of thousands of families across the country barely able to make ends meet, doing the best they can with that they have. What I am suggesting, however, is that most Black-identified Americans have a choice. We can choose to create health-supportive lifestyles that take cues from our cultural heritage—communal living, susus,[2] bartering, creating relevant community-based businesses, potlucks, daycare co-ops, eating locally and seasonally, establishing food-buying clubs or food co-ops, and growing our own foods. Or we can sit back as we lose access to local food systems, neighborhood food markets, and experience an ever-declining state of health and well-being.

Many Americans dream of winning the lottery or otherwise coming into large sums of money. Visions of green paper dance daily in their heads as they move through life. But if the law of attraction (which many have bought into) states that "Like attracts like," then why is our diet more reflective of a garbage dump than a pasture? Wouldn't logic dictate that to attract money, one's life must symbolize those aspects that would attract the desired object? Most Black people are experiencing a daily poverty of the mind, body, and spirit but relentlessly hope, wish, dream, and pray for material riches. This is an example of insanity.

Another woman has been arrested and thrown in jail because she refused to get up out of her seat on the bus for a white person to sit down. It is the second time since the Claudette Colvin case that a Negro woman has been arrested for the same thing. This has to be stopped. Negroes have rights too, for if Negroes did not ride the buses, they could not operate. Three-fourths of the riders are Negro, yet we are arrested, or have to stand over empty seats. If we do not do something to stop these arrests, they will continue. The next time it may be you, or your daughter, or mother. This woman's case will come up on Monday. We are, therefore, asking every Negro to stay off the buses Monday in protest of the arrest and trial. Don't ride the buses to work, to town, to school, or anywhere on Monday. You can afford to stay out of school for one day if you have no other way to go except by bus. You can also afford to stay out of town for one day. If you work, take a cab or walk. But please, children and grown-ups, don't ride the bus at all on Monday. Please stay off all buses Monday.[3]

In December of 1955, Jo Ann Robinson, head of the Women's Political Council, circulated this statement on flyers throughout the Black community in Montgomery, Alabama. The next morning, the Montgomery Improvement Association, newly headed by a young reverend (Dr. Martin Luther King, Jr.), proposed a citywide boycott to protest the city's discriminatory practices on the public transportation system. The proposal was passed, and a boycott was advertised at Black churches during Sunday service.

For 381 days, boycotters carpooled, walked, rode bicycles, mules, horse-drawn carriages, hitchhiked, and did everything to get to and from their destinations but ride the bus. Some boycotters were attacked by angry white opponents, had their homes and churches firebombed, and were even arrested for "hindering" a bus. The event literally shut the city down (economically). This boycott would go down in history as the signifying event for what would be called the Civil Rights Movement. Not only did this boycott cripple Alabama's economic status, it showed how Black people, when compelled to action, will come together for collective progress.

Now, imagine you came across a flyer that reads:

Another Black woman has died today of complications from diabetes because she refused to make healthy changes to her diet. She was 123 pounds overweight and was on blood pressure medication in addition to what she was taking for her diabetes. Just before her death, she was scheduled to have part of her right leg amputated, due to loss of circulation (a complication of diabetes), and her eyesight was failing (another complication). She was 43 years old. This is the 7,395th death since 2000 that is related to diabetes. This has to be stopped. Black Americans have to take control of their health, for if they don't, they may cease to exist in America by the year 2060. Thirty-thousand Americans of African descent die each year from food-related illnesses and diseases, consuming foods not native to their ancestral diets. Yet they go on, business as usual. If we do not do something to prevent this, we risk losing out on all the civil, social, and economic progress we've made over the past 50 years. The next time it may be you, or your daughter, or mother. Don't wait until tomorrow. The future is now. The next bite you take may be your last. We are, therefore, asking every Black American to break free from the chains of slave food in protest of your ill health. Don't buy from any fast-food restaurants. Don't deep fry your chicken or fish. Bake or steam them instead. Prepare your greens without animal remnants. Today, just say no to the "itis." You are not supposed to feel that way after you eat.

If this were posted throughout a Black neighborhood, would we see the same call to action? Would there be outrage? Yes. More than a few people would get indignant at the suggestion that they are responsible for their health instead of having outside forces to blame. More than a few would be upset at the idea that they'd have to cook for themselves instead of the more appealing task of creating catchy slogans to chant and wear on T-shirts, rap songs, securing book deals, or holding rallies and protests.

On August 29, 1997, seven thousand demonstrators staged a Day of Outrage Against Police Brutality and Harassment in response to the assault and brutalization of Abner Louima, following his arrest outside a Brooklyn nightclub. Similar protests and marches were held for Amadou Diallo, the Jena Six, and Sean Bell. Protests, marches, and press conferences to address police brutality and discrimination have replaced the grassroots tactics of the Civil Rights and Black Power movements with broad, top-down approaches that most resemble dog-and-pony shows. Speeches, songs, T-shirts, MySpace pages, posters, and marches are the new activism.

But homicide deaths, however disproportionate in communities of color, rank only sixth in the leading causes of death among Blacks in the United States. Cardiovascular disease, cancer, stroke, and diabetes are in the top five. African-Americans make up less than fifteen percent of the population of the United States, but are two to five times more likely to die from food-related diseases. The collective outrage remains unseen.

The Back to Africa and Black Nationalist movements have built a pedagogy based on a rejection of so-called whiteness, which scrutinizes everything from education and employment to hairstyles and dress, but there is very little critique on the authenticity of Black American culinary history. Fried chicken and potato salad is to Africa as blond hair is to Lil' Kim, but try hosting a function without one or the other and you may find yourself being asked to turn in your Black card.

Four hundred plus years ago, our ancestors sowed southern soil with their blood, sweat, and tears to produce commodities from which they reaped no return, and today we continue to be a slave to systems that do not reinvest in our communities and our health. A close relative of mine believes that maintaining her plantation diet is about paying homage to her ancestors who had no choice but to consume the entrails and scraps of their masters—slave food that sustained a people through generations of hardship and unspeakable cruelty. But when I ask if the poor quality of her health is worth the sacrifice, she dismisses my reasoning and concern for her well-being with the statement that she's "enjoying life." She is also quick to remind me about her "healthy" friends who have passed away "before their time."

Is it preferable to live a long life that requires drug therapy to eat food or to loosen joints so that one can walk, stand, or sit, to sleep soundly, to prevent a premature death, or submit to invasive surgeries that create lasting trauma and insufficient healing? Is that really how one "enjoys life"? Have we become a culture that self-medicates with food, to numb our pain and learned helplessness? Or do we believe our culinary traditions are the only positive, life-affirming practices we can claim as our own?

These questions, along with broader dialogue regarding the connections between food systems and environmental issues and how they affect Black communities, are missing from the Black Nationalist and Afrocentrist agendas. Social change is not possible without personal transformation, yet we continue to act as though we are blameless for much of what is happening to us and in our communities. The struggle for social, economic, and political justice must include awareness of food security and procurement. Where our food comes from, how it gets to the places we buy it from, and what is in the food we eat are just as important as having full access to housing, health care, jobs, and the polls. What good is independence if we are still a slave to food? How can we fully embrace progress if we are not in control of our bodies?

6

YOUNG, BLACK, AND VEGAN

Joi Maria Probus

The day I became vegan began like any other. I woke up and showered with soap that more than likely contained tallow. After showering, I used lotion that contained lanolin and then I applied cosmetics that contained insect particles, as well as ingredients that had probably been tested on animals. For breakfast, I had eggs and turkey bacon. I dressed in a wool skirt and silk-blend shirt, and then slipped my feet into leather shoes. I drove to work, where I had a cup of coffee with dairy cream and refined sugar. I went to lunch and, although I do not remember what I ate, whatever it was consisted of meat and dairy. I thought nothing of these choices. I certainly did not think of them as having any consequences beyond the nourishment, routine, and convenience they represented for me. And then by happenstance, my world changed.

Later that day, I spent some time with the new girlfriend of a close friend. I liked her immediately. She was friendly, quick to laugh, and engaging in conversation. We spent a long time talking and getting to know each other when somehow the conversation turned to food. My friend's girlfriend said that she was vegan. I'd heard of vegetarians, of course, and had probably heard the word *vegan*, but I did not know what it meant to be one. I asked her and she was gracious; she even stomached hearing me say "vay-gan" a few times as I tried to wrap my mind around what it meant to avoid not only animal flesh and animal-derived foods, but also not use or wear *anything* derived from animals or testing on animals.

I was fascinated. The commitment it took for these vegans to adhere to such a strict diet and lifestyle amazed me. I told my friend's girlfriend that I'd dabbled in vegetarianism myself as an adolescent because "I'd always loved animals and didn't think it was right to eat them"! I thought better of mentioning that my childhood vegetarianism forbade me only from eating animals of the cute and cuddly variety, that is, cows, pigs, and lambs. Chicken and fish, however, *were* on the menu. I disclosed that peer pressure and a single mother who was not about to cook separate meals to sustain my cute-only animal-free diet made my veggie days short-lived. I concealed the fact that, frankly, after a year of dining on chicken and the sides of family meals—canned vegetables, potatoes, beans—I missed hamburgers.

Still, I sought to understand my new friend. I wanted to know the *how*, and especially the *why*? In addition to answering my questions, she gave me a list of websites and encouraged me to research these issues on my own. I wasted no time, immediately seeking the answers to my questions. I was pleased to find a wealth of well-researched and documented information on the Internet, the most compelling of which were undercover photographs of animal cruelty, factory farms, and intensely graphic videos, such as PETA's *Meet Your Meat*. These images pierced my heart and took my breath away. I was filled with despair, disgust, and anger—emotions directed not only at the "civilized" societies that condone this systematic torture and the inevitable, untimely deaths of so many innocent lives, but also at myself for my own complicity.

I was a twenty-something, intelligent, Black woman who was extremely sure in her beliefs. I thought I already stood for and against everything worthy of my convictions. Only a few years prior, I had reigned supreme as the exemplar of young sistahood on my college campus. Whether I was penning articles on racism for the campus paper, holding my own as a speaker on student/faculty panels to address campus diversity, serving as student government secretary and vice president of the campus NAACP, or attending anti-death-penalty vigils at the nearby prison, I was full of ideals that could not, *would not*, be compromised. After graduation, I'd entered the "real world" with a confidence that resulted from a collegiate career built on knowing that *if you didn't stand for something, you'd fall for anything*. And yes, at times I was arrogant. I thought I knew it all. Yet, as I continued my research into veganism, I could not fathom how I had been so blind to these issues of oppression, enslavement, torture, and death. All I knew was that I could no longer support it. When I went home that evening, I was vegan.

But I was a far cry from the hippie chick girlfriend of my friend. For one, she was white. She was also a lesbian and an undergraduate at a local university, working part time. Black, heterosexual me had been out of school for two years and was one year into a nine-to-five job. I had recently been promoted to head up a division of the human resources department at a major art museum, and I was often recognized by my colleagues and superiors for my talents. An aspect of my job I loved was that it allowed me frequent contact with older women, whom I hoped to mirror as I carved a place for myself in the world. The women I looked up to were involved in charity work and community activism. They were prominent in African-American organizations like the Links and stood out as the few women of color in local chapters of more mainstream philanthropic organizations, such as the Junior League. They represented all that I, as a young, Black, professional woman, aspired to achieve.

When I became vegan, however, my priorities shifted. My new friend became my mentor and the person I sought to emulate. She gave me her own worn copy of Peter Singer's *Animal Liberation*, which I still thumb through regularly (but especially when I need to remind myself why I won't be purchasing the Christian Louboutin pumps, fabulous as they are!). Although those first days were occasionally challenging, I was undaunted. I readily accepted that my care-free past—the days when I could order food at any drive-thru window or pluck a shampoo from the shelf, concerning myself only with whether or not it would add moisture to my tresses—was behind me. Nonetheless, having the support of an experienced vegan was encouraging. She not only cooked for me on several occasions, she also showed me where and, more important, *how* to shop for foods and sundries, as well as which local restaurants were vegan-friendly. Although we have lost contact over the years, I will always be thankful for her inspiration and guidance.

Six years later, I am still astounded by the lack of compassion toward animals. I am aware of the controversial PETA display, "Animal Liberation," which incited controversy for using images and language that simultaneously address contemporary animal suffering and the human suffering that has occurred during some of the most abominable periods in human history—among them African enslavement, the Jim Crow era, and the Holocaust. Critics of this display believe that there is no comparison to be drawn between these horrific crimes against humanity and the appalling treatment of nonhuman animals today. To them, not only does this comparison diminish the significance of the historic events, it is racist, insulting, and culturally insensitive. After all, haven't the dominant cultures always considered us less than human and compared us to animals as a way of humiliating and dehumanizing us?

Sadly, PETA's critics have missed the point. PETA's intent is not to imply that Black, Jewish, or Native American people are viewed by PETA or *should be viewed by anyone* as subhuman. The desired result of these images is to evoke compassion, to help people empathize with the experiences of animals as victims of oppression, just as they would, and for some of the same reasons, with the humans depicted in the display. As a Black woman, I am at once angered and deeply saddened by the negative reaction to the "Animal Liberation" project by the African-American community. After all, it is the appalling treatment of nonhuman animals that should offend, not the perceived comparison of people to the animals. Unfortunately, many of those who have taken issue with PETA possess the same type of mentality that enabled the atrocities against their own ancestors and other cultures throughout history. By viewing animals, as with cultures or "races" of people, as *less than*, it is impossible to empathize with their pain and suffering. This lack of empathy is a pathway to the atrocities committed against the oppressed, and in most instances is a justification for the perpetrators. Cruelty and exploitation enrage when applied to people, but why not nonhuman animals?

The dumbed-down arguments—among them that unlike humans, nonhuman animals cannot talk or reason—distract from the only thing with which we should be concerned, which is the question, *Like humans, do animals suffer? Do they feel pain?* Perhaps only a prehistoric caveman would have cause to argue otherwise, but in modern times, with our vast resources and diverse options for food and clothing, the continued use of animals is unnecessary. We simply have no need, let alone the right, to eat their flesh or wear their skin. It goes without saying that, as entertainment, their use is even more frivolous. Furthermore, we have no right to use animals as test subjects for consumer products and medical research.

I am the only African-American vegan I know, male or female, who chose this lifestyle for purely ethical reasons. To nonvegan African-Americans, I am an enigma. After all, we are a culture for whom animal-derived foods are dietary staples. Sure, we have learned to accept the occasional Islamic brother or sister who does not eat pork, but for a Black person to shun chicken and fish, leather and wool? And for what? Animal rights? Hell, we're still working on *our* rights! I've heard it all. I've been mocked with laughter, incredulously stared at, and dismissed with a condescending shake of the head, more times than I care to recall. Still, I remain patient with these reactions because I know better.

Among African-Americans, a great deal of politics is tied up in the foods we eat and the clothes we wear. We created Soul Food out of necessity. We learned to eat, albeit with a large amount of spices and seasoning, what *massa* didn't want. This is how we survived. We have also come to equate *material* equality with *racial* equality. We covet and, if we are lucky, acquire luxury items like fur and exotic skins. These goods say to the world that we are worth something. We are valuable when we can possess things of value. Not to mention, minks and alligator shoes represent wealth, a component of the American dream that we have been denied for so long.

The few Black vegetarians with whom I am acquainted are more concerned with health than with compassion for animals or concern for the environment. Still, their reasoning, though dietary, helps support the case for veganism. Furthermore, it is not important *how* people come, as long as they come. This is one of the reasons why I am heartened when a new Black-owned health-food store or vegetarian restaurant emerges in the 'hood. As Black vegans and vegetarians, we should particularly educate our own about the benefits of exclusively plant-based diets and holistic health practices. Indeed, we *must* educate that these diets, and these diets alone, are proven to significantly reduce the risk of getting heart disease, diabetes, kidney disease, hypertension, obesity, and more. It is no secret that these conditions are widespread in the African-American community.

Of course, when presented with evidence of animal abuse and suffering, I wish everyone would have a *School Daze* "WAKE UP!" moment like I did—one that causes them to immediately "go vegan." But I accept that even vegetarians, who consume dairy and eggs, wear animal-derived fabrics, go to circuses and rodeos, and don't police the ingredients in their household products, still spare billions of animals from suffering and death. I may advocate for absolute veganism, but I'll take what I can get.

I have been vegan since 2002 and have noticed differences in myself beyond the benefits of my healthy diet. Overall, I am more compassionate. I have more respect for life and care more for the environment. I am at peace, knowing that the everyday decisions I make will do no harm. Still, I possess a small degree of guilt that will probably never go away. A part of me will never forgive myself for the suffering for which, in my vast ignorance, I have been responsible. My only comfort is that I am now armed with knowledge that I cannot ignore. And thus, I am changed.

7

VEGANISM

STEPPING AWAY FROM THE STATUS QUO

Venus Taylor

For me, eating meat is just one more in a long list of mainstream behaviors I've chosen to question. After marrying my husband, who'd been vegetarian for years, I dropped meat in order to simplify our meals as a couple. I'd never really felt attached to meat; I ate it merely because I'd been taught, growing up, that it was the most important part of any meal. Years later, after reading *Your Health Your Choice* by Dr. Ted Morter (now published under the title *Fell's Your Health and Wellness*), I was inspired to begin my new life as one who questions mainstream philosophies. It was exhilarating to find a book containing truths about the ills of protein-based diets not publicized on television, not accepted by traditional Western medicine, or shared by the majority of Americans, yet so undeniably valid that they resonated with my soul.

I began, from that point on, to base my lifestyle decisions on reading and research that "felt right" and rang true in my heart and mind, regardless of the objection or approval of the mainstream. I happened upon books like *The Continuum Concept* by Jean Liedloff and literature from the La Leche League when I was pregnant with my first child, and I determined that attachment parenting (including not spanking and breastfeeding beyond the first and even second birthday) felt right to me. Despite howls from my parents and in-laws, we breastfed until the kids were nearly four years old, and we chose not to practice corporal punishment. Twelve years later, we have the most well-behaved, emotionally secure, intuitive children you'd ever want to meet.

During my first pregnancy, I questioned the chemicals I'd used all my life to straighten my kinky hair. I decided—again, against a backdrop of family howling—to dreadlock my hair and my children's hair.

My husband and I read alternative spiritual writings found in the occult section of bookstores and, finding answers to our questions about faith, relinquished our practice of organized religion and are now more spiritually free and empowered than ever before (much to the dismay of my father-in-law, who is a Baptist pastor).

As my kids neared school age, I read about homeschooling (prompted by my daughter, who rejected the entire concept of school after three weeks of preschool). I knew by the tingly waves of joy undulating through my body that homeschooling was the right choice for our family. Beyond that, I read further about coercive/passive learning versus interest-led/active learning and decided to unschool my children (life-based learning led by child and family interests instead of curricula and textbooks) rather than practice school-at-home.

Raising my children as vegans from birth caused some concern among the in-laws, but I didn't care. I listened to my instincts, read and researched what I felt was appropriate for my children's health and education, and trusted that what made sense to me was what was right.

People have often asked, "What does your doctor say about it?" I look at them quizzically and reply, "Who is my doctor to tell me how to live my life and raise my children?" I also inform them that, first of all, we rarely see doctors, because we're rarely sick. In fact, we are visibly thriving. Second, I add, "If I ever I consulted with a doctor who believed a vegan diet was unhealthy, I'd simply choose another who reads and knows better."

For the past three or four years, I've practiced vegan raw foodism, which is another subject I came across through reading and research. Though my family is not completely raw, I am, because it makes me feel energized and healthy. Also, I look younger every year, without working at it.

Veganism is about questioning the status quo, bucking tradition, and choosing to live in accordance with your own values—trusting your own mind and spirit over the beliefs of the larger culture, your ethnic culture, your family, and your friends. Veganism is just one more way that I've taken ownership of how I define myself. I took back my hair from hairdressers.

I took back my spirituality from ministers. I took back my children from institutions. I took back my health from doctors.

Black folks are not unlike others—we feel safer with the status quo. We prefer doing what most others like us are doing. Some have argued that it is an evolutionary instinct to stay with the herd. There is safety in numbers. Standing alone, one risks attacks by wolves, wildcats, gossips, and other predators. We are also taught not to question authority or tradition by those who wish to retain control over us. Ministers need us to depend upon their understanding. Doctors need us to value their advice. Pharmaceutical companies beg us to ask our doctors to prescribe their drugs. If we think for ourselves, these people lose their income base.

However, when the paths the masses are following lead us to destruction—when our schools educate us just enough to trail the rest of the world in math and science; when our diets lead us all to cancer, obesity, depression, dis-ease, and pharmaceutical dependency; when our churches don't help us break the cycle of oppression, depression, and suppression—then the wisest, most species-saving, survivalist track is to strike out from the herd. Question all assumptions. Do something different.

Choosing veganism (or homeschooling), especially as a Black person and most especially as a Black woman, means choosing to trust yourself over the teaching of men, doctors, ministers, white people, and other Black folk. Because it is such a countercultural choice, veganism means living life in accordance with your deeply pondered, deeply held values— whether you choose it for health reasons or animal-rights reasons. It is one step on a path to an authentic life.

8

BEING A SISTAH AT PETA

Ain Drew

In April 2006, I found myself at my dream job. I had converted to vegetarianism right after graduation, and after two years of service at a Detroit charter school, I was about to put my college degree to use by pushing vegetarian ideals.

PETA hired me as their Urban Marketing Coordinator, and I packed my Motown bags to settle closer to the ocean. Norfolk, Virginia, was to be my new home. My job at PETA was clear: take PETAWorld, the urban campaign that had been all but swept aside, and bring it to life. I was hired as the sole writer, marketing guru, and human link between PETA and the urban community at large.

Initially, I embraced my position. I was shuffled to different events to educate people about animal-rights issues from the Black and hip-hop perspective. I pushed literature in Los Angeles and New York City, from Detroit to Atlanta, all the while dodging open hostility. However, those challenges also began to present themselves loud and strong in my inbox, and it became difficult—given my natural desire to want to educate—to ignore.

Almost daily, I was verbally reprimanded by members of my own community for holding my position. I'm Black, and with all the discrimination that my mothers and I have endured and continue to suffer, how dare I spend my days standing up for animals? Furthermore, how dare I campaign against the diets of our foremothers and forefathers? These were among the less subtle taunts. Others insisted that PETA is a terrorist organization or an extremist group out to obliterate all traditional practices. The emails that fit within the latter bunch were much less annoying.

When I decided to adopt a vegetarian diet, the idea struck quickly and effectively. I'd picked up a PETA leaflet in a restaurant after devouring a delicious fish sandwich, had looked at my sister, and confidently had told her that I wouldn't be eating any more poultry or sea-food (I'd given up red meat two years prior). Admittedly, I indulged in a spoonful of my momma's turkey chili a few weeks later, but the hurtful images from the leaflet were replaying in my mind like a perpetual slideshow. That was my last taste.

I gave up meat for one clear reason: animals in factory farms are treated despicably. The conditions they have to live in resemble nothing that nature intended for them. Most chickens in factory farms will never touch a blade of grass, breathe fresh air, or enjoy fresh water. Spiritually, I couldn't support a system that treated any living being with such disregard. Taking the job at PETA was an opportunity for me to work a standard nine-to-five job, make decent money, experience life away from my hometown, and work toward a cause I believed in.

My decision to spend my days working toward animal liberation wasn't a calculated one. Furthermore, I never imagined that I would have to defend it. I couldn't fathom being attacked for my career choice or my sociopolitical beliefs because I had chosen to stand up for animals rather than being a human rights activist. The fact that very few people could actually grasp the concept of PETA being a place of employment and not a cultlike institution was ridiculous to me. Each workday, I rose at eight in the morning, got dressed, and then would lazily walk to my desk just like a very large portion of the American population. However, my mission was one that people are rarely introduced to and that is less frequently spoken about in public forums. Besides, my induction to the world of animal rights was guided by a simple leaflet left on the windowsill of a quaint diner.

The unsolicited scoffs from people who questioned my allegiance to my race begged the questions: Do people chastise veterinarians for choosing to cure and aid animals versus the numbers of sickly people? Does the Humane Society receive threats from people demanding that they shelter humans versus nonhuman animals? This is all very doubtful. But PETA's vibrant and boisterous bravado attracts those who would rather ignore or be ignorant of our treatment of animals. The fact remains that for every injustice, there will be an organization in strong opposition to that injustice.

Because I was attracted to a vegan lifestyle due to industry practices that I hope will soon end, it was also necessary for me to educate myself about the health benefits of abstaining from consuming animal products in order to ensure a solid commitment. The diets of my foremothers and forefathers kept bellies full in a time when opportunity to maintain a healthy lifestyle was extremely limited. In many low-income areas, they still do. Beyond lacking adequate healthcare, if you're not in the desired tax bracket, quality food is not easily accessible or affordable. This perpetual cycle keeps the community down, stricken with high cholesterol, obesity, and suffering from conditions that could easily be avoided. What better way to destroy a people than to keep them in lackluster physical condition?

With this knowledge, I was ready to take PETAWorld on with a passion. I was prepared and excited to teach my people about healthy eating and how to avoid the ailments that are prevalent among the Black community.

I updated the website with a bevy of health-related information and constantly brainstormed new ways to introduce the concepts of veganism and vegetarianism to people who were engulfed within a culture of Soul Food. In understanding that PETA's overall mission was to help animals, I made sure to reference how an improved diet could alleviate the pain and suffering of factory-farmed animals. My goal was to be sure that everyone came out on top and that people were aware that the choices they made concerning their diets were a huge benefit to themselves, as well as animals who needlessly suffer in the name of our tastebuds.

Unfortunately, after a few months, I found that PETA wasn't as concerned with helping Black folks overcome our health issues than they were about getting us to stop wearing mink coats or promoting dog-fighting. Apparently, Black folks wearing furs to the club was more of a problem than the health problems that plague us. In marketing meetings, there was a constant discussion about how to make fur "less hip," which celebrities to approach, and how we could come across as more "urban." After repeatedly being ignored when I mentioned tackling issues that were more pressing, I knew that my time with PETA was running out. This was not how I wanted to make a difference.

I am all too aware of the growing health disparities in the African-American community. While there is a disproportionate number of fast-food chains and liquor stores in neighborhoods where low- to middle-income families reside, the lack of health care and adequate insurance is even more alarming. Ongoing discussions about fur, among other albeit horrible animal atrocities, were taking away from relevant issues that would have made PETA more approachable to the Black community I'd been hired to represent. Even when PETA did take the initiative to address vegetarian issues and the benefits of adopting a vegetarian diet, they opted for shock tactics that didn't directly address the health issues of the community they were trying so badly to reach.

After a trip to Atlanta, during which I was reluctant to approach artists at a hip-hop film festival and reel off facts about animal mistreatment and disgusting them with some harsh realities in what I deemed an inappropriate venue, I was fired. It was November, seven months after my big move, and only six months after I'd settled into an apartment.

The truth is, PETA will exist as long as animal abuse exists. They have a knack for what they do: creating a media frenzy to bring attention to the animal injustice of the moment. Who's going to care if an animal is purposely drowned, hanged, or electrocuted while conscious unless someone makes a lot of noise about it? Although I harbor a little resentment toward PETA, the largest and most effective animal-rights organization in the world, I have to give kudos where kudos is due. In spite of the attention-whore tactics of their marketing and communications department, there are a host of people there, all nine-to-fivers, who help animals daily in a multitude of ways and make people happier and healthier in the process.

9

HOSPITAL-SPONSORED JUNK FOOD AT A "HEALTHY" BIKE-RIDING EVENT?

Robin Lee

One Sunday in October 2007, I went with a dear friend to an event billed as a "Bike Ride along the Grand Concourse" in the Bronx. To put this location in perspective, this aptly named grand thoroughfare cuts through the center of the borough.

Before Mayor Giuliani came into office, Bronxites enjoyed the entire concourse—six to eight miles—closed off to traffic on six Sundays throughout the year for either walking or biking. This was immediately nixed by the Giuliani administration solely because he didn't like the Bronx borough president, who was Fernando Ferrer at the time. So much for the progressive power of politics! But I digress: that was during my pre-"vegetarian/getting fit for myself" stage of life.

So, imagine my delight and anticipation, after discovering the energy of fruits and vegetables and having learned how to ride a bike, to participate in this great event. What a disappointment! It spanned only three blocks, *not* the entire concourse as in previous years. There were various activities for kids and families, but many didn't show, and the planning was so poor that there was limited space to "reclaim" the roadway from cars. What was the point?

One good thing was that I found a group of riders who are on various committees to increase greenways in the Bronx, and they gave a great tour of areas I didn't know existed, in a twenty-mile trek around the South Bronx. (Fear not: the days of "Fort Apache" have receded into the mist of the past, as luxury apartments sprout up all over the place.) This would have been a wonderful bike ride if more community members could have participated.

The ride consisted mostly of people on those various committees and one unaware community member—me. I'm not the thinnest crayon in the box, by any means, but I'll bike up inclines or at the very least give it the African Woman 200 percent attempt until foiled by physics (need that momentum!) and biology (fatigued thighs and legs) [*smile*]. As I rode, I noticed how many young people are grossly overweight and how few places provide healthy snacks in many neighborhoods. (An aside: I'm becoming increasingly pessimistic about the access to good health in this country; the knowledge that could "free" people seems only available to the educated and the rich.)

As I was coached effectively by a generous fellow rider up one steep incline, a young girl remarked, "That hill is really steep. You can go another way." I went up and up, slowly, but reached the apex nonetheless. My fellow rider, Ed (a multiple 100-mile–bike-tour veteran/ vegan), was invaluable and great company. I humbly send a *gassho* his way.

Now for my rant. A local hospital, Bronx Lebanon, was one of the cosponsors of this event, and they set out a table with information about hypertension, diabetes, and asthma in a sort of *Wheel of Fortune* set-up. Participants got free treats when they either inquired about the information at the table, "played the game," or just approached the table. The treats pissed me off: Oreo cookies, Chips Ahoy, and Nips (all in snack-sized packages) that seemed to predate the anti–trans fat trend currently running across the nation.

Hackles raised, I went over to the table and declined the free treat offered. I asked if there was a nurse or dietitian at the table I could talk to. The table was run by nonprofessional volunteers. I was aghast. I asked if any of them lived in the neighborhood. The answer was no, but they were aware of the rampant diabetes and asthma in this community. I even asked if any of them ate those treats they were giving out. Two were twenty-somethings who admitted they neither ate these snacks nor much fast food. I noticed them munching on apples they'd brought with them. One other woman was the mother of one of the twenty-somethings, and she confided that she'd never had these snacks in her home when her children were growing up. The Latina at the table was munching on some Oreo cookies and drinking *café con leche*.

Then I went off: *How dare they hand out these items, which clearly are counterproductive to the very information they are trying to convey.* And so came the lame excuses:

1. *The treats lure the community to the table to get the information.*

My response: You have a community that, for the most part, has cultural ties to countries that have many lush fruits and vegetables that could have been incorporated into a healthier diet. Just a bit of research about papaya, mango, and root plants could have gone a long way. Ad agencies have sold us on the idea that *free* or *low-cost* will lure people, but the biggest draw is acknowledging you "see" people by showing them their familiar culture.

2. *These are mostly for the kids; this is like a pre-Halloween event.*

My response: Kids need the most help in eating healthy. Like reading, writing, and 'rithmetic, this information stays with them their whole lives. The real horror of Halloween is the sugar pumped into kids.

3. *They can burn off the sweets while playing at the various activities.*

My response: And then crash hard or have an asthma attack if they are susceptible. These things can't sustain energy. I wouldn't have made the twenty-mile tour on my bike if I had eaten those "treats."

At this point, one of the thin twenty-somethings looked at my 5'10", 210-pound frame and was "amazed" at my feat. I brushed that off, explaining that at 240 pounds I'd completed a thirty-three-mile Tour de Bronx a year previously. He inquired how I'd done it. I told him by eating vegetarian, getting on my bike, and walking more. I'm not even focused on losing weight anymore; the process recedes into the background of my life as other things take my attention.

I ended with the notion that, while I applauded their efforts to provide healthy information and activities, this sort of thing was "one step forward, two steps back" that served no one and fostered stereotypical notions of what true health is and isn't. Isn't it a shame that the agency at the center of this mess is, of all places, a hospital? Then the truth: As the other ladies in attendance moved away from the table and the discussion, he confided that the treats were free for the hospital, leftover from other events, and that they had "no budget" to set this up.

I looked at him, pointed to his face, and asked him to examine the brown/Black faces of the community he was "serving." Then I stated: *You probably think racism isn't as bad as it was before you were born; think about that again.*

I wonder if he gave it any thought.

10

BLACK-A-TARIAN

Ma'at Sincere Earth

I don't eat swine, but yeah I got a big behind
You don't eat any meat; you look at me with deceit
With your chicken from Tyrone's you don't feel alone
It doesn't make any sense that you look at me like I don't exist
Sis, I don't like slave food, dude I don't eat the white man's scraps
I love my godly naps, my body is a temple,
shouldn't what I place in it,
be a symbol of some serious thought
instead of whatever that is man-made or brought
I sought, to be queen-like original, but like Chris Rock says niggas love to not know
You say, "Shit I eat anything." It doesn't matter
the dirtiest, the fattest, as long as you can put hot sauce or ketchup on it,
it's the bomb diggity
Forgive me for coming so hard on you meat-eaters
but as a group, you laugh at me and question me like I eat rat or
any other meat, whitey, Asian, or anybody else throw at my feet.
All I'm saying is don't give me a hard time for not eating meat
Cause I got a million intelligent reasons why than your shit
Like "its good, u wish you could"
Damn stop being a nutritional Uncle Tom cause being a vegan is not wrong

(circa 1997)

was a little angry back when I wrote that. You know I was your usual "fight the power" sistah in the midst of Black faces with white paint at the local university. No one understood me. I encountered a lot of debates on my choice to be a vegetarian with many of my peers. It wasn't as popular for a Black person to eat healthy back in 1997 as it is now. Vegetarianism's popularity has come a long way. It's getting much easier to eat and live among the masses of meat-eaters. Vegetarian spots and vegetarian-friendly additions to menus are popping up everywhere. Through the muffled cries of sick people, the government saw the opportunity for the economy to prosper off the need to live a healthier life. Hence you have the new vegetarian era. My options are still limited, but at least I've got two vegetarian markets and a number of vegetarian- or vegan-friendly restaurants to go to. So that's good for Baltimore, being that this is the home of the best crabs and seafood in the world. But even though more people are interested and accommodating when it comes to me being a vegan, there are still a lot of misconceptions.

Yes, I'm a vegan but I'm not an animal activist.

People assume that just because you are a vegan, your front is animal rights, and they think they should never see you in a leather coat or shoes. But that's not what motivates me to not eat meat. I'm not a walking PETA advertisement. I don't even understand animal rights. As much energy as these organizations put into animal rights, if they put the same into human rights, these animals wouldn't be mistreated in the first place. It's just an ongoing cycle of lack of compassion for each other that has developed in the relationship with the world. Animal cruelty is just the byproduct of human cruelty and is not the equivalent. One just perpetuates the other.

The recent death of the crocodile man, Steve Irvin, showed an example of someone who showed so much passion for animals that it was reflected on everybody he came in contact with or who watched his show. Now, *that's* making a difference. I agree that they should pass laws regulating and limiting the unethical treatment of animals and the unnecessary use of them in everyday products and foods. But it's the consumption of animals that's getting out of control, that's hurting people and animals, not the wearing of them. Most people can't afford real leather or fur; there are so many leather and fur imitations, who knows who is really wearing it? PETA seems to know.

I don't choose to wear leather or fur, but if I happen to wear it, it doesn't contradict me as a vegan. A vegan is one who doesn't eat any meat or dairy or products and that's what I do. Of course, I don't support the purchase of, nor do I use, animal products. But I won't sacrifice a nice leather coat at the thrift store on sale or rip a fur off a person's back in broad daylight because I'm a vegan. I would like to see a PETA supporter scream at a brother in the 'hood wearing a fur. Being a Black woman, you have to be conscious of the things you support, because self-preservation is most important. If organizations don't support the growth and development of my people, then what am I really fighting for? They have distanced themselves as the elite, middle class. I think PETA does a good job with producing those slaughterhouse movies and getting the word out, but they don't connect with the average minority. Being a vegan is a usual characteristic of PETA supporters, but not all vegans are PETA members or are white.

I ate fried chicken before, but no more.

I don't think humans in general should eat meat, but I definitely don't think Black people should eat meat. With the problems of blood pressure, diabetes, obesity, and, yes, just plain racism, current-day Soul Food could be one of the culprits for the race's downfall. The rate of blood pressure among African-Americans in the United States is the highest in the world. Over eighty percent of all Black people are lactose intolerant and most don't even know it. We have accepted another race's diet for our own. Our bodies are not reacting well to the diet of the masses. America's diet is an example of sweeping racial differences under the door. We all have differences, and we have to acknowledge that those differences play a part in everything we do, including our diet. Recently, the food pyramid had to be changed because it doesn't work for all races. That, in itself, was a lesson to let others know that we all have different cultural dietary needs and that they need to be addressed. Diet is the racial oppression that Black people have to get over in order to survive.

Even though as a child I constantly suffered from headaches after eating pork chops, I ate meat all the time. In the eighth grade, a Muslim classmate did a report on the harmful effects of swine. I looked into the subject and found a lot of information about pork and the connection with the headaches I would get. Right away, I stopped eating it. Gradually, year after year, I would learn more and more about different meats and would stop eating them. I was a long-term vegetarian. It started out as youthful disgust and became a lifelong and growing commitment not to eat meat. I wasn't a good vegetarian, with the various years in between, but every New Year I would go "cold turkey" with a new meat. I wasn't as focused a label reader as now and that probably resulted in me eating a lot more meat in my food than I knew.

It was Sister Souljah's autobiography, *No Disrespect*, that got me serious about being a vegetarian. When I read it, I was in search of my racial identity similar to her journey in the book, where she writes that her dietary habits improved during her growth. I, too, wanted to align my mental growth with my diet, because they are one. I understood what it meant to be holistic, and how your mind, body, and spirit have to be aligned in order to have optimal health.

An unexpected journey actually drove me to being a vegan; it turned out to be just an elevation from being a vegetarian. While I stocked my pantry with the essential things I needed to be a better vegetarian and was doing my scheduled fasts, I felt it was important for me to be in the most natural state, which symbolized going back to my original state of existence before the enslavement of my racial identity. I happened to come upon the books *African Holistic Health* and *Nutricide* by Dr. Llaila Afrika. Those books gave me yet another freedom, one I'd not yet encountered, which was the nutritional liberation from mainstream America. The theory of not accepting another race's diet for my own was revolutionary and profound to me. The idea of freeing myself nutritionally from the oppressors' diet motivates me to avoid meat. I soon became a vegan to solidify my nutritional commitment.

Must love tofu and hip-hop . . .

That same commitment is extended to my dating life. I do compromise with vegetarians and soft-core meat-eaters, those who don't eat meat that much, and are very open to being a vegetarian. All my meat-eating friends say I'll never meet a Black man who's a vegetarian, and definitely won't meet one who's vegan. I think it really depends on where you live; the more culture a city has, the more opportunity there is for people to be exposed to vegetarianism. I've been out with hard-core meat eaters (those who don't ever want to become a vegetarian or may even not like vegetables), and it simply doesn't work. Food is centered around everything: ceremonies, celebration, cookouts, and meetings of every sort. It ends up being the insensitive joke and issue in the relationship. Diet affects the way a man smells and definitely tastes; being physical with your mate is inevitable. Some things just can't be compromised.

Currently, I am single; so I might not be average. My nine-to-five life as a vegan is filled with work lunches, a happy hour or two, and an occasional nightclub or date. I'm very creative with my food choices. I look into popular restaurants' drinks and acknowledge what is vegan-friendly. These social interaction outings are important to a healthy state of mind. Who wants to turn into the old vegan cat lady?

One day, if I do reproduce, I want to have a vegetarian household, so having a mate who shares the same feelings is ideal for me. Being a vegan is more than a choice; it's a lifestyle. My ideal mate would have to embrace the lifestyle that comes along with being more conscious about food choices and everything he does. I don't think it's a lot to ask a man to divorce a diet of slave food and embrace a more kinglike diet with healthy foods. I can respect a man who knows how to eat to live and loves hip-hop; he might be the man for me.

A psychic told me one time that if I wasn't a vegetarian, I'd be dead. My grandfather had diabetes, my grandmother had diabetes, and my father has diabetes. Now, whether the psychic just made an obvious acknowledgment of the growing number of Black people dying from diet-related diseases, or was really tuned in, either way, I still took it as a valuable piece of information. I'm one month away from becoming thirty years old, and one of the things I'm satisfied about in life is my decision to be a vegan. It feels good to eat good foods. My decision to go the road least traveled with my diet reflects my evolving journey of cultural refinement and my lifelong commitment to being in my most original state.

I am what I eat, what I think, and how I feel.

> *I am busy living in the right now and trying to do my best every day.*
> *That to me is success.* —YOKO ONO

That's where I am right now.

11

IDENTITY, FREEDOM, AND VEGANISM

Melissa Santosa

"Self-righteous." That's the customary description I've been labeled with since I became a vegan. Refusing to consume animals and their by-products as a way of life is often misunderstood as impractical and impossible, even after a full explanation of your reasons, and even if you walk what you talk. It's equally annoying opposite is the word *righteous* when it is used as compliment. People at poetry readings, old college friends I run into at the grocery store, and well-meaning white leftists constantly refer to me and that word in the same breath.

Most self-proclaimed vegans I know have heard one or both words used to describe them, and for me, it's a misconception that I've chosen veganism because "it's the right thing to do." More than anything, veganism has chosen me, and the more I live, the more I believe it is a lifestyle that sustains the existence of our world. The main reason I undergo life-altering epiphanies is that I have serious problems with dissonance. Once a seismic shift has occurred in my worldview, it's time to clean shop.

People who don't fully understand veganism harbor a dual curiosity of lure and loathing. The most common insinuation and the direct question that I get is, "How can you do it? I know you must cheat once in a while. Oh come on!" It's as if only absolutes are valid and that the regimen of eating only certain foods is the only motivation. Yes, like many vegans, I am not one-hundred-percent all of the time. Sometimes it's out of genuine ignorance, especially in my early days. But once in a while it's because I haven't had a bean pie in eight years, and by eating a regular one I can figure out how to adapt it to be vegan. Occasionally, these slip-ups lead me to feel guilty, and often it's a reminder that it's okay to be human, no pun intended.

No one asks, "How has your way of life sustained you?" We think in terms of logical limitation and skip the leap of faith, the uneasy journey of the spirit. I am not looking for

73

perfection, but my perfect substitute is looking. Our existence often means the extinction of another being. There is a great responsibility and challenge in that philosophy. My life has broadened to an antiviolence perspective that sees institutional/cultural abuse and violence toward women and children.

I became a vegan even before I knew the full meaning of the word. I was at a summer camp for the Forum to Advance Minorities in Engineering (FAME) program, where we would prepare debates, write essays, do SAT practice tests, and hear lectures by professionals in the field of science and engineering. Both of my older brothers went through the program, and I was basically forced to go by my mother and chauffeured there by my father. However, there was great comfort in being in a place where I was expected to be young, gifted, and Black.

I was reading Gandhi's *All Men Are Brothers* and Dick Gregory's *Natural Diet for Folks Who Eat: Cookin' with Mother Nature*. The concept of *ahimsa*, or "non-injury" in Sanskrit, was a doctrine of consciously doing no harm to any living being. I am reassured by the fact that we can make an active choice to embrace the interdependence of life rather than destroy it. *Ahimsa* is a whole vision of interconnected struggle that provides no easy answers nor a one-way approach. It made me aware of privileges we take for granted as humans living in the global North and the responsibility we have for the ecological, animal, and human costs of our way of life.

At that point in my life, I had reached the apex of quirky awkwardness and adding one more piece of kindling to the fire didn't hurt. In the cafeteria, I stood in line behind a tall and patchouli-scented man, and asked him if the rice he was piling onto his plate had any dairy in it. "Yes," he replied. "It's not vegan, it has a little cheese." And there I had the word and the pronunciation. When a dietitian came to give us a presentation on healthy eating and proper exercise, I mentioned to her that I was a recently converted vegan, and she explained about getting enough protein and calcium from beans, legumes, and tofu. When I arrived home for the weekend, just a month before eleventh grade, I told my parents at the dining table that I would pass on the chicken and just eat the plantains, "and, by the way, I no longer eat anything coming from an animal."

My parents went through the stages of confusion, shock, denial, anger, threats, and misguided advice. My mother resorted to making things up such as, "It's against our religion to go on diets." And my father would offer up odd alternatives, "Here, eat fish, is no meat!" My mother finally suspiciously concluded that I was under the influence of some hippie teacher or classmate.

While they certainly wouldn't take credit for inspiring my veganism, my parents do bear some responsibility for my unique identity and emergent worldview. From Guyana and Indonesia respectively, my mother and father are from two different ends of the world. They met in graduate school, married, and had my eldest brother in a matter of a few years. They studied at the University of Guyana in the era of Walter Rodney and had experienced the independence struggles of their countries. I grew up hearing about the post-colonial struggle in Africa, Asia, and the Caribbean as much as I heard about the Black Liberation struggle in the United States.

At a recent panel discussion on revolution in the twenty-first century held at a Training for Change workshop in Philadelphia, I listened to young activists describe the fact that the global South is leading the world in liberation strategies. I grew up never knowing that people could think otherwise. Becoming vegan was one of many awakenings to an authentic life of informed interdependence and respect for all life. After being a vegan for two years, I learned about the fair trade movement and attended a regional conference for United Students Against Sweatshops.

Veganism cultivates an attention to minute details of food ingredients, clothing labels, and how the things you consume are produced. This mindfulness leads to the deeper investigation of all things you consume, not only as to their material content but also the conditions in which the products are manufactured, their ecological impact, and the standard of living they create for all those on the chain of raw material, manufacturing, selling, buying, and disposing.

Being as obsessed with food as much as we vegans are, I wanted to know where the food I eat comes from, who grew it, and how it made it to my table. So it goes for clothes, shoes, jewelry, cleaning supplies, stationery, cars, appliances, home, and even the places where we shop for these items. Part of my tenure as a vegan has been spent eschewing much more. During our four years of marriage, my husband, Sahr, and I have not worn rings, as a way to draw attention to the exploitative diamond industry in Sierra Leone, where he was born. Veganism has spawned my interest in antiglobalization, antiviolence, organic agriculture, voluntary simplicity, and faith systems indigenous to West Africa and South Asia.

My first vegan friend was a white girl in my high school named Kristin. When we met, I had been vegan for six months, and the more we talked, the more I realized we'd met before in elementary school. "You went to Highlands Elementary, too!"

"Yup, I think I remember you. They used to call you Peanut," I said, feeling surprised by memory. Kristen became a vegetarian as a thirteen-year-old mainly as an animal-rights activist. Then a few years later, she started a vegan lifestyle. My journey into veganism came the summer that I was sixteen. As with our personalities, our journeys were quite different. Monkish and introspective, I became vegan through reading, revelation, and reluctance. Fast forward eight years, and my father has passed from heart disease, and my mother sends me articles from the February issue of PETA's magazine about Black vegetarians, and brags to people about her hip daughter.

Of course, it's not all happy endings. There's the matter of instant gratification. People see difference and immediately want to grasp it, or more precisely, an explanation of your state of being in their language, from their frame of reference, and in terms that seem justifiable to them. A friend who shall remain nameless was especially skilled at plucking my nerves, over-analyzing and criticizing what little she knows about my lifestyle with questions like, "How are you going to be vegan when the revolution comes?" It isn't a bad question; but I believe that being vegan *is* part of the revolution.

Sometimes I struggle and think, "Fuck this, if I could choose another life, I would." If it were in my logical power to deny the call to action from wherever it summons me, I would. For me, there is both choice and obligation. In many ways, life is a series of responsibilities, and it is our right to choose how we fulfill these obligations. There is a voice in my head that both motivates me and paralyzes me. It keeps telling me that I have to hold it down. Like professor after professor at the historically Black university I attended, it says, "To whom much is given, much is expected."

Although I also have Asian ancestry, I have lived all of my life in Black communities, and often self-identify as Black. But I am tired of the generational guilt of Black people that seems hereditary. My mother's family has a history of breast cancer, diabetes, sickle cell anemia, heart disease, hair loss, and cataracts. But the disease I fear the most is the feeling that I've failed every generation before me. The revolution we struggled for to own ourselves has also become the struggle we owe to ourselves. We owe it to ourselves to open our eyes to a future we never imagined and to see liberation in ways we did not think possible. To some degree, we are all throwbacks, just trying to make lemons into lemonade. Our elders think that we have forgotten their pain, but we remember theirs every day as we try to struggle through our own.

My journey to connect more deeply with my Indonesian heritage is something I have taken very seriously in recent years, and my experience in conflict-resolution work and peace-building has been a foundation for that.

My home state is the second smallest in the nation and arguably the most incorporated. Delaware is one of the capitals of the nation's poultry industries. We have Allen's, Tyson, Mountaire Farms, and Perdue. If you have spent a day in Kent or Sussex County, you will have seen at least one truck packed with cages of soiled, restless chickens. New Castle County, the northern part of the state, is the land of banks and chemical industries such as MBNA, Chase, and DuPont. I grew up in an apartment complex that stood alongside a creek with a chemical plant on the other side. As kids, my two older brothers and I would wade thigh deep through the murky water and return home to our parents' scolding. In retrospect, I wonder what could have been in that water and how that could relate to the fact that two of us have chronic asthma.

Living in an environment that has a stronghold on factory farming, militarization, anti-immigrant attitudes and legislation, and environmental racism has been a constant source of sadness, but is also a source of opportunity for transformation. That is one of my biggest challenges right now.

In a time of war, genocide, ecological disasters, and xenophobia, the need for a worldview that anchors daily life to the calling of hope and transformation is undeniable. My life is a continuous search for wholeness, which means healing my body and my heart, and renewing my reverence for my origins in the spirit and on earth.

12

TERROR

Tara Sophia Bahna-James

There is something
About you
That seems so young,
So trusting

This is the part of you that I most love
And the part that I am most frightened to hurt

Do you think the German poets
When speaking of the terror of love
Meant the terror that comes
From knowing
We can be harmed
Or from knowing
We have the power to hurt

Of these two terrors
The second is the greater
Humanity's deeper fear

Perhaps it is so
Even with Americans
Who arm their leaders
Not for fear of being destroyed
But because in disarming them for a moment

All the harm done would be exposed
Leaving the people
Limping homeward in shame
Like Oedipus
Who was haunted by mirrors

The terror that comes
From knowing you have the power to hurt
This is the greater fear

Perhaps this is why our dogs
Can look into our eyes
Unflinchingly
With unconditional love

It is not because they are too stupid to know that someday
We may casually break their hearts

But because they are wise enough to know that
They will never break ours

13

EYES OF THE DEAD

Mary Spears

I saw a dead body today
I was coming from work
As I came face to face
With the carcass of an adult pig
Someone had him slung over his shoulder
And was carrying him into a restaurant
The pig's eyes were wide open
As if he were shocked to death
I was stuck in my tracks
For what seemed like hours in my mind
But minutes in reality
Those eyes . . .
Those eyes must have looked at his killer
Begging for his life
Those eyes
Must have said to someone
"I have the right to exist"
So why was he dead?
I passed by
Clutching my heart
My eyes grazed the dead roasted fowl
Hanging by their necks in the window
As I neared the end of the block
There were tears in my eyes
I couldn't understand

How could people be so heartless?
How many have to die
For someone else's pleasure?
How long will it take for everyone to notice
That slavery of animals
Should not be accepted?
How many of my ancestors
Were treated like today's farm animals?
How many of us look the other way?
When I hear of calves
Being taken from their mothers
To be sold as veal
I can hear the wailing voices of mothers
Crying for their babies
As the slave master takes them away
The mother cow breastfeeds the human race
My ancestors breastfed the white race
So when I looked into those stunned eyes today,
No one could have said to me,
"What's the big deal?" "It's just an animal."
I could have remembered a time
When someone might have said the same about me

14

I AM SISTAH VEGAN

Tasha Edwards

I am definitely not your Aunt Jemima.
I am Mother Earth, Daughter of a New Day,
Sistah Vegan.

Even in my days of playing hide-and-go-seek with
Fresh produce in the local store,
Even my earliest delicacies were cruelty free,
Sunflower seeds soaked in vinegar, French fries,
Pickles with peppermint sticks,
Peanut butter and jelly.

And this is in the projects,
Where healthy eating is chased away like a suspect
And free milk and cheese was supposed to put our minds at ease
About the disease that towered above our existence in the
Absence of trees
And, even now, I knew the government was pleased to keep
So many of us, caged away from our ancestral pride,
"Giving" us food stamps to buy things that were killing us inside
While they were eating squash and eggplant and discussing
Peace in the Middle East,
While the Black population decreased and decreased because
We kept cooking with the same grease (you know the can on the stove)
Over and over again.

Did you know that the first Black mayor of Chicago was Harold Washington?
Yeah, he died from a heart attack in the middle of a meeting after being known for
Eating two pizzas at a time
Did you know that Martin Luther King was on his way to a personally requested
"Soul Food" meal when he was struck down at the hotel after
Sharing a catfish plate earlier with Ralph Abernathy?
When he spoke of being "Free At Last," did our Americanized palates ever
Come up for discussion?
Was anybody rushing to say "We Shall Overcome Cancer and Obesity"
Or are we still holding on to our story about how "Massuh" fed us the scraps
And that's all we know how to eat?

Then, who educated Dick Gregory?

So, no, I'm not Aunt Jemima and I do honor compassion and love on my plate.
Hardly am I ever haunted by what I ate.
Yes, you can eat peacefully on a small amount of change
But the question is how long you plan to maintain the lie to yourself,
Your people and health?

I am Sistah Vegan.

15

GOURMET CHEF AT McD'S

Olu Butterfly Woods

what if I can't depend on u when I need u most
which is so long ago
my people my people
I wanted to make the freshest organic cuisine
with the most delicious soulful spices
at a very affordable price
I set the table with candles and flowers
but u didn't want to come over to my place
and I wanted to be with y'all so I had to go over to where u was at
welcome to McDonald's may I take your order?

I wanted to cause u nourishment of the highest order
but u prefer ghetto take out
bone burgers & bubble-injected syrup
have u seen what is in the milkshake?
sorrow tears and blood
and what's in those nuggets?
it's not chicken
try sludge and complacency
I swear it on the yellowing of uneaten broccoli florets
on the flight pattern of fruit flies around rotting bananas
on all the grain used to feed the cows instead of starvin people
could u go to bed hungry when all that is bein served
is edible genocide
& the FDA approved abused skulls of children

Mad Chattel Disease
Over 1 billion served and growing

u non going to da phone booth superheroes
if I catch u standin on the corner again when I need all this help
how many times did u think I was gonna stand for this
5,972?
what is the smallest tragedy that can bring the sirens out?
y wait til Michael shoots Donte?
y not when Michael was in the eighth grade and didn't know how to read
and was not even eatin one vegetable a week?
what is the smallest emergency that can alarm us?
if u only pause for my squeaky wheel, my outrageous tantrum
and my too much of me hangin out of my skirt
or my grease special
and not my finer elements?

my people my people
got me feelin like a gourmet chef at McD's
I keep givin u a knife to slice the bread or cut yourself from the noose
but u keep tryna cut me up
I say can I take your order?
but u are in the middle of a drug transaction
so I repeat myself
and u hold your hand up to my face
while u proceed to tell the person in line with u
that they are ten times less than nothin
dumb as a doorknob made out of chewin gum
and they never gonna be even a roach motel receptionist
then u both proceed to look at me like my birth is the reason y
today is not a good day
and with the meanest look
order happy meals
o no

u are reading this as if this is just a poem
what if I can't depend on u when I need u most which is so long ago
they keep makin it lucrative to destroy ourselves
cuz they don't love u like I love u
call me in 2050
after your third triple bypass surgery
and the food from the dumpster, which has so many preservatives
that it will outlive our grandchildren, has been recycled
I hope I still remember my good cookin
after everything tastes like styrofoam

let's see
hot grape soda and peanut butter frankincense tea,
furry apple juice or a glass of guinea pig?
it's all Moet to me
pickled jellyfish, fermented chocolate spinach fondue, enema marmalade,
moose eyelash soup, cotton candy stuffed onions or BBQ phlegm?
as long as it tastes like chicken right?
what is worth savin?
so I saved a dirty napkin to dry my tears with
I am almost finished with my addiction to your well-being
but I will keep my heart on vibrate
nothin compares to me
standin here still holdin a free cup of water
that will not kill u
tell the children some random chick on a microphone
that they never met
sends her love
she made it from scratch

16

TO EAT OR NOT TO EAT

Thea Moore

To eat or not to eat
That stuff that we call meat
What's really goin' on
When you suckin' on the bone
Pullin at the marrow
Might as well just shoot an arrow
Straight thru your heart, your stomach, and your bowels
Why shorten your life for the taste of some cow?
Well you could just "Eat mo Chikn"
Or better yet you could be lickin
Your fingers from the juice of a cherry
Fresh mango, watermelon, or strawberry
Yet you constantly fiend
For some pork in your greens
But did you ever notice that it sho' make you mean?
You should expect some frustration
From the constant constipation
Of meat sittin' in your body for days
Yet you still act amazed
Buckin' and rollin' your eyes
Actin' so surprised
When folks ask, "Man, what crawled up in you and died?"
Well it was dead when you ate it
So that when you defecated
I passed by the bathroom and man I almost fainted

It makes me wanna holler
Smoked turkey in my collards
I won't be buyin' sickness with my hard earned dollar
How much will you pay
To have it your way?
Yeah, we know you deserve a break today
Buying self-destruction
Overlooking filthy production
Cause what happens when it's processed is anybody's guess
You can ask what they put in it but the truth they won't confess
You're better off trying to figure out what they put in Spam
Come on, ya'll do know that it's more than just spiced ham
It looks good in Kash and Karry
But it's really kinda scary
Got you believing eatin' flesh is something ordinary
But let's not forget
About suckin' on the teat
Naw brothers not your boo
But the beasts that moo
Drinking milk and eating cheese is killing you too
Yeah I know you a breast man
But I'm tryin to help you understand
Killin' you with animal products is part of the master plan
While you sippin' animal secretions
That's furthering your deletion
They're taking plans of mass genocide to the ultimate completion
Propaganda machines so well built
That you don't even feel no guilt
As you consume the trash they feed you and then you ask if they "Got Milk?"

It's by their orchestration
To remove our population
Don't think it's only rumors

Profuse bleeding in her bloomers
Meat and dairy that she's eating feeding fibroids and the tumors
Sisters dying, and there's no room
For new life in her to bloom
Suffering pain and agony of assault against the womb
Doin' all they can to prevent the birth
Of yet one more from the Mothers of Earth
Ain't no mercy for those who menstruate
But my brothers ya'll ain't safe
As you chew upon that steak
That's jackin' up your prostate
You'll be tryin' to bust a nut when you can't even bust a grape
Meat will kill and weaken you mind, body, and spirit
I'm tryin' to tell you true but you still ain't tryin' to hear it

They tell you that pork is the other white meat
Don't fall for the okey doke but after me repeat
Lips that touch swine will never touch mine
Open up that third eye and quit walkin' around blind

For me it's plain and simple
Animal products defile the temple
As I look at that pot belly
Ain't no way that you can tell me
Veganism is not the solution
To rid your body of pollution
It's time to take some action
To eliminate the putrefaction

I'm not here to try to scorn ya
Just don't say I didn't warn ya
You may laugh at what I'm eatin'
But hear the truth in what I'm speakin'

17

STOP FEEDING ME YOUR BULLSH*T

Tishana Joy Trainor

every time I hear a commercial
telling me milk does my body good
i become physically ill

every time i see signs for
Whopper with cheese
i wanna throw up

i am lactose intolerant
i am also bullsh*t intolerant

doctors told my parents
to keep feeding me the milk
even though dairy made me ill
and my parents felt obligated
for the sake of my health

i suffered for years
being forced to
drink the milk
eat the cheese
and even though I liked yogurt
it still tore me up

one day i got over it

when I heard myself tell my children to
drink the milk
eat the cheese
and i was buying yogurt

i put it all back
researched alternatives
found out it wasn't meant for us
and cut that bullsh*t out

as our health improved
i vowed to never let the pressures of media
affect my health or
the health of my children

drinking 3 glasses of cow's milk
can't help you lose weight
eating cheese on your salad or yogurt
can't help you slim your waist down
it's all bullsh*t

don't drink the milk
don't eat the cheese
don't buy the yogurt
don't believe the media hype

18

"WHAT YOU COOKING, GRANDMA?"

Nia Yaa

I had just come inside from playing and saw my grandmother in the kitchen doing her thing. She loved to cook, but this time I was surprised by the odor coming from the kitchen. She just gave me a funny look and kept on working. She knew what was coming; I was known for asking a million questions and not stopping until I got to the truth.

"It's chitlins, baby."

I had never heard of that, so I asked, "What is chitlins?" I knew my grandmother ate things that I had never heard of before—pig feet, tripe, fatback, gizzards—all of which my weak stomach could not tolerate.

She said, "It comes from a pig."

I had to ask, "So why does it smell like that?"

She went on, explaining that it was pig intestines and that she was cleaning them. I said, "It smells like poop," and she said that was what it was. That was enough for me. I went back outside into some fresh air, thinking that was not something I would be eating. I just never had the desire to eat that kind of stuff. Later that evening, when I saw the chitlins on the table, they appeared to shake like Jell-O, and I had to fight my nausea. After a few prior episodes, my grandma knew not to push certain foods on me. Once again, she bent the "you have to try everything at least once" rule. Thank you, Grandma.

I refer to myself as a natural vegetarian, because I was a "picky" eater and have always eaten more fruit than candies or pastries and more veggies than meat. When I was thirteen, my mother announced that she was going to eat only chicken and fish—no more pork, beef, or other red meat. A friend of hers told her the truth about the meat industry and that it is not healthy to consume meat every day. My mother passed the message on to me. She said that pigs carry worms and that the Old Testament says we should not eat animals with hooves. She said the pig was made of a cat, a rat, and a dog, and that all meat is processed with hormones and injected with drugs and steroids. She said meat was full of diseases because of the way animals are raised and mistreated. After hearing this news, my mother said, the next time she saw a piece of beef on her plate, she could see the cow's eyes looking at her, and she decided then that she would not eat beef again. I have seen my mother eat pork only once since then: it was at a holiday dinner, and she paid for it the next day.

Vegetarianism was a natural transition for me. Not eating red meat was no problem, since my diet as a teenager consisted mostly of fruit, salad, French fries, and Oodles of Noodles. I did eat chicken, fish, and cheese about twice a week for the next five years. It was hard to resist Harold's chicken, pizza, and other fast food as a teenager, but I stopped eating burgers. I remember hearing rumors that they were putting weird things in the fast-food burgers at the time. I was never too crazy about steak, and my mother did not raise me on fast food or snacks (thank God). She was from the country, so we ate plenty of fruits and vegetables every day. I am grateful that I never became a sugar addict and still eat very few sweets or other junk food to this day.

Right after I graduated from high school, my grandfather passed away from colon cancer. I didn't know much about a colon until that time. When it was explained to me what colon cancer was, I thought about the amount of food I saw him consume after a day of hard work. He loved biscuits in gravy and grease, fatback, and ham. He raised pigs sometimes, and there would be two different meats, plenty of vegetables, potatoes or yams, biscuits, and more on the dinner table every night. I was always amazed at the amount of food my family in the country ate compared to us in the city, where we had three-course meals for dinner. I think it was money and access to the variety of food, as well as the need to adapt to the different culture, in the city. I now understand that in the south they had the eating habits of our enslaved ancestors. Those habits are different from the American habits that we were introduced to in the north. They were both very different from the eating habits of our ancestors, who lived from the fruits and greens of the earth. My grandfather did heavy labor, so I know he needed plenty of energy to keep him going. Peace be with you, Papa. There was a lesson for me in his transition—I remembered what we learned about beef and pork, and I realized there was truth to it.

Soon after my grandfather's demise, my mother and I decided we were going to stop eating all meats and their byproducts, and become vegetarians. I went to one of her Rastafarian friends to learn how to cook vegetarian food. I learned to make tofu, gluten, banana pudding, stir-fry, natural salve for my skin, and more. I learned about living *Ital*, which you could say is a Caribbean word for "vegan." Being Ital is about being natural and in tune with the Most High and all of nature. Some of the main principles of being Ital that I learned and adapted are:

1. Your body is a holy temple made in the image of the Most High; therefore, you should not put any flesh, chemical, poisons (drugs), or other foreign substances in it.
2. Don't eat anything that can walk, swim, fly, or crawl, or anything that has eyes.
3. Live in harmony with nature; stay outside as much as possible.
4. Be kind and take care of Mother Earth and her gifts: the animals, plants, insects, water, land, metals, etc.
5. Be one with the Universe and live with respect and love for all.
6. Support individuals and businesses with this similar mindset, so a righteous Ital community can grow.

These lessons helped me to understand the animal-rights aspect of being a vegetarian. I remembered seeing animals packed on farms and in trucks. They were being treated just like our enslaved ancestors. I began to research preservatives and how they are used for mind control and genocide. I began to read all labels and buy foods with the "K" for kosher (no pork). I learned about organic food and how to farm for myself as well. I started with a small herb garden of peppermint, sage, and lavender. Each year I would experiment with greens, slips of cucumbers, tomatoes, and okra. I had entered into a new world, and I loved it. I made a commitment to buy things that were not tested on animals or full of preservatives and chemicals. I stopped buying commercial soap, deodorant, toothpaste, skin and hair products, and began to make my own or buy from other Black businesses, which provided better quality goods. My life was gradually transforming, and I began to feel the benefits of the change. I gained more energy, and I didn't experience the congestion and sore throats I had suffered since childhood. This was a journey that led me to go deeper and learn more.

My vegetarian menu was enhanced with an East Indian cooking class. One thing the teacher said that I will not forget was that this is the only country that makes gravy out of flour and water. She told us that Americans have the worst eating habits and more overweight people than any other country in the world. She went on to show us how to make a spicy and delectable gravy by simmering onion, garlic, tomato, and spices, which was the base of many of East Indian dishes. The food was so colorful, saucy, and just plain good. I was motivated to learn to prepare foods from other countries in Africa, Asia, and Latin America, where the people have more natural lifestyles and eat more vegetables. I began to study spiritual systems from around the world and found that dietary laws exist in all of them. I learned that, in many countries, meat is traditionally eaten only after a community ritual where an animal has been sacrificed. So there is a large variety of vegetarian dishes to try from around the world.

At first, it was difficult to find tofu and other organic foods. You could not buy tofu at the grocery store back then. It took determination and creativity to endure this challenge. I learned to shop at Asian, Latin, and farmer's markets. I find the food is fresher, there's more variety, the food has fewer pesticides and GMOs, and it's less expensive than the regular grocery stores. The health food stores were always in white neighborhoods, difficult to get to, and very expensive. However, you may not be able to find anywhere else certain things you need as a vegetarian. I would occasionally participate in food co-ops, where a group of us would get together to order food in bulk. It was a great concept, but difficult to keep consistent for one reason or another.

More challenges came from family members, who seemed to believe I wasn't eating enough. They would offer meat to me as a joke, and it was a few years before they began to offer alternatives for my family at the family gatherings. Many times I had to prepare food for myself, which was cool, because it gave the others a chance to taste something different. It didn't take me long to learn that if I cheated and ate something I hadn't eaten in a while, my body wouldn't accept it easily.

One outstanding memory I have was the last time I ate eggs. I was taking a six a.m. flight from a visit with my father, and he decided to make me an egg sandwich for the ride to the airport. I thought I needed to put something in my stomach, because I had a long flight ahead of me, so I just ate it. It was definitely the worst airplane ride I have ever had. My stomach grumbled, gurgled, and griped for the entire ride. Needless to say, I learned a valuable lesson: once you clean your body and stop eating certain foods, your body will not easily accept them again.

I found it a blessing to have the knowledge of living naturally and to be able to pass on this lifestyle to the next generation. I breastfed my four children. I never understood why a mother would make a baby wait while she fixed a bottle of cow's milk when God gives it to mothers ready-made. I feel that breastfed and organic vegetarian babies tend to be less fussy, have better coordination and movement, and learn faster than many children raised on animal products. I didn't feed my children baby food from the store, either. Instead, I steamed and mashed fresh fruits and vegetables for them myself. I have raised them on fresh, mostly organic fruits, vegetables and legumes, with an occasional treat followed by some cleansing tea.

I've heard enough comments about my children at the park and other places to support my beliefs, though I didn't get much support from my family in the beginning. They gave me a hard time about breastfeeding, saying I needed to give them a "bottle of regular milk." They would sometimes give them meat when I wasn't around—especially my older sons. I never bought candy for my children, but many people would offer it to them at the bank, the store, at friends' houses, and so on. (You'd be surprised at how many people think they are doing good by offering candy to a child.) I didn't like going to the store with my children because we had to pass so many aisles full of stuff we don't eat, but they thought they wanted to try. When they got older, I taught my children to read labels and learn about the preservatives we must avoid. This made the store trips much easier.

My older sons, however, have ventured off the path. They eat some meat, but only occasionally, because they understand what it does to their bodies. My oldest son went to visit a relative and called me to help him ease his constipation after a week of heavy eating. He learned to take more caution with what he puts into his temple. I'm grateful that my second son is quick to catch the smell of animal in any food we are served. My youngest son is very proud to be a vegetarian and will tell anyone what he cannot eat. I am so pleased with his attitude and strength.

My children rarely get sick, and I give thanks and praise that they have no health problems. They have not gotten vaccinations because it is against our beliefs, so they have a religious exemption for school. My Spirit will not allow me to let anyone violate their body temples with poisons. I did research on vaccinations fifteen years ago, before they began adding even more to the list of stuff they are giving our youth, and I could not let them be injected with a live virus, chemicals I have not heard of, and other preservatives at such a young age. It just doesn't make sense to me. Instead, I build their immune systems with garlic, lemon, hot peppers, vitamin C, echinacea, and other herbs on a daily basis. They take their herbs with no problem, even raw garlic and cayenne, because I started them off that way when they were little, and they don't know anything else as their medicine. We don't use any over-the-counter medicines and go to the doctor only for regular physicals.

I was told by my spiritual mothers that I was my children's first teacher and that if I wanted them to be like me, I should keep them with me at all times until they got older. I homeschooled them while they were young, and I worked with or taught at the private, African-centered schools they attended when they were older. I feel it is very important to raise my children with these "new ways" that help to break the cycle of oppression and are really the ways of our ancestors.

The lessons grew as I connected with more spiritual teachers. Becoming a vegetarian and living a natural lifestyle opened other paths in my life. I began to learn about African history and African spirituality. I chose to wear locks to express my natural lifestyle. I learned to make jewelry and other crafts I could sell, so I could be close to my children. I made a commitment to myself to do all I could to help our people, to buy everything from Black businesses when I could, and to stop supporting my oppression by continuing to make my oppressors rich. I saw that most of the stuff they were selling was damaging or full of chemicals, so I learned to make clothes, soap, oils for our skin and hair, tooth powder, deodorant, etc. I also learned to fast, which I was told was a way to make a sacrifice to the Most High and should be done often to keep our body temples pure and clean. My first fast was for three days, with three people, with my spiritual mother as a guide. It was a beautiful and transforming experience for me, and I knew this fast would not be my last.

I was introduced to raw foodism in Atlanta, while staying with a beautiful raw-food couple and their baby. I saw the sistah feeding her baby avocado and garlic, and that the baby was very healthy and happy and really enjoying it. The couple's five-year-old daughter had seen my five-year-old son eating chips (from the health food store), and asked him, "Why are you eating that garbage?" I was stunned and very curious about this raw-food lifestyle.

One day I was taken to a large house in the West End. We sat in a large room with three or four other people, just hanging out. Then, all of a sudden, folk just started arriving like someone had rung the dinner bell. The room filled up, and the sistahs came from the kitchen with trays of colorful, sweet-smelling raw food—seaweed salad, raw potato salad, nut pâté, carrot tuna, and raw blueberry pie—and I was hooked. I say that raw food is some of the best food ever, and raw-food people are some of the most beautiful spirits you'll ever meet.

Around this time that I got *Heal Thyself: For Health and Longevity* by Queen Afua. I went to visit my grandmother while reading it, and I couldn't put it down. She asked me what I was reading, and I told her, "This book is going to change my life." I felt that every word Queen wrote resonated with my spirit, and I'm so grateful to have found something that confirmed and contributed so much to my vegetarian lifestyle. It proved that you can be healthy and prevent disease, and I changed even more. I began to drink more herbal teas and consciously ate more fruit and vegetables. I began to eat a salad every day and used raw garlic like crazy. I acquired vegetarian cookbooks and herb books and began to be more creative and versatile with our menu. My children fasted, learned to do yoga, and began to meditate as well.

I was blessed to meet Queen Afua in 1997 at the African Street Festival in Brooklyn. She was (and still is) a bright and shining light. She shared her "Breath of Spring" formula with us, which immediately lifts your energy and opens up your air passages. Then she blessed me with encouraging words: to be strong and diligent and to continue on the path. Meeting Queen made a lasting impression on me, and I left feeling her presence and energy. Meeting queens who have been vegan, spiritual, strong, and beautiful has definitely influenced my lifestyle and let me know it is right. That memory continues to inspire and motivate me to grow and share with others about healthy living.

When Queen Afua's *Sacred Woman: A Guide to Healing the Feminine Body, Mind, and Spirit* came out, we started a Sacred Woman Circle in Richmond, Virginia. We met to pray, discuss, heal, dance, sing, meditate, and bless our dis-ease away. We fasted and sometimes had over twenty sistahs in a meeting. It was a beautiful experience and most of us from the core group became certified in alternative healing practices. I later went to Washington, D.C., to go through the Sacred Woman Gateways with the *Heal Thyself* priestess there. That was an uplifting and rejuvenating experience for me, and I recommend to all sistahs to go through the Gateways for purification of your mind, heart, body, and spirit.

In my opinion, the Gateways are like the rites of passage that we would have gone through if we had been raised in our traditions. We met for eleven weeks, including orientation and graduation ceremony. This time I fasted as a sacrifice to the Most High and for spiritual growth, cleansing, and purification. I found it to be more powerful to fast with a group. Having the support of other sistahs, chanting and praying together, is enlightening. We also went to New York City for a soul sweat and to New Jersey for a Kemetic full moon ritual. The highlight was the graduation initiation ceremony, where we revealed our lessons to our community and family and accepted the charge to stay on our throne.

There is so much to learn, I find it necessary to continue to take classes to develop myself. Through that experience, I have changed the way I look at life in a lot of ways. I was tested and still go through tests, but I remember to keep my heart light, fast, meditate, and pray through it all. Sacred Woman is a solution for many single Black mothers who have to do it all: dealing with the household, bills, and the children, and having little time for themselves. Sacred Woman not only helps you find balance or *ma'at*, it also gives you tools to help you in different situations as well.

I have gone through six months of training with Queen Afua as a fasting and detox therapist, a Heal Thyself Ambassador of Wellness. I am now on a fifty to seventy-five percent raw-food lifestyle (I don't like to say "die-t," because I want to live and eat live food). I've been teaching vegetarian cooking classes for about ten years. I've also taught holistic health to children at private African-centered schools and other private organizations. One of my favorite things is to share healthful eating practices with children, as well as information on yoga, meditation, and the environment. I've been known to help young people change their minds and eating habits, to stop eating pork and other meat as well. I have a cousin whose mother still hasn't forgiven me for telling her daughter the truth about pork. She refused to eat it when she got home after visiting my house years ago.

I've had the joy of watching other family members change their eating habits as well. My father has gradually stopped eating fried food and other junk, after years of persuasion.

He even had his first colonic this year, and he felt so good he recommended his friends have one, too. Even my grandmother has changed some. She reads about herbs and drinks her tea, and she loves Queen Afua's "Breath of Spring." She hasn't stopped eating meat, but she has changed her habits and challenges what the doctors tell her, too. She has been doing her own research. I give thanks for that.

We have a Sacred Ital family. I am raising my children to be strong and natural. They can see the positive effects our eating habits have had on our overall wellness. We strive to stay Ital and pure, even though the level of toxicity is very high in our environment and in the foods we eat (with the pesticides and GMO products, it is hard to find real food). We fast, pray, and take blood-cleansing and other tonics every week. We play and work in nature, recycle and take care of the earth. We look forward to the summer gardens and to the day when we can grow even more of our own food. I feel this lifestyle will make us stronger as people, because we have to overcome many obstacles to maintain our lifestyle. It is the same thing our ancestors have been doing for thousands of years—fighting to maintain their ways and culture while living among others.

My dream is to build a self-sustaining, eco-friendly African community, with a large farm and greenhouse, fresh spring or well water, solar-powered homes, and our own businesses and schools. There are several cities with European-based communities—Asheville, North Carolina; Santa Fe, New Mexico; and many others—who do this. We cannot expect others to do this for us. We have to create institutions for ourselves, our children, and our future. I feel it is important for our community to change our eating habits and lifestyle in order to prepare for the changes that are coming to the world in the future. Revolution means change, and we need a spiritual revolution that will bring an attitude of peace and Divine Love to replace the years of violence, aggression, and oppression that have threatened the balance of Mother Earth. We have to stop the raping and destruction of the land and nature for the meat, and other industries. If the masses of people embrace the vegetarian lifestyle, we have a chance to save the world and make a better living space for us all.

19

THE FOOD AND SEX LINK

Angelique Shofar

The aromatic fragrance of lemon, lily, and lavender drifted under my nose, while small chunks of pineapple, grapes, and bananas were teasingly popped into my mouth. Blindfolded, I savored the flavors and textures with my tongue and saliva. Maracas and the soft rhythmic thump of a drum penetrated my ears, and fabrics, flower petals, and jets of water brushed my skin. His lips touched mine. Soon we were both carried into the currents of the sea of love.

I was born and raised in a West African tradition and culture, and my desire to eat has always had an emotional edge. I often felt too overwhelmed to pause and discern what truly caused the pulsations below my navel or the tingling at the base of my neck. Instead, I sought comfort and sensuality through food. As I placed each portion in my mouth, my tastebuds would vibrate. My body was starved, but mostly it was not for food, but a yearning for the pure pleasure and satisfaction of human touch. My body was calling for the magical erotic moment that induces and seduces the sexy dancer within.

Food and sex can both be healthy and nourishing when consumed in balanced quantities and with utmost awareness. However, in contemporary culture, we have sacrificed quality for convenience and in doing so have missed out on experiencing and understanding the erotic nature of food. We have yet to seize, explore, and master fully the link between sex and food: to challenge ourselves to move beyond the advertisements and billboards promising sensual pleasure by simple over-indulgence, and the inevitable condemnation of society if we take too much. We need to recognize that food is perhaps the main vehicle for how we feel about our bodies and souls, how we respond sexually to ourselves and each other, and how we choose to interact with the world around us. When our choice of food is animalistic in nature, then our sexual nature will naturally conform. Like a hungry, aggressive animal in pursuit of its prey, our sexual appetite mimics the nature of our food through visible and not so visible acts of violence and destruction. With these considerations in place, is it not safe to declare that food and sex share a common ground?

As many societies have noted, eating can be highly erotic, akin in many ways to lovemaking. Preparing and serving our food, decorating and enhancing it with spices and mingling the different flavors, are like the foreplay that prepares us for the profound pleasures of the merging of two bodies. Saliva enhances the potency of those pleasurable moments in both lovemaking and eating. When we eat from the same bowl or calabash (a tradition with roots in African culture) we cultivate intimacy, trust, and open the way to deeper physical, emotional, and spiritual pleasure with our partner.

My first experiment with the voluptuousness of sensuality was with my girlfriend. I first placed a blindfold over her eyes and put on soothing music. I filled a bowl with grapes and poured liqueur into a small cup. (I chose peach schnapps, but any will do.) I speared a grape on a toothpick, dipped it in the liqueur, and raised it to my partner's nostrils, encouraging her to guess what it was. Her body glowed, and a ripple of energy coursed through her as I then offered the grape's soft roundness to the curves of her lips, leaving trails of the liqueur's sweet burn upon them, then pressed the grape against her lips until they parted and enveloped it. Finally, I dipped my finger into the liqueur and stroked the contour of my girlfriend's lips very gently. We said nothing as she absorbed the grape into her body.

By simply slowing down and creating ritual around eating, such as above, we can begin to nourish our physical body, temper our emotions, sharpen our minds, purify our energy field, and cultivate peace. We will be able to listen better to the the messages our body brings us every day. We need to return to the healing powers of food and sex as our first sources of medicine.

Slowing down to eat is a fundamental aspect of Tantric living. We can be much healthier physically and sensually if we chew our food properly and eat consciously. I used to have "dates" with myself. I would turn my telephone ringer off and take my own sweet time cooking dinner and preparing the table for me, I, and myself! While I was training to become a yoga teacher, we students practiced the art of conscious eating, which required total focus on each bite, chew, and act of swallowing while eating in complete silence. This combination allows the body to digest the food and route the nutrients—a process often disrupted by external distractions and activities while eating. Having a date with myself in the kitchen and conscious eating were both powerful and pleasurably quiet, where stimulation came from the senses rather than words.

The Tantric tradition favors eating in moderation and choosing food that is seasonal. When we are present within ourselves, we can hear and feel the body more clearly. Conscious cooking and conscious eating bring out the erotic power in food that may differ from person to person. In those moments, the messages we receive from our foods can open us to their erotic and healthy energies, allowing us to understand the unique language of each item we place in our bodies, and whether it's healthy or destructive.

The Hatha Yoga tradition says that one should refrain from eating excessively acid, bitter, salty, or pungent foods. Rishi Gheranda advises that "half the stomach should be filled with food, one quarter with water or other liquid, and one quarter should be empty to aid the practice of breath control" (see Gitananda Yoga Newsletter Downunder, June 2008, Vol 3. No. 2). How do you measure? you're probably asking. Your body knows: listen and trust it.

The mental attitude of the person preparing the food pervades each item like the herbs and seasonings that penetrate the outer layers of our edibles. Likewise, *how* we eat has a strong influence on the entire digestive process. Consuming food while we're upset or sitting before the television or behind the wheel takes away from the sacramental quality of eating. We can enhance sacred moments by creating purpose in the preparation of food and at the table. I always fill my food with light and positive words to raise its vibrations—blessing its source and the many people that played a role in its journey from the earth to my mouth. Borrowing Dr. Masaru Emoto's concepts in his book *The Hidden Messages of Water*, I speak the language of love and gratitude to my food to change its energetic condition.

Rushing to make quick meals deprives us of the healing and aphrodisiacal properties of cooking. Those moments of food preparation can be a meditation, where we savor precious seconds. Feel the texture of the greens, explore the rough surface of root foods; pay attention to the way yellow peppers or red tomatoes radiate their colors and how they make you feel;

add spices to awaken your sense of smell. All these acts will ensure you bring out the sensuality that abounds in food.

Having sex and preparing food are both alchemical processes that create soulful magic. Instead of beakers and flasks, the chef works with pots and pans; instead of wands, the chef uses giant spoons and forks to transform the elements of earth, air, fire and water, combining raw and/or non-raw foods in their concoctions. Set free to experiment and play, a chef can put together any two edible things and make something new and often tastier than each separate component. Like the alchemist, the cook transforms matter through the application of fire, blending, emulsifying, separating, coagulating, macerating, and aerating, while adding a pinch of heart and a deeper part of themselves.

Like all good spells, my meal preparation begins with the desire to travel. Do I have a yearning for something spicy, warm, light, or colorful? Or does my body need something cool and refreshing to balance the summer heat? Do I want to travel to Asia, Africa, the Mediterranean, Central America, or stay right here in the United States? And is my body in sync with the wild imagination of my mind?

The same applies to creative lovemaking: with my partner I can swim the depths of the oceans and climb the majestic mountains of the world. Conscious sex can reveal its alchemical dimensions when done intently and ritualistically. Parallel to the process of cooking, two lovers can utilize the elements of nature in their lovemaking to create anything their heart desires. When the orgasms of partners are in sync, a cosmic field is opened as the energies of both individuals merge. Though the results from the alchemy of sex may materialize only over time, two lovers can nonetheless generate love, compassion, and deep understanding; they can plant the most wonderful seed that will incubate and be brought forth as a child or manifest as a creative concept. The beauty of the alchemy of sex is that there is no before or after, only the eternal now.

One of my fun and easiest alchemies is a herb-y fruit salad that combines fresh lettuce and salad leaves of baby leaf spinach, red chard, green lettuce, and Greek cress, with strawberries, peaches, apples, and a dice of raw almonds, topped with a simple fresh lime and pineapple juice dressing. I begin with a prayer that honors the earth and all those who played a role in getting the produce into my kitchen. Then I fill the dish with light and love to raise the vibrations to awaken the flavors and purify each ingredient. Feeding each other is a great way to share and savor the magical taste of this sexy salad. Praying and eating together offer blessings and create pure intentions as the participation transmutes the ingredients or transforms the energy from something of one value into a substance of even greater value. Remember: pick both your foods and your sex/love partner wisely and intently.

APHRODISIACS

Meals rich in fruits and vegetables provide beneficial nutrients that keep organs in peak condition and energy at maximum levels, both of which are essential for lovemaking. Most directly linking food and sex are aphrodisiacs, which have been used for thousands of years to seduce, spice up a sex life, improve potency, and remedy infertility and sterility. They can be classified in two main groups: 1) psycho-physiological—visual, tactile, olfactory, aural; and 2) internal—stemming from food, alcoholic drinks, drugs, love potions, and medical preparations. There follow a number of vegan, aphrodisiac foods.

Almond
A symbol of fertility throughout the ages. The aroma is said to inspire passion in a woman. It is a major source of essential fatty acids, providing the basis for the healthy production of male hormones essential to regulating sex drive. Try adding marzipan (almond paste) or sliced almonds to an erotic desert for a sexual appetizer and treat.

Asparagus
Rich in vitamin E, this vegetable has been known to stimulate the production of women's and men's sex hormones essential for a healthy sex life. It is said that people who eat a lot of asparagus also have many lovers.

Avocado
The Aztecs called the avocado tree *Ahuacuati,* which means "testicle tree," because they thought the fruit hanging in pairs looked like the male's testicles. This fruit has a sensuous texture. Simply serve in slices, adding a small amount of olive oil, sea salt, and freshly ground pepper.

Bananas

Bananas are rich in potassium and B vitamins, necessary for sex-hormone production. The banana flower with its amazing phallic shape adds to the popularity of the banana as an aphrodisiac food. Many women are friends with this fruit as their masturbation tool.

Basil (sweet basil)

Basil is said to stimulate the sex drive and boost fertility, and to produce a general sense of well-being for body and mind. Most curiously of all, its scent is supposed to drive us wild! In fact, basil oil was once employed by Mediterranean prostitutes as a perfume to attract customers! Take me to Asia, and it's no wonder why I go crazy for Thai food. The popular spice basil (*Ocimum basilicum*) also possesses aphrodisiac powers and contains essential oils, tannins, and vitamins.

Cardamom

Cardamom cools the body when it is hot and warms it when it is cold. Ancient queens such as Cleopatra used to take baths in it.

Chili Peppers

Capsaicin is the chemical ingredient responsible for the hot effect of the chili pepper. It stimulates nerve endings, raises your pulse, and makes you sweat. It is believed that eating hot foods such as chili peppers can evoke the release of endorphins, which create a natural high conducive to the feelings you have during lovemaking. It contains a lot of vitamin C and also has irritating effects on membranes and the urogenital area, so avoid overdosage.

Cayenne Peppers

Cayenne peppers also contain capsaicin. When cayenne is ingested, it dilates blood vessels, which allows increased blood flow throughout the body, especially in the major organs. The male penis benefits greatly from the ingestion of cayenne. It is a widely held belief that cayenne aids in longer lasting erections, with stronger ejaculations and more intense orgasms.

Celery

Celery is considered an excellent food to ramp up sexual stimulation since it boosts a powerful substance known as androsterone—an odorless hormone released through male perspiration. If you are partnered with a man, I bet you forgot that your man's sweat has driven you wild many times: perhaps the same effect that a dozen red roses and a bottle of Champagne apparently have!

Durian fruit

This fruit has an intriguing reputation in Southeast Asia as having aphrodisiac properties. It is not clear whether this is attributed to some substance in the fruit pulp.

Garlic

It may be bad on the breath but it's surely good on the sex drive. It is better if both parties love and enjoy the benefits of garlic. This way there is no clash of the breath. Garlic contains high levels of allicin—a compound that can improve blood flow to the sexual organs. Note: Don't just munch on big cloves of raw garlic. Allicin is only produced through the enzyme reaction, once garlic has been chopped.

Oats

Oats are known to increase your libido by the time you go to bed. The key is to eat oats each day for breakfast. Oats have been proven to stimulate the human libido in both males and females. The common group of oats is from the grass family. The oat family includes rice, whole wheat, rye, and barley, to name a few. Oats are not only known to lower cholesterol, but also to aid stamina and longevity in the human libido. Last longer with oats in your diet.

Pineapple

Diuretic invigoration! Pineapple has a great digestive and purifying effect and is high in bromelain. Use fresh fruit juice. For aphrodisiac effects to work, eat pineapple with chili powder or mixed with agave nectar and rum. A small glass taken daily will suffice.

Pomegranate

The pomegranate with its many seeds has been a symbol of fertility (and a well-known aphrodisiac) for thousands of years in many ancient cultures. For example, in China, the pomegranate stands for wealth and a large, healthy family. The pomegranate was discovered around 1000 BCE, making it one of the oldest fruits on the planet. From China it found its way to Italy and then to Spain and England. The Spanish planted the first pomegranate tree in the U.S. Not only was the fruit of the pomegranate used, but the ancient Romans also employed the husk as a kind of leather.

Sea bean

Found in South America and Africa, the sea bean is a psychedelic edible, and the beans have aphrodisiac qualities. They are ingested or smoked instead of marijuana. In ancient America, these beans were used in magic and rituals and have been found in prehistoric graves. The active substance is L-betonicine.

Squash

Squash has a diuretic, invigorating effect, and the seeds are an aphrodisiac for women. In Ayurvedic and Tantric systems, squash seeds are eaten during love rituals. The seeds contain fatty oil, protein, and vitamin E that is important for healthy sexuality.

Sweet potato

Another invigorator! Excessive consumption stimulates the woman's sex drive.

Thorn apple

Thorn apple is considered a strong psychedelic, very erotic, a plant of prophesy and witches. Leaves or flowers are brewed into tea, the seeds are eaten, the herbage smoked. All species and all parts contain highly active tropane alkaloids.

Wild lettuce

Found in Europe and North America, wild lettuce has a narcotic effect and the dried sap is smoked for ritual purposes and as a sexual stimulant. Wild lettuce contains an alkaloid lactusin, which has qualities that are similar to morphine.

DECLINING LIBIDO

Diets low in fat cause low libido because fats are building blocks for hormones. Hydrogenated oils and fats interfere with pleasure and a good life. Good fats are essential to pleasure. In addition, sugar overload causes blood sugar fluctuations that decrease energy and overall well-being and sexual health. Sugar may also compromise the neurological and circulatory actions that are vital for healthy performance. The good news is that there are many delicious and healthy sugar alternatives. Do watch out for crash diets, as they will certainly collapse your sex drive. A sudden drop in daily caloric or nutrient intake will confuse the body and cause a decline in sex hormones, along with a lagging libido.

Stay away from fried foods and rich cream sauces. They can leave us feeling more sluggish than sexy. Too much sugar, salt, saturated fat, and highly processed food is linked to frigidity, difficulty reaching orgasm, and lack of interest in sex. Scaling back on these foods will help revive and preserve sexual vitality and enhance total well-being.

Put a cap on the overindulgence of alcohol and coffee, and skip tobacco completely. These "pleasure drugs" take away from the depths, experience, and authenticity of feelings and the lovemaking act. Some indulgences are beneficial. The rich, delicious decadence known as chocolate contains phenylalanine, an amino acid that raises the body's endorphins—our natural antidepressants. Enjoyed in moderation, a few pieces can lift libido, providing a tantalizing prelude to sex. A sexy diet is one that is filled with vibrant foods to increase libido.

Indulge in a blend that is out of this world: eating and making love. Use food creatively while making love! The key is to slow down and allow oneself to savor the feelings and sensations that each moment brings.

Sensuality and peace begin on the plate!

20

JOURNEY TO VEGANISM

Ajowa Nzinga Ifateyo

PART ONE: TIPS FOR SELF-OBSERVATION

1. In bed, while you're still in the back between sleep and awake—before you open your eyes—ask yourself how you feel. Put your attention generally in the body. If you have time, you can put your attention on every organ and ask the same question. Or say, since we're working with the liver, you can just check in with that one. Notice where you see a flash of color, a thought, a picture, or you get a feeling. You may not get anything the first several times; that's okay. Keep trying.

2. In the bathroom, after you urinate, smell the toilet paper after you wipe. Notice the smell of your urine. Does it have a smell? Is it subtle or loud (when you eat asparagus your urine will be very loud!)? What color is it? Is it clear, pale yellow or neon yellow (if you take B vitamins it will be very yellow)? If you defecate, notice the consistency. Is it hard and dry? Or soft or "medium"? When I don't drink enough water, I get a dry texture. This is how I know I am not getting enough water. Before you flush, look at it. Do you have little hard balls of shit coming out, or turds? The "rocks," as I call them, mean I am constipated. I also have mild diverticulosis (probably developed when I did the liquid protein diet in the 1970s and became badly constipated because I didn't eat for thirty days). Is it brown, golden-brown, green, or black? Supposedly, the healthy color is golden brown, but if you eat greens, the stool will be green, and if you eat beets, the water will be tinged red. Black stools could be an indication of a problem (possibly a sign of internal bleeding), but I notice when I take iron, my stools are dark brown, nearly black. Notice the smell. Is it putrid? If so, you may need a colon cleanse. When you're cleaned out well, you'll be able to smell onions and other foods you eat. As a rule,

your stool should not stink loudly. Is there undigested matter in there? Chew more. Eating more nuts on this diet, I noticed my stools were more "grainy."

3. Look at yourself in the mirror. Look at your face overall, then into your eyes. Are the whites clear, dull, watery? Are there red veins? Brown spots? Is there a yellow tinge? Look deep into the pupils. Meet your Observer, the higher self, the one who records everything you think, say, hear, and feel. Supposedly, this is available to us if we learn to access it. While you're checking her out, tell yourself "I love you." Check the corners for crow's feet. Smile to notice more. Look under the eyes. Are there bags? How full are they? Are they a different color than the rest of your face?

4. Look at your nose. Is the tip full, shiny? On the side creases, are there little white fat deposits? Take your nail and scrape. Look around the nose, particularly under the nostrils. Is the skin puckering?

5. Look at your lips. Are they wrinkly? Fat? How's the color? If you've got anything else on your face, such as moles, DPNs (the growths that look like flesh-colored moles but aren't), scars, etc., look at them. Are they any different?

6. Now look at your overall face again. Anything stand out? What sense do you get from yourself? How do you think other people would see you?

7. If you have full-length mirror in your bedroom, notice how your body looks. Never say negative things about yourself because that Observer records everything. Your thoughts are a command to the unconscious mind. If you say you're fat and ugly, then the unconscious continues to manufacture those states because that's what you've told it. Words are very powerful. Tell yourself how beautiful you are (even if you don't believe it). Tell your body how much you love it.

8. Before you step outside your door, determine what kind of day you're going to have. Remember the Observer. She's listening to your thoughts. Even if it's raining or you know you're in for a busy day, say, "I'm having a wonderful day." Notice your attitude during the day.

9. During the day, notice how you feel after you eat. Are you sluggish or energetic? Simply notice what does what. Around three o'clock or so, are you sleepy? If so, notice whether or how many carbs or much sugar you've eaten. If none, note what you *did* eat. This

way, it is like biofeedback. You start to notice what makes your body feel good and what doesn't. Keep notes if that helps. (A food diary is wonderful for this, noting what you eat, but also what you drink, urination, bowel movements, etc.—yep, it's a lot of work, but whatever you can record is helpful because you'll start to notice patterns.) Also notice if certain emotions make you eat. If you're angry, do you go buy chips to chomp on or some sweets to make you feel good? (Of course, this is for later when we get to eat those things again…if we want to.) Repeat for dinner.

10. Before you close your eyes in bed, check in. How are you feeling? Are you stressed out, angry, disappointed, dead tired? Did anything contribute to those things? Tell yourself again, "I love you." Notice what effect, if any, this has on you.

Once you start looking, the body gives you all kinds of information. Your intuition will increase. You'll get flashes of information (a quick thought or image that disappears) that might seem way out, but pay attention. Sometimes we can't believe some things the body tells us about ourselves. Sometimes we can, as when we get a strong feeling of not liking or trusting a person. Trust that. In time, something will surface in that person or situation to explain why. But you have to remain alert. The body talks to us all the time through heart palpitations, hunger, binges, cravings, constipation, sneezes, nausea, etc. When these things happen, just ask, "Okay, what brought that on?" Sometimes it's obvious: it's your period (hormones dropped); someone walked by wearing some expensive chemical (perfume) that your body doesn't like; you ate that deep fried food; you bit into some rancid nuts, etc.

Our bodies are amazing computers. They record data and give them back to us. We just have to know how to look for them. I first learned about some of this stuff from my own body: when I was sick; when I became a vegetarian (my blood pressure dropped ten points); when I stopped smoking (I could get out of bed instantly instead of sitting on the side for ten minutes); when I was a member of Black Women's Self Help, where we looked at our cervixes and monitored our mucus to determine when we were fertile; when I read books such as *Alive to the Universe* and Gabriel Cousens's works on diet and health; and when I have watched my own intuition. It's not hard; it's just that nobody has ever told you about it. You haven't shared your own experiences because you doubted yourself. Now you know you're not crazy. Now you know some things to look for. Go for it!

Part Two: Health, Sweet Sex, and Spirituality

In my younger days, I was a die-hard pork fan. I loved my pork chops with the fat fried to a golden brown crisp. I hated the smell of chitlins stinking up the house, but loved them after vinegar and seasonings transformed them into a Christmastime delicacy. However, ham hocks were my absolute favorite. The three textures—the stringy reddish meat, the soft melt-in-your-mouth fat, and the slightly tough skins—were just the prize in a pot of greens or black-eyed peas with okra and corn on the cob.

Today at age fifty-four, I sometimes ponder how in the universe I managed to transform myself from lover of the hog to spiritual vegan—one who does not want to support the killing of animals by wearing clothes, shoes, and accessories made from them.

Looking back, I can see that my decision to eschew eating meat was incidental. Later, I made a conscious decision not to eat animals or the products of their death, such as dairy products, or utilize bags, shoes, or clothing made from their bodies. That decision made by chance put me on a path to a twenty-five-year journey that has informed so much of who I am today as a U.S.-born African woman. That initial step evolved into a transforming force in my life and has led me to be exceptionally health-conscious (some would say "obsessive"), intuitive, environmentally and spiritually aware, and a crystal lover (I definitely own the "obsessive" label here). The genesis of this journey is in the culture in which I grew up.

Flesh Culture

I was raised in a South Florida Bahamian-American family. Every Friday, we deep fried snapper, serving the crispy fish with the Bahamian staple—pigeon peas and rice—along with sautéed okra or cabbage. On Saturday nights, we always ate broiled steak. On Sunday mornings, we had big bowls of boiled or stewed grouper, a meaty fish, with grits—another Bahamian standard. For Sunday dinner, Mama always cooked a ham in addition to whatever other meat she'd have, such as turkey wings or chicken, fried or stewed. A pot of greens was simmering on the stove every Sunday, chock-full of those luscious ham hocks. Fried bacon seasoned the string beans and squash and the rice, whether it was cooked together with sweet peas or pigeon peas or tomatoes (another staple, this is called "dirty rice"). In all we cooked, meat was central to the seasoning, not to mention on the menu. Lots of meat on the table—mostly pork—meant you were living good, or "high off the hog."

Today, I realize that with so much of that hog in my diet, it was no wonder that sometime in my late teens I started having an unexplained "sickness to my stomach." It was a sort of uneasiness or queasiness—not quite nausea, but a slightly ill and uncomfortable feeling. Through trial and error, I noticed that if I drank hot beverages or ate hot soups or noodles, the discomfort went away. Knowing today what I do about how hogs are raised in filth, and because of some health issues that developed later, I suspect that I was suffering from a serious case of parasite infestation even then. The discomfort I felt all the time was so bad that I constantly drank coffee from those fat 16-ounce Styrofoam cups popular in the 1980s. (I know now that the strong acid in the coffee and the Styrofoam no doubt reacted to create quite an unhealthy chemical cocktail that only contributed to the problem.)

By that time, I'd gone away to the University of Florida in Gainesville to study journalism. I became involved with the African People's Socialist Party (APSP), a radical group that published a newspaper and harassed the governor of Florida about the false imprisonment of Freddie Pitts and Wilbert Lee, two Black men railroaded for killing a white gas station attendant—a murder they didn't commit.

During my travels across the country, I met people whose serious politics also included food. One brother from one of the Party mass committees in Atlanta pulled out his copy of the Black Muslim leader Elijah Muhammad's pamphlet, "How to Eat to Live," to explain to me how horrible meat was; how rotten the dead flesh is and how the butchers used dye and lighting to make it look healthy; how the pig was the filthiest creature on earth because it ate garbage, excrement, and everything else; and it was full of parasites to boot (I hadn't a clue about parasites at the time). I'd half glance at the pictures in the pamphlet, but then say, "Uh-huh. I love pork too much to give up meat." And I'd laugh, thinking to myself, "I'll never quit eating meat. At least not pork."

But then one day, years later, after I'd gained more weight than I wanted, I fasted for three weeks. I'd heard Dick Gregory speak at the University of Florida and had started the one-day fasting as he suggested. I'd learned that fasting was a quick way to lose weight. I had worked my way up to a two-week fast trying to lose weight, and had done it enough to go on juice for three weeks.

After fasting for that long, you gradually work your way back to eating solid food—first with fruit, then vegetables, then soups and soft foods. Later, you add fish and chicken and then, last, you eat the hard-to-digest meat. Well, after working myself up to eating a piece of steak, I got a punch in the stomach. The sick feeling that I hadn't noticed the previous four weeks came back so suddenly and strongly that it was obvious the meat had something to do with my queasy feeling. To test it out, I went off the pork, beef, and chicken. I noticed I didn't have that feeling. I ate beef and pork and noticed that I got the feeling again. I didn't get the feeling with chicken. Oh boy! What a blow! My whole world seemed to change. I weighed my options. I could continue to be sick, or I could give up the meat I loved so dearly and enjoy a calm stomach.

I'd had an experience of how good it felt to be free of that feeling and that, thankfully, overruled any desire to cling to meat. Quitting meat was the beginning of sensing the wonder of my body. One week after giving up meat, I went to the doctor for an already-scheduled checkup and noticed that my blood pressure, normally around 120/90, had dropped to about 110/80. I was stunned. Could not eating meat do that?

A more dramatic change in my body happened when I quit smoking. I'd started smoking in 1972 when I went to the University of Florida at seventeen years old. I worked myself up to a pack a week. As the editor of the Party's newspaper, I worked long hours, and smoked and drank coffee and beer to handle them. By 1981, I was smoking two packs of Salems each day. Totally stressed out, my 5' 6" body weighed 215 pounds. I was twenty-seven. After I became tired of coughing and having mucus dripping into my throat at night, I freed myself from my enslavement to the cancer sticks. I quit on a Sunday, and threw the remaining two cigarettes in my pack of Salems out rather than smoke them.

Then, a second surprise entered my life. The next Monday morning, after the alarm clock went off for me to get ready for work, I was up and out of the bed before I realized something profound. I didn't have to sit on the side of the bed for ten minutes with my head cradled in both hands while I "got myself together." When I realized this, I had to ask myself a serious question: Had cigarettes really been stealing that much energy from me, and I didn't even know it? As the days of abstinence increased, and my energy grew, I became convinced of this sad truth.

Though I had conviction and great experiences to support quitting for good, I also decided to cleanse my blood of the nicotine to make sure I didn't go back to smoking. (I'd quit two years before for a year after seeing a smoker's lung on display. Amazingly, I started again.)

As part of my new health consciousness I started reading *Back to Eden* by Jethro Kloss. I read that burdock root was a rapid blood purifier. I made the mistake of buying the tea instead of the capsules and had to mask the horrible taste by mixing in peppermint tea. It worked. Then, in order to sustain my freedom from nicotine poisoning, I knew I had to quit beer and coffee at the same time. I couldn't drink coffee or beer without wanting a cigarette. I got those out of my system and then started drinking teas and juices. In practically one fell swoop, a matter of a week or so, I rid myself of all my bad dietary habits—meat, coffee, beer, and cigarettes.

I was on a roll then. I started shopping at a health food store that had opened in Hallandale, Florida, where I lived, and learned about brown rice, fertilized eggs, and "exotic" vegetables. Soon, I cut from my diet almost everything all at once: milk, sugar, butter, eggs, cheese, and chicken. I kept eating seafood because it was so much of my Bahamian culture that I couldn't give it up. I promised myself I'd do it in a year. But because I'd made too drastic a move at one time, I found it difficult to eat anything such as pancakes (I didn't know anything about egg substitutes then). So I swung back toward the middle and allowed myself to eat cheese, and I compromised and started using brown sugar and honey. That was 1981.

With my new diet and exercise, I lost fifty pounds. I became a fanatically charged-up "health addict," which is what we were called then. Hallandale had a wonderful little vegetarian restaurant that I loved eating at, enjoying my new lifestyle. My male friend Bruce, who'd helped me jog and lose weight, ate health food too, but continued to eat meat. Whenever we ate out at the restaurant, we were always the only two Black people there.

I felt better than I ever had in my thirty years. My body was lean; my head clear. This transformation was also shortly after I suffered great grief and disappointment in the APSP. I was disillusioned because of a betrayal by the chairman and felt that I'd wasted the best years of my life. Getting myself back in shape, physically, emotionally, and mentally enabled me to find my center.

When I moved to Washington, D.C., in 1982 and later to Los Angeles, Allentown, Pa., and Miami, I discovered that the vegetarian lifestyle became much richer with curries, veggie pad thai, and udon noodles. I could go to an Italian restaurant and get an order of sautéed spinach, one of sautéed mushrooms, and garlic pasta and bread. I was thrilled when I discovered Indian food, and of course, Thai and Korean and Japanese cuisine, where I could eat tofu and sea vegetables or fermented veggies, vegetarian sushi, and other interesting foods. Food and health had now become an adventure.

For thirteen years I continued to eat seafood and cheese, telling myself "next year." During the years I lived in Washington, D.C., I joined feminist causes and enjoyed an even greater array of health-food restaurants, such as the now-defunct Food for Thought in Dupont Circle, and Naturally Yours on P Street. Memories of the stir-fried noodles and cakes have never left my brain cells, or wherever memories are stored. However, it was 1994 before I could tear myself away from seafood. That was the year of the mercury scare. The news was full of reports of deformed fish turning up everywhere containing large amounts of mercury. There was talk of other chemicals and needles and biohazardous blood being dumped in the ocean. Those news stories were the final kick in the butt I needed to give up seafood. Because I was still having problems with mucus dripping from my nose, I decided I had to give up cheese, too, which was hard. I absolutely adored Cracker Barrel sharp cheddar and would eat two packets a week.

Becoming a vegan in 1994 was exciting and difficult. I had no idea what a sacrifice I was making. The meat substitutes available now hadn't been made. There were some canned Worthington meatless products, but I eschewed them in the beginning. I didn't want meat and told myself that I didn't need to "pretend" that I was eating it. I had learned to cook with herbs and eat vegetables that I'd never heard of or hadn't ever eaten fresh—like spinach, mushrooms, and artichokes. As a kid, my mama had always bought frozen spinach; mushrooms and artichokes were new to me. So while the new foods made life interesting for a bit, after a couple of years I got bored and started eating meat substitutes for variety. I also started to enjoy their texture.

Eating out as a vegan was nearly impossible. It was hard to go into a restaurant and find a meal without cheese on it, even when it wasn't mentioned as part of a dish on the menu. I'd order pasta with garlic, and cheese would come sprinkled on top. Garden salads arrived with cheese or eggs in them. And sometimes the waiter wanted you to just remove the offending animal product. One had to quiz waiters about what was in a dish and push them to go ask the cook if they didn't know. There was a natural resistance to finding this information out. I always got the impression that they thought I was some weird spoiled freak.

For years when I ate out in a restaurant, I'd eat only Chinese food because I could always get tofu and vegetables. Eating out at first was difficult in a place like Allentown. Luckily, it had an Indian restaurant where vegan dishes abounded and an Italian restaurant where I could get pasta with marinara sauce. Later, the town acquired a health-food restaurant and, later still, a veggie pizzeria.

In December 1994, I moved to Miami-Dade County and was disappointed that Miami, the "big city," didn't have the vegetarian resources that a small town like Allentown had. I couldn't find one health-food restaurant in Miami or the surrounding communities. There was only the Whole Foods deli, and I made special trips to Whole Foods in Aventura, closer to the Broward County line, which fortunately was where I lived with my mother before moving to Miami-Dade. I would stop by on my way to work in Miami and buy lunch so I wouldn't have to come back north. Later I discovered Koinonia, a "no meat sold here" takeout in North Miami run by Jamaicans who made wonderful dinners, veggie pies, and smoothies. I always got a dinner with rice, a veggie mix, a meat substitute, and salad along with two veggie pies and a smoothie. I was a stressed-out reporter for the Miami *Herald* at the time, and I always needed extra food with me for those times I worked late in Miami Lakes and Hialeah. Fortunately, this isn't a problem today, as most restaurants now have finally learned to have vegan items on the menu, even only a soy or vegetable burger.

Veganism was hard on the sex life, too. Bruce, the man who helped me to make a big change in my life by jogging with me and teaching me how to meditate, ate meat. I didn't want to kiss a man who ate meat. I eventually left Bruce for other reasons and moved to Washington, D.C. I dated a couple of meat eaters but wouldn't kiss them. One man I dated asked me outright: "Why is your pussy so sweet?" He was genuinely curious.

"Must be those fruits and vegetables," I said, never missing a chance to extol the virtues of vegetarianism. Then he begged me not to wash for a week because he liked "pussy with a bite." I put two and two together when I heard several lesbians talking about preparing for their first sexual encounter with a new love by drinking fruit juice for a week so that they tasted really sweet. Eating fruit and a vegetarian diet made all the difference in the world. I noticed that I didn't have body odor even if I didn't bathe for an entire weekend and certainly didn't feel a need to douche to stay fresh smelling. I realized that eating meat contributed to body odor.

It was interesting to be confronted with the perceptions of meat-eating men about sex with vegetarian women. A friend of an uncle was adamantly trying it on with me, and repeated often, "I know that veggie pussy is some good pussy." It was ironic that they were attracted to me and I was repulsed by them because they ate meat. Black vegan men were hard to find. I tried to be okay with men who were fish eaters.

Once, a man I like a lot tricked me into believing he was converting in order to become involved with me. I made it clear that I didn't want to get serious with anyone who ate meat. I met him at the Miami Book Fair when he was selling his book. We talked for three hours the first day and exchanged numbers. After that, we talked every day for three months. He told me how he was practically a vegetarian, only allowing himself a pastrami sandwich once a year. He'd been a Muslim, so he didn't eat pork and only ate one meal a day. He promised me that he would eat like I did and he was anxious to learn how to eat healthy from me. He even nicknamed me "Vegan"—he was fascinated with the word I'd used to describe my diet—and started calling me that instead of my name. Anxious to finally find someone whom I could feel free with, I ate it all up. Finally, we planned a trip down to Florida. I went shopping and bought seitan, tempeh, textured vegetable protein, tofu, and veggies to make enticing dishes that would further enhance his desire to join the vegetarian lifestyle.

On the morning I was to pick him up from the airport, I cooked a meal of chickenlike seitan over brown rice and veggies and had it ready to feed him after picking him up from the airport. He took one look at my masterpiece and asked, "What's that?" After I told him, he said "I'm not eating that" and insisted we go out to eat. I couldn't believe it. "I thought you said you were going to be a vegetarian." He cut me off. "I was just talking trash," he said. I was speechless. He had had no qualms about lying to me. He waited till he'd flown from New Jersey to tell me to my face. It was a big joke to him. I had no qualms about not kissing *him*.

My dates with vegans and vegetarians also turned out to be problematic. Even vegetarian men could be full of it, too. I met a vegan at Koinonia, an alleged Muslim whom I found out was trying to tip out on his girlfriend and rush me into bed on the first date. Another vegetarian man I met in a Black study group was so secretive and different from me that it didn't work. Another was an acupuncturist whom I was extremely attracted to, but he apparently had some issues that he didn't communicate fully about, creating a great distance between us. Finally, I realized that just because a man was vegetarian didn't mean we'd get along any better or that that commonality would overshadow other problems. All of this came after a vegan I'd fallen for in Washington dumped me without any explanation.

I concluded that I needed a break from men, vegan and all. Men were just too much of a distraction. I decided to focus on being a kick-ass reporter covering the city of Opa-locka, Fla., which had enough social heartache, crime, and corruption to keep me not thinking about men for a long while.

One persistent man, however, managed to bring me out of my self-imposed isolation and convinced me to go out with him. We went to Denny's Restaurant in North Miami Beach. When I ordered a salad and fries, my date exclaimed to the waiter that, because I was a vegetarian, I was a very cheap date. The waiter, a young Black man, looked a little confused and squirmed a little. He then whispered to my date, and they broke out in the most uproarious laughter.

After the waiter left to put in our order, my date told me he'd said that he didn't like to date vegetarians because they didn't like to have oral sex—their definition of "meat" included penises. I found this hilarious and enlightening. My date was trying to find out if that was true. I just laughed. He was a meat eater. We weren't even going there. Later, I noticed that at times he had a funny "smell," even after he'd bathed. I later came to identify it to some extent as coming from meat. It reminded me of the smell I'd pick up in my mother's kitchen. I'd come in from a city council meeting sometimes at midnight or one in the morning, long after she would've cooked, cleaned up, and put up the food. I'd smell an odor that I came to identify as chicken, after asking her what she'd cooked that night. My friend smelled like that. I knew then that I didn't want to have a relationship with a meat eater. Before, I had been wavering, telling myself that I had to compromise on the meat question, else I wouldn't find a relationship. But after identifying that chicken smell on men, I decided I'd go without.

But what I lost in male company, I gained with God. As a result of becoming a vegetarian, I came more spiritual. I looked up one day and found myself in love with trees and with an insatiable desire to be outdoors all the time. I felt oppressed if I were indoors on a nice day, and wherever I lived I had to do some activity outside. When I lived in Allentown, I walked along the water every day in Leigh Park and did tai chi among ancient trees that I started to feel a special closeness with. When I was in South Florida, I walked and performed tai chi and Qigong on the beach under brilliant blue skies to the roar of the ocean. In Washington, D.C., I walked for hours in Rock Creek Park, losing myself in that patch of forest in the middle of the city, scaring my friends and neighbors who were bothered that I'd walk there alone.

Noticing how not eating meat caused my blood pressure to drop and how quitting smoking gave me more energy was just the beginning of a process of self-observation that led to even greater learning about my body and health and spirituality. One's intuition becomes stronger and more powerful. You recognize more cause and effect between what you eat and how you feel, what you believe and what you end up doing. Being vegetarian made me calmer and centered—something I noticed in other vegetarians. It was enlightening one day to be around meat-eating friends who drank, who acted wild and called it fun, and who soon became uncomfortable if you didn't drink with them.

Noticing your body, and observing the effects of food and positive thinking, naturally puts one in touch with God, the universal power. Pretty soon, you notice other vegetarians—mostly sisters—and you see an energy and excitement and spirituality that are common to us. When I shopped at Whole Foods in Aventura, I couldn't help but notice the Unicorn shop next door where I discovered crystals and all kinds of books linking our food choices to health and spiritual wellness. Soon, I felt a real love of the earth that went along with being in touch with earth energy from crystals, taking herbs, and body movements such as tai chi, Reiki, and raising my consciousness.

How can one eat the variety of foods—especially the fruits and vegetables that we have at our disposal—and not know there is a power greater than ourselves? Or look at the billions of stars in the sky and have doubts? I feel the power of God when I'm among the trees with my hands raised or can feel the energy of the earth when I stand doing Qigong.

It's fascinating to learn that authors like Gabriel Cousens, M.D., believe that the body is just one big crystal. In this regard, veganism was a step toward more physical health as well as a journey to a more spiritual life that is constantly evolving. I'm reminded of novelist Alice Walker, who revolutionized my thinking when she wrote about the enslavement of animals on the planet. How could we kill another being for food or enslave them to make them work for us? Once we understand this and practice it in our daily lives, then we're on a path to a greater life, just by our choice of foods. Even making a choice of not indulging in sex at times because I couldn't stand the effects of animal-eating was a sacrifice that resulted in greater love of, and learning about, myself. I believe people know this on some deeper level. How else does one understand the anger meat eaters feel because a vegan refuses to eat meat? Why else would it matter to them, if not for them feeling it is something that they should be able to do, or wish they could do? That to do so is a form of justice in the world?

Becoming a vegan, or more conscious about food, makes one more aware of life and living and the earth and love. You just can't eat meat with consciousness. For me, it truly has been a revolutionary and transforming journey—one still going on. I discover more about myself, food, herbs, crystals, energy, and love every day.

And just think: becoming a vegetarian at first wasn't even planned!

21

THE FULFILLMENT OF THE MOVEMENT

Adama Maweja

Growing up in Detroit during the 1960s was very intense for me. My sensitivities more than likely stemmed from the fact that I was born with a hole in my heart that was not discovered or corrected until I was four years old. I underwent two major open heart procedures, a forty-pint blood transfusion, and had my brain starved of oxygen for over twenty minutes when I literally turned blue and was comatose until my mother promised God that if I lived I would do God's work.

The sounds of ambulances and sirens would always send me into prayer for whoever was hurt. I'd have nightmares from the eleven o'clock news: "Parents, it's eleven o'clock. Do you know where your children are?" followed by mug shots of the top five "wanted" people (all of whom were ugly and scary to me). The footage of America's racism and hatred of Black people, the sit-ins, the hoses, dogs, police brutality; the assassinations of President Kennedy, Robert Kennedy, Dr. King, and Malcolm X; Vietnam; the riots, military tanks rolling up and down our streets, curfews, looting, shooting, and dark, thick black and red smoke from the city burning—all had a serious effect on me. I remember watching the March on Washington at six years old and everything in me knew that somehow I was to be an extension of the Civil Rights Movement.

At the age of seven, I watched my mother prepare dinner one evening. As she was preparing the meat, I asked her, "Momma, what's that?"

"Lamb."

"But what is it?" I asked again.

A little more firmly, she says, "Lamb!" still not understanding.

I asked more forcefully, "But what is it?"

She looked at me and responded as intensely, "Lamb!!"

"Like a baby lamb?" I mused.

"Yes, like a baby lamb."

I asked, "So what's chicken? Like a real bird?" Momma said yes, and for the first time I realized that meat was the flesh of dead animals. I loved animals. I'd just recently been to the Children's Petting Zoo and to a farm on a school field-trip. As I thought of how dear the little lambs were to me, I vowed I wouldn't eat meat anymore. I told my mother, "Well, I'm not going to eat that anymore." Of course, she shared my refusal to eat meat with my father, to which he replied at dinner, "You better eat everything on your goddamn plate, or I'll beat your goddamn ass." I was never the same after that.

Another of my most significant memories as a child was riding in the back seat of my father's Buick, with both he and my mother smoking cigarettes with the windows rolled up, and me complaining because I literally felt I was about to die because I couldn't breathe. "Please let the windows down!" I was pleading for my life! It's amazing how the seemingly most intelligent people just don't get "simple" things.

During the next few years I was beset with profuse nosebleeds and midnight emergency-room visits. An automobile struck me when I was ten years old, and I was hospitalized for two weeks with internal hemorrhaging from bruised kidneys. In the meantime, I would throw my parents' cigarettes away and fuss with them about their drinking. My parents were college graduates, my mother a teacher and my father a Morehouse College graduate and a manager with the Detroit Housing Commission. My mother drank socially; my father would have his daily wind-down with a beer or pink Champale with Spanish nuts or pistachios. He would go out on weekends and come home to my mother's complaints about how he smelled from the alcohol.

Tensions between my parents increased to the point where they decided to divorce when I was eleven, and they asked me which of them I wanted to live with. I replied, "I don't want to live with either one of you." I was sent to Jacksonville, Florida, at the end of sixth grade to attend my family reunion, and I remained there, living with my maternal grandmother from seventh through tenth grades; after that, my grandmother, grand-aunt, mother, and I all moved back to Detroit where my mother was based as a national representative for the American Federation of Teachers.

I did well in seventh through tenth grades, learning clarinet and performing in the marching and concert symphonic bands for the duration. I was salutatorian and class graduation speaker of my ninth-grade class. I even received an award for being an outstanding student from the University of Tennessee. Tenth-grade band activities took up most of my spare time. I was told we'd be moving back to Detroit after the school year, and I was livid. I didn't want to go back to Detroit. I began losing focus and received my first C and D on my report cards.

I did fairly well in school after returning to Detroit, despite being hit by a car in my junior year and spending four months hospitalized. I managed to graduate with a decent GPA, receive recognition for Class Couple, and was once again a commencement speaker. Unfortunately, my speech had to be rewritten because it was too extreme in my counselor's view. I wrote another and delivered it to a graduating class of over four hundred and our families.

I decided to apply to Spelman College and the University of Florida. I was eligible for a scholarship at Spelman but there was no on-campus housing available at the time of my application, so I chose University of Florida, which I entered in the summer of 1975. Having looked at many options, including business, advertising, pre-med with interest in psychiatry, journalism, and broadcasting, I decided to major in psychology. I managed to get through my first two years smoothly, pledging Delta Sigma Theta sorority as a freshman, moving off campus after my first year with a couple of my sorors and boyfriend, and doing what we do as a part of the "maturation" rituals of becoming an "adult" (short for "adulterated"...no longer what the Creator intended).

It was in my junior year in 1977 that I really began to pay more attention to the world and the issues of the day, as well as the significance of the information my studies were providing me with. As a psychology major at the University of Florida, I realized for the first time the importance of the interplay of diet, food, substances, education, and capitalism on the bodies, hearts, minds, and souls of people.

The staggering statistics of the disproportionate percentages and the rates at which we African-Americans were sick, diseased, imprisoned, dysfunctional, obese, and dying inspired me to pray more intensely than I ever had in life for answers to our problems. Of course, my instructors claimed ignorance as to the causes and admitted having no solutions. Hence, because I was both Black (minority) and female, as well as very intelligent with an academic record to back it up, I could get funding for doing research on these important matters.

So, in effect, the message was that no matter how much education, money, opportunities, talent, credit, jobs, access, experience, wealth, or whatever else we may have won after Civil Rights and affirmative action programs, we'd continue to die prematurely and in disproportionately large numbers from so-called incurable diseases. Stomach, lung, uterine, and prostate cancers; tumors and cysts; sexually transmitted diseases; mind- and body-altering and recreational drugs and substances; stress, dis-eases of the mind; criminality, insanity, suicide, homicide, and AIDS/HIV at the time were not a consideration: but the overall effect and reality is, and was, genocide.

Inundated with statistics from the urban laboratories (our city hospitals, clinics, etc.), dissatisfied with speculation, theories, and hypotheses, and totally appalled at the staggering numbers of African-Americans dying by the tens and hundreds of thousands annually from diseases that the scholarly, educated, researched, and degreed could find neither cause nor cure, while every disease becomes a multimillion-dollar institution under its own name, I took to praying with an intensity that became all-consuming. I asked to be shown what the causes and the solutions were.

My soul was disturbed. I had no peace, and I reached a point of disillusionment with everything I was doing, everyone around me, and myself. I cried; and a part of me drowned in my tears—the part of me content to excuse it all by ignorance of my youth, by being in pursuit of knowledge and an education. Having matriculated through two years of a four-year degree, I still had no knowledge, no answers, and no truth, only facts, figures, studies, tests, scores, statistics, and the realization that being stamped with a B.A. degree in psychology would leave me ill-prepared to do anything of significance to improve the condition of my people or society in general. And wasn't that the whole point of becoming educated? So I could make a difference and to insure the progression of my lineage?

The intensity of my prayers, tears, and commitments to the Creator catapulted me into immediate lifestyle changes as the desperation of my longing for truth inspired me to do several things right away. Though I'd worn my hair natural since the age of eleven, I had permed it at the urging of my boyfriend. I cut the perm from my hair into a short, brushable natural.

It was as if someone began to speak to me through my own thoughts. I was inspired to look deeply at myself, and I realized that I was matching a few things that my parents did that I really hated: 1) smoking cigarettes; 2) drinking alcoholic beverages; and 3) eating the flesh of dead animals. Of course, I wasn't alone in these behaviors, being in college, but I subsequently realized that I was supporting businesses perpetuated by white people. Even though Black people buy into these businesses and are employed by them, they are staples in Black communities. They can be found on almost every corner across and or down the street from every church.

A particular phrase continued to resound loudly in my head, "The rich get richer and the poor get poorer." I began to listen for the answers as to why this was the case. I realized that many of the rich were rich because they were the ones making all of the products being distributed throughout the African diaspora. I began a personal economic boycott of the businesses and their products, which I have subsequently labeled "death industries" or "corporate deities of death"—that is, purveyors of tobacco, cigarettes, alcohol, meat, dairy, sugar, and fish (seafood), in particular. My oath at that time was, "I will not give you motherfuckers another goddamned dime of my mother's money!"

To stop smoking, I sat in my apartment alone one evening with a brand new pack of Benson & Hedges menthol cigarettes and began to smoke one after the other, putting each one out halfway. I inhaled slowly and consciously, speaking to myself, "With each puff you're taking two minutes off your life. Do you want to live or die?" I literally cursed myself out as the ashtray began to fill with ashes becoming blackish-gray, the room filled with stench, and I imagined my lungs and my tissues.

I remembered riding with my parents in the car with both of them smoking, the windows rolled up. I felt like I was suffocating, I gasped for my breath, my life, and here I was twelve years later fighting for my life. I didn't have to smoke the whole pack before I'd had enough. The body has a saturation point for any chemical or substance; once you reach it you can release the addiction. I reached mine that night without any physical sickness or nausea.

Alcohol was not a big part of my life, although it was readily available on a predominantly white campus. I lost all desire to consume any form of alcohol with the thought of how many people's lives and livers had been destroyed by it. My parents drank, and I knew as a child that it wasn't right. As my parents went through changes with each other, they would sometimes drink more, which led to a couple of serious arguments and fights between them. I detested their drinking of alcohol and the arguments that escalated because of it.

Twelve years later, I was receiving the spiritual guidance and strength I needed to do what I'd initially wanted to do at the age of seven. I ate on campus for lunch but would prepare dinner at home (even though I'd eat out when I didn't feel like cooking). I continued to buy meat until I couldn't eat it. I would look at it and tell myself, "You're about to eat the flesh of a goddamned dead animal, are you out of your motherfucking mind?"

Soon I was eating fruit or having juice in the mornings before class. I would have a large salad, a bowl of soup, vegetables, whole-wheat crackers, toast, or cornbread. Over the next sixty days my weight decreased from 127 pounds to 103 pounds. I ate no chips, cookies, ice cream, or any other junk food. Not only did I lose weight, I also noticed better mental clarity. My mind opened up. It was as if I'd been in a dark room or tunnel, when suddenly a bright and brilliant light was turned on. I went to class, paid attention, and understood things at another level. I no longer had to labor over my books as before. I began to ask questions and make points that could not be countered. I could hear what wasn't being said and could read between the lines.

My heightened awareness, fueled with the intense desire to know the solutions to the problems facing Black people, contributed to my being able to bring all of my professors to tears as I challenged them to see the futility of continuing to perpetuate an educational agenda or curriculum that didn't empower its students to do anything different from those who'd come before. It became clear to me that whatever curriculum or subject a student majors in, nutrition, diet, and health should have been prerequisite courses, just based on the fact that we were destined to be parents. I challenged my professors to see that as long as we were fed off the flesh of dead animals, sugar, sodas, cigarettes, coffee, and the myriad of other junk foods with artificial colors and flavors that were sold on campus and in every store, it would be impossible to think clearly.

During these changes in my body, heart, and mind I continued with intense prayers, and received counseling to assist me in processing all that was coming to or through me. However, it was during a party I attended that I had a most significant experience. I was sitting with a brother who was an associate professor of history, a martial artist, and politically intense. As we were sitting at the counter, he said to me, "Gina, there is no God!"

"What do you mean there is no God?"

"There is no God," he responded. "Everything you know about God the white man taught you."

"No," I said. "My mother taught me about God."

"Well, everything she knows, the white man taught her."

"No," I continued. "My grandmother taught her."

"Well, who taught her?" he asked.

"Her mother," I said.

"And who taught her?"

"*Her* mother."

"Well, if you go that far back you're going back to Africa," he said.

I responded: "That's where the white man learned about God, and then he took it and created formal religions."

In the process of this conversation, it was as if I'd left my body and was suspended somewhere in space looking at the earth and seeing its polarities, dualities, good/evil, black/white, hot/ cold, south/north, and so on. I could hear the elders saying, "Beware of the blue-eyed devil" and other things. As I returned to the conversation, I asked the brother, "If there is no God, then what is it in you that makes you fight the wickedness of this system the way you do? What is it that separates you from them if it is not God?"

He no longer tried to argue the point with me after that, but as a result of my having to defend my knowing of the presence of God, I came into another depth of thought that stopped me from eating or sleeping for the next three days and nights; I was on fire. I began to see things I hadn't seen before. My energies became so intense that conversations I held with people had them crying in the streets.

There were over 30,000 students at University of Florida, of which 1,500 were African-American. While president of the Lambda Psi chapter of the Delta Sigma Theta sorority, I began to realize the need to move into other realms of campus political involvement. I began to work in organizing the Black Student Union. I decided to campaign for a seat in the UF

Student Government Senate from the College of Arts and Sciences and won with an overwhelming majority of the votes. I became the first Black person and first woman to be elected to the Student Government Senate, which appropriated its three-million-dollar budget to student activities. I organized the Progressive Student Organization, which was comprised of members from each of the Black student organizations on campus.

As a Black Student Union organizer, I picked up Stokely Carmichael (Kwame Touré) from the airport when came to speak at the campus. I had no real political or historical depth at that time; my studies were centered in the areas of psychology, sociology, spirituality, and sexuality. So, meeting with Brother Touré was very empowering for me, and I had one-on-one time with him.

His lecture was very powerful; the auditorium was filled overwhelmingly with white students. I listened, and observed during the question-and-answer portion that he spoke very confidently and authoritatively. But what was most significant and life-changing for me was that no one could dispute him. I cannot say that everything he said was true, but I realized in that moment what was to be gained: that which should be fully valued, to *know,* to be indisputable, the truth, was most important. "Know ye the truth and the truth shall set you free."

I quickly abandoned my desire to continue on to graduate school. My administrators were encouraging me to go to law school; they were so impressed with my transformation. It had been my initial desire to have my Ph.D. by the time I was twenty-five. I told my administrators that I wouldn't go to law school because man's law differs from place to place, and that if I studied law in Florida and then moved to Montana or Africa, I'd have to study law again.

I realized that I'd be better off in the long run if I studied God's laws, for they were consistent and could be applied through every situation and circumstance and would be in effect regardless of where I stood upon the planet. I also realized that some of those closest to me, my sorors particularly, as well as other students, were not perceiving the truth of what I was beginning to share with them. My advisor told me, "It's obvious that you have been 'saved'! You cannot force your opinions or beliefs on others!"

Of course, I wasn't telling anyone I'd been "saved," so my response was, "*Saved?* Saved from what? You all elected me president of this chapter, and now that I understand truly what pledging is and everything this organization stands for, you're telling me that I don't have the right to tell you? If you all can't step with me in the name of God, I certainly won't step with you in the name of Delta Sigma Theta." I continued my activities, realizing that I didn't want to alienate those I most wanted to touch. So, as disgusted as I was with my wardrobe and popular clothing, I went out and bought clothes that fit me, so I could continue to look somewhat like my girls. But I was never the same. If I hadn't been so close to graduating, I wouldn't have bothered.

I had no fears about unemployment; my concerns were that I was growing and understanding so much, and having such a major effect in other peoples lives with my intensity, that I realized I wasn't ready to become a target of the FBI or CIA. Nor was I ready to spend the next few years arguing with professors or having to study the thought, theories, and opinions of those who had yet to come up with true solutions to the problems and issues of the world.

The revelations were continually pouring forth so much so that I was driven to call my mother one night from a pay phone in the pouring rain to tell her I'd come to know "the truth." I thought she would be delighted as she, too, was ready to change her life. My mother financed my education, out-of-state tuition and all, from her pocket, employed by the American Federation of Teachers. As my graduation approached, she decided to quit her job so she could pursue a divinity degree with Unity School of Christianity.

As I stood there getting soaked, she asked me, "What truth?" I told her about the conspiracy to feed people a diet that doesn't allow for the true thought, comprehension, or clarity necessary to create a better system. But when I told her that I knew the truth of who *I was*, she began to tell me that I needed to read the Bible, and other books that I can't remember the names of.

Disappointed that she wasn't receiving my news as I thought she would, I listened to what she was saying for as long as I could, then I replied, "Momma, you're trying to tell me that if I had been born blind, deaf, and dumb, where I could not read the scriptures or hear the story of Jesus or the teachings of this man or the other man, that I would have no way of knowing who I am as a child of God? I don't believe that." I expressed to her that I really didn't understand why it was she felt so compelled to go to Unity School of Christianity at this point in her life, or her need for white people to teach her about God, when God had already revealed itself to her through me sixteen years ago when I awakened from that coma after my brain was starved of oxygen for over twenty minutes—and having turned completely blue after the second procedure of my open heart surgery at four years of age. However, it is what she wanted to do with her life, as she had completed her responsibilities to my sister and me. Oh well!

My mother, sister, niece, and grandmother came from Detroit to attend my graduation. They were very proud as I graduated with presidential honors, and organizational, scholastic, and leadership awards. When I got home to Detroit, however, no one wanted to listen to what I had to say. I told my mom that I thought it was strange that she could have supported me all that time and invested so much in me, yet not want to hear my thoughts or know what was on my mind. Her response was that I had no right to come into her house and tell her how to live. I told her I had more right than McDonald's, Burger King, Merrill-Lynch, Jesus, and the rest of those whom she'd been giving her money to, because I came through her womb, loved her, and would be there if anything was to happen to her.

To make a long story short (until the autobiography), my mother and I fought for seven years over the issues of diet, health, nutrition, etc. She became a devoted ministerial student, then a minister in Jackson, Michigan, and always justified eating the flesh of dead animals and all manner of other things with scriptural tutelage... until she had her sixth heart attack (not realizing she'd had the first five, thinking they were gas pains). She was scheduled for a triple coronary bypass, so I traveled to Jackson from Atlanta and began to facilitate her healing by initiating cleansing of the colon and bloodstream with enemas, herbs, and fresh juices. I'd taken quite a few of my health and wellness books with me, only to find that my mother's library contained all of them. It was then that I realized that just having the information or the books was not enough. My mother didn't have anyone around her who was consciously seeking to live or apply the information contained in the books.

I stayed with my mother for four months during her recuperation from the bypass surgery. I'm sure she was truly appreciative of my efforts. I know my grandmother was, as I was the only one of the family who had a lifestyle that was free enough to be with my mother for those months, and I had been applying myself consistently over those seven years since college to learn about health, healing, and being well.

My mother lived for another seven years after that heart attack. She made great strides in eliminating some things from her diet and incorporating herbs, supplements, vitamins, and such. She continued to justify some things by quoting scripture to the effect that it wasn't what you put in your mouth that defiled you, but what came out of your mouth. Ministerial programs issuing divinity degrees and licensing people to preach, teach, and/or have churches need to offer life-support service by assisting their candidates through and over their addictions to dead flesh (meat), alcohol, tobacco, coffee, sugar, and pharmaceuticals. Unfortunately, my mother, though a very faithful woman committed to the service of lifting others up through her ministries, never received the inspiration to let go of all flesh foods, dairy, sugar, alcohol, and cigarettes. Therefore, she never accepted the fullness of the blessings of healing that were available to her.

She passed on November 3, 1993, in her sleep, from seven years of incomplete healing from heart disease, diabetes, and hard-headedness. I'd seen her three months earlier, during our family reunion in Baltimore, where we stood almost face to face, which means she'd lost height and stature. I gave her a red-clay facial, back walk, and massage. As we hugged and kissed each other, I knew that our healing was complete. Though it wasn't a fully conscious thought, I knew within myself that that would be my last time seeing her alive. There was a real peace between us, a quiet acceptance of who we each were in the continuous succession of the lineages that came before us.

She lived as she wanted to, and touched the lives of many people as an educator, a union organizer, minister, mother, woman, and friend. My mother was my salvation. It was by virtue of her commitments for my life that I survived the heart surgeries, car accidents, near drowning in the Atlantic Ocean, falling asleep at the wheel of a Camaro, and more, long enough to receive the inspiration to make commitments for my own life. It was by virtue of Momma's prayers with and for me that I learned to pray. My mother's commitments and prayers for my life were supported with and by the prayers of family, those who offered their blood for my four-pint blood transfusion, those who were on the phones with Unity prayer lines, church members, and coworkers with her, praying for my recovery through open-heart surgery, that allowed me to awaken from the coma that held my life in the balance all those decades previously.

One evening in my social movements class, I made commitments for my own life, after listening to a reel-to-reel tape of all the voices of rage and reason in the Civil Rights and

Black Power movements. The messages of that era were projected into my consciousness from that tape player and filled me up as nothing ever had. By the time I got as far as the traffic light leaving the campus, I'd opened up and tears streamed from my eyes. Every atom and cell of my being was charged with my affirmation, "IF I CANNOT LIVE TO MAKE A DIFFERENCE IN THIS WORLD, THEN LET ME NOT LIVE AT ALL!"

What was revealed to me three decades ago is still very much the order of the day. Sickness, disease, dysfunction, and premature death are the results of not living harmoniously with the elements and forces of life, and that which is the law of existence. It is indeed tragic that the government and its agencies, the educational systems, the religious orders, and the business sectors have seemingly conspired against the well-being of babies, children, and all the lineages that were before them and are destined to come through them. That's like conspiring against God and its intelligence. My grandmother was seven years old when it was mandated within the educational system that eggs, cheese, milk, and meat were the staples that everybody needed to be healthy. It was not true then and is one of the biggest lies told now.

The move from farms to city life, from fresh foods to canned and frozen foods, pot pies, and TV dinners, from home-cooked meals to fast foods and now genetically modified organisms and terminator seeds, constitute a progression of errors and lies. It is the result of "educated" people who became scientists, doctors, researchers, pharmacists, and the like, who were probably themselves fed and continue to eat the flesh of dead animals, the aborted fetuses of chickens, and the pus and mucus of cows; who smoke cigarettes, drink coffee, and have to take all manner of over-the-counter medicines and pharmaceuticals to move their bowels, wake up, perk up, go to sleep, get rid of headaches, and so on.

Living one's life simply—with a real depth, love, and appreciation for the Creator's presence as it is manifesting and womb-manifesting as All There Is, including our Mother Earth, her creatures, and her children represented as the descendants and ascendants of the aboriginal, indigenous, and native peoples of the planet—is the true key to a healthy, peaceful, and harmonious life as individuals, families, communities, nations, and a global village. In truth, we are all interdependent on the resources we are and those that lie beneath the soils of where our souls originated upon the planet.

Many people refuse to think that there could be life with no wars, no sickness, and no disease. These very same people speak about how they love Jesus or God or any of the saviors, saints, prophets, or gurus, and then fill their mouths and stomachs with the flesh of abused, violated, and dead animals, choked down with degerminated bleached flours or starches, and then pour carbonated, sugar-laden, alcoholic beverages down their throats, ending with a belch, and then smoke a cigarette, cigar, or marijuana spliff afterward. The diseases of the mind, heart, and soul have their source in following the examples, urgings, and teachings of the corporate deities of death rather than our Creator's.

It is no wonder that with all of the technological advances, modern medicines, and discoveries that scientists, researchers, and the "higher" echelons of educational prowess profess, no one has told the people that there could never be "cures" to any of the multiplicity of diseases that our communities are beset with. The only real cure is in real living and observing the laws that govern life, which are consistent with honoring the intelligence of existence, the human body, and nature and all her creatures. The real cure to all disease requires a true commitment to life, law, cleanliness, and love for and within oneself, and toward everything and everyone.

There are far reaching consequences to changing our lifestyle, diet, and habits that include: better health; more clarity, potency, power, and peace; and greater ethical and moral consistency, as well as the redistribution of the wealth that we make and receive. It is indeed unfortunate that the business interests of the meat, dairy, sugar, and beverage industries have, at their heart, the idea of profit instead of genuine concern for the well-being and health of people, children, and sustainability of the earth. A result of the proliferation of the interests of these businesses is devastation upon the planet, and in her waters, air, and within her soil. These affect the bodies, hearts, minds, lives, and souls of people who live and depend upon her.

During my initial awakening, cleansing, and lifestyle change over twenty-nine years ago, I had the acute perception that the depth and scope of the world's problems would require that every living being take the time to get centered and focused in prayer twenty-four hours a day, seven days a week. Now the government and its agencies, the religious systems, educational establishments, political organizations, and the multibillion-dollar institutions that under the name of each disease claim the lives of millions of men, women, and children annually still don't have love, light, wisdom, or care enough to cleanse themselves or call a moratorium on the licensing of the corporate deities of death—the alcohol, tobacco, meat, dairy, sugar, chicken, and fish and their affiliates, the artificial flavor, artificial color, sweetener, and additive industries—from distributing their poisons on every corner, across and down the street from every church in Black communities particularly and disproportionately.

I mentioned earlier that I knew from when I was six years old, watching the March on Washington, that I am an extension of the Civil Rights Movement. Forty years later to the day, I was in Dr. King's house in Atlanta providing food service to Coretta Scott King. I knew this was no coincidence. Mrs. King had given up meat at the urging of Dexter her son, and had fallen into the thinking that "going raw" was what she needed to do to get healthier. I was the second or so in a progression to provide her with raw food. I tried to encourage her to see that it wasn't so much raw food that would give her the greatest leverage in reversing conditions established from fifty years of consistently following the lies of the educational and medical establishments, but the cleansing and revitalization that would come from "not" eating—getting quality and quantity of high mineral and herbal supplementation that would facilitate giving her digestive system sufficient rest, help open her eliminative system, and nourish her at the cellular level.

Mrs. King was two years older than Mother, but there are some things that that generation and those who've outlived them have in common, and that is their respect for and appreciation of white people and their assessments and recommendations as to what to do. While a psychology major at UF, I explored in a communication class the methodology of creating credibility for a message, messenger, speaker, presenter, etc. We've been socialized through the whitewashing of Black history, and the blue-eyed, blond Jesus and his disciples, to see white as right regardless of how much we've actually witnessed that demonstrates that much of the world's devastation, as well as that of our own ancestors, came at the hands, hearts, and teachings of white people. They, as well as so many others, have yet to realize that the answers to Black people's plight will and have come through our own people.

It was truly my honor to spend quality time speaking, serving, and sharing with Mrs. King, It was my opportunity to assure her that the Kings' works, efforts, and sacrifices were definitely not in vain and that there were others, like myself, coming forward with what they missed: you cannot be a "free" or liberated people when you continue to feed from your slave master or as the slave master feeds, or to feed from his scraps. I had time to share with her that a boycott of the death industries would be the most expeditious means of creating a national and international revivification of our truth, destiny, light, and purpose as a global family. She had no disagreement with me but was too tired and weak after assisting her sister back to health for several months and being called upon by so many to lay the foundation for everything else.

The "movement" cost her and others dearly, for people to have acquiesced to the point of not even being able to have regular and consistent movements (bowel); the laxative business is a billion-dollar industry. Very few of those on the front line of the Civil Rights and Black Power movements (who are still alive) look well. The eldest, the Rev. Joseph Lowery and the Rev. C. T. Vivian, look healthier than all their juniors whom they mentored. If they had truly perceived the issues of pertinence, then the death industries would not be so prevalent throughout our communities and the incidence of dysfunction, distortion, disease, discontent, dissatisfaction, divorce, divisiveness, despair, desperation, and devilment would not be as intense as it is.

The commercial meat, dairy, and "not food" industries are laying a foundation for the modern-day slave camps that lead to the disease, degradation, and dysfunction of the animals being bred for human consumption. Once these abused creatures are slaughtered and their body parts processed as "food" for children, the etheric energy of their pain, aggravation, discomfort, and distress is permeated through the flesh and body parts and absorbed into the etheric body of the human that consumes them, which creates apparently inexplicable fear, stress, mood swings, and other mental, emotional, and physical imbalances that facilitate them being labeled as some sort of socio/psychopath. The real psychos are the ones who run, monitor, and provide for the licensing of these businesses in the United States: FDA, USDA, AMA, and any and all of their affiliates in the meat, chicken, dairy, fish, seafood, pharmaceutical, and additive industries.

The body is truly fully intelligent and is the temple of God, where the spirit is housed in a physical home that becomes permeated in filth, thereby creating the first point of breach of integrity, which leads to the inability to function in the integrity of what and who one is in truth. Decades of living inharmoniously contribute to the inability to think, care, and do what is in the best interest of oneself and others. This lifestyle lays the foundation for the myriad of diseased states and the immaturity of those who are physically older in years. Therefore, people excuse the utilization of the intelligence of existence to work against the intelligence of existence. No other being does it. Every being works toward the perpetuation of itself, its kind, or has purpose directly related to the continuation and contribution to the well-being, sustenance, and maintenance of the earth and her creatures.

It is truly our time and we must realize that we need to respond appropriately to being under siege. A boycott of the death industries manifesting as a serious, deliberate, and all-consuming fervor and fever for life and life-giving, life-supporting, life-sustaining and life-renewing foods, supplements, thoughts, and activities will allow each of us to be in a dynamic state of progressive self-realization. Hence, this will facilitate our greater potency and efficacy in any and all fields of endeavor to which we may apply ourselves.

We must apply our talents likewise, in cleansing and nourishing ourselves, and facilitating integrity with the True Self of all Selves…the Intelligence of Existence, which some call "God." I give praise, prayer, and thanksgiving that I am ever renewed, reborn, and revivified so that my life is a continuous testament and living testimony to the glory of the cosmic whole and the establishment of the eternal laws, eternal order, and the eternal government.

22

MA'AT DIET

Iya Raet

I am one hundred percent vegan in diet only. My veganism is for physical, cultural, emotional, and spiritual reasons. As a divine being, I choose to eat a divine diet. I do not like to label myself as vegan. Not only must my food be vegan, but it must be whole. I prefer to call my diet a holistic or Ma'at diet. The diet I choose is based on the principles of Ma'at: order, balance, and harmony. I choose to eat the diet of my ancestors. Eating vegan foods will not provide mental clarity, well-being, and self-healing. However, eating vegan *whole* foods will provide the body with the wisdom to heal itself.

When I was twenty-one, I had a polyp on my colon. People over fifty are screened for polyps, not twenty-one-year-olds. After the polyp was removed, I never thought to change my diet. I didn't until December 2000, when I read *Sacred Woman* by Queen Afua in one day, and decided to become a vegetarian. It was clear to me beyond a doubt that vegetarianism was a way to achieve Afrikan liberation, mentally and spiritually. The next day, I ate no flesh. That day, while eating a cookie, I thought to myself, "Why am I eating this? Why am I eating dairy and eggs?" This was the last day I had dairy or eggs, and went vegan immediately. Consuming toxic foods unknowingly is ignorance; eating them with full understanding is either stupidity or addiction, and my thirst for enlightenment was stronger than any addiction. I certainly wasn't stupid. So, here I am today, almost six years later, a healthy, healing, and spiritual Nubian woman.

My son was blessed to have experienced a holistic, vegan diet from the womb, since I had a vegan pregnancy. My diet consisted of whole grains, fruits, and vegetables. I made sure I ate raw, green, leafy vegetables daily. My supplements included liquid chlorophyll, vegetarian Omega-3, -6, and -9 fatty acids, B complex, calcium, magnesium, B_{12}, and blackstrap molasses. I delivered a healthy baby boy, 7 lbs 13 ozs, in a planned home birth. I had no vaginal tears and an easy recovery. I know my vegan diet provided me with the discipline to endure the pain and to stay physically and mentally balanced. It also gave me the courage to believe in myself as a healer and encouraged me to learn more about the medical system. The more I learned, the more I realized I wanted to heal myself and stay out of the system. This knowledge led to my home birth. Birth is not a sickness. I do not live a life of sickness, but of healing and detoxification.

My son, Sun-Ra, was breastfed and cloth-diapered. He was neither circumcised nor vaccinated. Only vegan products were placed on his skin. I choose to cloth-diaper my son because it is healthier for baby and the environment. Cloth also saves money. Eating a Ma'at diet creates a closer connection to the earth and the spirit. You become an earth mother, thinking twice about placing waste upon the land. The laws of Ma'at state, "I will not lay waste on the plowed land."[1] The diet affects all aspects of life. It opens one's ear to the spirit of the earth and the universe. The Ma'at diet enabled me to come full circle, to feel the vibration of the universe. Holistic living puts you in tune with your oneness with the universe, and you have no choice but to respect and protect it. This results in a greater awareness to protect your family. Through nutritional healing, I protected my newborn baby like a hawk.

When my son began eating solid foods, they were vegan, organic, and homemade. When I bought ready-made baby foods, they also were vegan. I never placed foods in the microwave, but simply ran them under hot water in a container or storage bag. Microwaves are toxic. By the time my son was one year old, his favorite foods were raw tomatoes. When we went to the market he would grab green and leafy vegetables from the cart and eat them. He also loved raw green peppers and garlic. Yes, raw garlic; my baby is a hardcore green baby! When I make raw meals he begs for more. He is an inspiration to me, a beautiful testament to the Ma'at diet. He is a child who never consumed toxic foods, receieved toxic vaccinations, or experienced doctors poking at him. When he had his first fever, he was healed holistically. I placed onions in his socks and on his body. I also used herbal teas and tinctures. The fever vanished by the end of day. I only used the elements of the universe for healing:

- Earth—herbs.
- Water—herbs are placed in water.
- Air—the steam and moistness of the air is present when cooking the herbs.

- Fire—fire is used to cook the herbs.
- Ether—I ask the spirits for guidance. I listen to the spirit of the plant. I ask Osain, the Yoruba Orisha of herbs, for guidance.

The universe and us humans are made up of the elements; therefore, I use them for healing my family. I use my own healing intuition, not those of the Western medical industry. A diet free of waste and toxicity allows the connection to the healing powers of the universe. The vegan diet is safe for pregnant and breastfeeding mothers. It is also safe for children. But it is imperative that whole foods be consumed. I encourage mothers to feed their families foods that are organic whenever possible. Read labels, stay away from artificial colors, additives, MSG, and preservatives. If you don't know what an ingredient is, don't buy it. Being vegan is not enough. There are many dangerous chemicals in foods that are free of flesh, eggs, and dairy. Refrain from white rice, white flour, and other bleached foods. Instead of feeding your family the standard rice and potatoes as the starch for your meal, try grains such as millet and quinoa. Millet is an extremely healthy ancient African grain. It is highly digestible and very high in protein. It is also a great source of B vitamins, potassium, lecithin, vitamin E, magnesium, and iron. Quinoa contains all eight essential amino acids! Strive for more than veganism; adopt a whole-foods diet to secure your family's optimal health.

Holistic Parenting from the Pan-Afrikan Perspective: The Womb

The womb is the primordial waters from which all life comes. The *netert* (goddess) Nu represents these waters. Ra, the life force, is the fire element, which rose from the water element. His children are Shu and Tefnut, air elements. Shu and Tefnut gave birth to Geb, the earth element. Afrikan spirituality reflects the cosmology of the universe. The watery womb created the Neteru. Neteru is the name for the Kemetic (ancient Nubian Egyptian) deities. Ask yourself, "Is my womb suitable for bringing forth the next gods who will walk this earth? Am I using the elements of the universe to create and heal?"

The Afrikan woman's womb is attacked by hormonal birth control, pesticides, and other toxins. Women also have womb issues related to holding on to emotional hurt and pain. They sometimes curl their bodies up into a fetal position with their legs and arms close to the womb. Women take the hurt and give it to the womb. A woman will never be healthy if the womb center is holding pain and emotional baggage; she cannot bring forth healthy children if the children have been created in a womb that is dysfunctional. The mother and father must cleanse their whole being before conception. Once the child is conceived, parents must begin nurturing the child while in the womb. Mother and father need to send the child loving and healing light daily. Parents must be conscious of the energy being sent to their unborn child. They should send only the divine and positive. The child is encapsulated in water. Water carries emotions, so the baby can receive both positive and negative energy. Whether the mother is feeling joy, anger, or sadness, the unborn child will feel it, too.

The unborn child has the ability to hear when he or she has been in the womb for about four and a half months. This is when the ear becomes functional. *Iyas* (mamas): Sing Afrikan cultural songs to your babies and read to them in the womb. *Babas* (fathers): The child can hear your voice, too. While there is some evidence that the child hears the father's voice and that his voice has a calming effect on the newborn, the link between the child's ear and the father's voice is not even remotely as direct as the mother's voice. Hence, the greatest contribution that the expectant father can make is to love his child's mother.[2] In Senegal and Mali, the father takes his special bond seriously; a father may loosen his belt during the mother's pregnancy to help establish his connection with the child. Sometimes, during the mother's labor, the father will have his belt loosely wrapped around the mother's waist as an offering of his own *nyama* (life force) and support for the child's entry into the world.[3]

It is obvious that unborn children have an outside connection even while in the womb. Kings, love your queens. Hold them up to the highest position. Rub their feet and back. Help out with the cooking and cleaning around the house. Make her feel special. Prepare her an herbal bath. Take time out each day to show her your appreciation. Send her love so that she may pass this love on to the child. Sending love to the womb is essential because so many toxic energies are present. The Environmental Working Group published a report stating that unborn babies were stewing in a toxic soup.

The Red Cross took ten samples of umbilical cord blood and found an average of 287 contaminants in the blood, including mercury, fire retardants, pesticides, and the Teflon chemical PFOA. Also found were polyaromatic hydrocarbons, or PAHs, which are produced by burning gasoline and garbage, which may cause cancer; flame-retardant chemicals called polybrominated dibenzodioxins and furanes; and pesticides including DDT and chlordane.[4]

Mercury can damage the fetal brain and nervous system. Polyaromatic hydrocarbons increase the risk of cancer. Pesticides can cause fetal death and birth defects. Flame-retardant chemicals can hinder brain development. Some European countries have taken notice and are beginning to use fewer flame retardants. The United States, however, has not taken heed. The same group analyzed the breast milk of mothers across the U.S. in 2003 and found varying levels of chemicals, including flame retardants known as PBDEs.[5] The bedding many pregnant mothers and children sleep on contains flame retardants and toxic dyes.

Mothers can do many things to keep their babies safe in the womb. The universe balances negative and positive energy. Mothers can counter the negative energy with the following positive energy:

- Be peaceful. Surround yourself with peaceful energies.
- Keep your surroundings in divine order so you are in divine order.
- Refrain from gossip.
- Meditate by sending healing light, energy, and colors to the womb.
- Eat as many organic fruits and vegetables as possible.
- If you are not a vegan, eat meat and dairy that is organic, hormone-free, and free from antibiotics if possible.
- Stay away from animal foods that come from the ocean. Unfortunately, the oceans are highly polluted with mercury.
- Avoid exterminators coming into the home; use other options such as boric acid for fleas and roaches. Pure peppermint oil keeps mice away.
- Avoid unnatural air fresheners.
- Use only natural home cleaning products; avoid chemicals such as Scotchgard in your home. Scotchgard is highly toxic.
- Use all-natural personal body care.
- Avoid chemical relaxers, perms, and texturizers.
- Eat foods that are natural antioxidants to combat toxins.
- Avoid constant television watching and music that is not conducive to healing.
- Protect yourself from EMFs (electromagnetic energy fields) and ELFs (low-frequency electromagnetic energy fields) caused by kitchen appliances, cell phones, televisions, microwaves, etc. Crystals such as black tourmaline, fluorite, and clear quartz can be used to combat harmful energy fields. Diodes can also be used to avoid EMFs and ELFs.

- Avoid lipsticks with lead.
- Avoid nail polishes with formaldehyde and phthalates. Water-based nail polishes are available.
- Sleep on an organic mattress.

Vegan Diet During Pregnancy

A proper vegan diet is safe during pregnancy and lactation. Vegans do not eat the flesh of animals. Nor do they eat animal byproducts, such as milk and eggs. Many animals are pumped with antibiotics and hormones that are passed on to the womb. Dead animal flesh and its byproducts also carry adrenaline and poison. Adrenaline is produced when the animal experiences fear right before its death. This poison is not healthy for the unborn child. Dairy also can be problematic because it creates mucus. Mucus causes disease, tumors, and cysts. Milk also contains pus (white blood cells) and bacteria.

A mother's caloric needs rise during pregnancy. According to John McDougall, M.D., mothers will need 200 to 250 calories more a day. However, physically hardworking pregnant women from the Philippines and rural Africa take in no more, and often fewer, calories than before pregnancy. Fortunately, their foods are primarily nutrient-dense vegetable foods that easily provide the raw materials to grow a healthy baby.[6] Afrikans are able to eat fewer foods, but consisting of more vegetables, and still provide for their babies. There is great value in plant-based diets. Mothers do not need to consume large amounts of animal protein for a healthy and fit pregnancy.

I was successful maintaining a vegan diet during pregnancy and the lactation period. I know the vegan diet was vital in creating a smooth pregnancy. However, mothers should not change their diet drastically during pregnancy, because it will result in the body rapidly detoxifying. These toxins can be released to the baby. Vegan mothers concerned with whether or not they are eating correctly should consult a vegan nutritionist to provide nutritional counseling and answer questions related to weight gain, caloric intake, fats, minerals, and vitamins needed.

When I was pregnant I was told I was anemic. I didn't believe I was truly anemic because I felt great. My midwife suggested I take a popular herbal supplement that helps to make most people's hemoglobin counts rise. However, my count did not rise. She then suggested the herb yellow dock, which didn't work either. I also drank a lot of chlorophyll and added blackstrap molasses to my nondairy milks. My midwife then suggested that my hemoglobin count might be what is normal for me. Hemoglobin tests are not always effective. As a matter of fact, this test cannot diagnose iron deficiency because the blood volume of pregnant women is supposed to increase dramatically. The regrettable consequence of routine evaluation of hemoglobin concentration is that, all over the world, millions of pregnant women are wrongly told they are anemic and are given iron supplements.[7]

I didn't abandon my vegan diet of fruits, vegetables, and whole grains. I made sure I ate a lot of live foods daily. I found that fruit kept my stomach at ease and helped me avoid morning sickness. My lunch always included raw, green, and leafy vegetables, which contain many nutrients, including vitamin A, vitamin C, calcium, and fiber. To keep up my good fat intake I ate a lot of avocados and added liquid vegetarian omega-3, -6, and -9 fatty acids to my meals. Many vegans worry about vitamin B_{12}. I'm sure for some vegan mothers this worry may escalate. Most vegan mothers rely on B_{12} supplements, fortified foods, fermented foods, and nutritional yeast. Do not rely on nutritional yeast alone.

Nutritional Chart

Vitamin A	Dark green leafy vegetables, carrots, sweet potatoes, broccoli, cabbage
Vitamin B_{12}	Nutritional yeast, sublingual B_{12} supplements, fortified foods
Vitamin B_1	Whole grains, brown rice, navy beans, kidney beans, oats, nuts, seeds, wheat germ
Vitamin B_2	Green leafy vegetables and nuts
Vitamin B_6	Raw fruits, plantains, bananas, hazel nuts, spinach, potatoes
Vitamin B_9	Beans, whole grains, legumes, dark leafy vegetables
Vitamin C	Broccoli, oranges, papaya, guava, tangerines, kale, collard greens, kiwi fruit
Vitamin D	Sunlight, torula yeast, fortified foods
Vitamin E	Wheat germ, spinach, broccoli, kiwi fruit, almonds, green leafy vegetables, sweet potatoes

Vitamin K	Alfalfa, parsley, spinach
Protein	Nuts, beans, tofu, potatoes, wheat germ, oatmeal, kelp, dulse, Irish moss, nori, and spirulina
Iron	Blackstrap molasses, yellow dock, alfalfa, nettle, figs, watermelon, raisins, dark leafy green vegetables (kale, collards, spinach, etc.)
Omega-6	Safflower oil, sunflower oil, vegetables, fruits, nuts, whole grains, soybeans
Omega-3	Spirulina, flax seeds, green leafy vegetables, hemp seeds, pumpkin seeds, avocados
Omega-9	Avocados, peanuts, olive oil, sesame seeds, peanuts, pecans, cashews, macadamia nuts
Calcium	Kale, collard greens, okra, blackstrap molasses, tofu, broccoli, oatmeal, parsley

Meditation

There is a Malawian Chewa proverb that says, "Mother is god number two." She is a Mut (pronounced *moot*), mother goddess. Afrikan women are divine earth mothers who have been blessed with the ability to create. Afrikan mothers, sit proudly on your throne. The name Auset means seat or throne; this great Netert (Kemetic goddess) was the ultimate mother. She was devoted to motherhood and marriage. Auset was a healer who brought her husband back to life, and who birthed a divine son who would bring order and righteousness to the world again.

Auset lives within us all. Afrikan mothers must have the confidence to birth in their own images. The birth experience will be remembered for the rest of the mother's life so it must be made a blessed event. Mothers are in control of their births and bodies; no one should interpret what the birth should be for the mother. This is her blessed experience. The divine spirit manifesting in the womb should be protected. In the same way Auset protected her son Heru from Set, mothers have the right to question and say no.

Mothers can begin meditating on the birth as soon as they are aware that conception has taken place. She must prepare her body, mind, and spirit for a celestial birth. I visualized and meditated during my pregnancy. I sat in my bathtub of salt water and talked to my son, guiding him through our birth experience, which was soon to come. I reassured him that it would be safe to leave the womb when it was time. I visualized him leaving my womb in a peaceful manner, the cervix opening slowly like a lotus flower, allowing his head to enter the birth canal. I envisioned him crowning slowly and then pulling him up with my own hands onto my belly. I also sent healing colors and light to my womb. I massaged my womb, and let the water caress it. While in the bath I read the book *Coming Forth by Day* to my son. This title, also known as the *Egyptian Book of the Dead*, is one of the world's oldest books. It is essential that babies are exposed to enlightening literature. Music is also important; choose musicians such as Nina Simone, Sun Ra, John Coltrane, Pharoah Sanders, and The Wailers. Give your baby music and words that shine a healing light on the womb. Sit still, be at peace, and find your center. Take time to imagine your birth and what you need to do to create this heaven.

Altar work can also be used to connect with the baby. My altar included candles, seashells, plants, water, blue cloth, and crystals. The altar was organized around a doll of the Yoruba orisha Yemaya, mother of the orishas. She is the protector of mothers and their babies. Parents can create any type of altar that resonates with them and their baby's spirit. My altar was the special place where my baby and I could connect with each other. The women of the Dagara culture create shrines for their unborn babies from things such as plants, water, food, and medicine bags. A shrine is and will be a sacred space that holds the baby's identity. Each time parents need to strengthen their bond with the baby or each other, they can return to the shrine.[8]

Pregnant mothers should not underestimate the power of bonding with their babies through the womb. Mother and baby are literally one, complete harmony. The parents have the power to tune into their unborn child's needs and must find a quiet and still place to communicate with their baby. Parents may ask the child if there is anything that he or she needs, and some ask the child why they have been so divinely chosen to be their parent. Parents may also choose to find out the child's destiny or life path. They should communicate daily. So, when the child comes to the earthly realm the parents and child are in tune. This will enable them to meet their baby's needs and be in accord.

Preparation

Mothers can prepare their bodies physically. Some women prepare the perineum for birth to avoid tears; commonly, oil is rubbed on the area to increase its elasticity. Traditionally, the Buganda women of Uganda would sit in shallow baths of herbal preparations during the last few weeks of pregnancy to relax the tissues of the perineum. In nearby Sudan, the women would squat over a pot of herbs on the fire; this form of steaming moistened and softened the perineum and was widely believed to make labor easier.[9]

The community can also help the mother prepare for birth. Everyone is responsible for respecting and honoring the mother's queendom. Within the Afrikan community rituals are usually performed for the mother and baby. Every Afrikan mother and child should have a "blessing way," a rite of passage for the expectant mother. Blessing ways usually have only females in attendance, including the doula and midwife. Men are sometimes in another room, drumming. In Somalia, a ceremony takes place when the mother is eight to nine months pregnant and only women are invited. Food and beverages are served and prayers are said. The mother is also pampered: "We will put some oil in her hair. Then everybody massage around the stomach, massage the muscles there."[10] The Dagara culture also has rituals for the mother-to-be:

> A shrine is created for the baby during this ritual to facilitate communication between the parents and the child. The shrine usually starts with a gift of a medicine bag the grandparents bring to the ritual. Water, earth, plants, and fabrics are used to create the shrine; the shrine can also contain precious items that others at the ritual may have brought for the mother-to-be and the baby. Contents of the shrine and the medicine bag increase as the parents-to-be are guided to bring items the incoming soul will point out to them during the duration of the pregnancy.[11]

Blessing Way Ideas

- Begin the ceremony by opening the way with a libation to the ancestors.
- If possible, have a traditional Afrikan priestess attend. She can call on deities and ancestors and give divine information regarding the child's destiny, mission, and much more.

- Each sistah should be smudged with sage, myrrh, and frankincense.

- Set up an altar for mother and baby. Use colors such as blue and white to represent mother deities such as Nu, Yemaya, and Auset. Place fresh flowers, plants, stones, crystals, and candles on the altar. Have guests bring altar gifts for mother and baby, such as stones, poems, shells, and flowers. As each guest places their gift on the altar, they should explain its significance.

- Each sistah should introduce herself, beginning with the mother-to-be, by lighting a candle and stating, "I am _____, daughter of _____. The mother-to-be will light the next person's candle. This will create a lighted circle of unity.

- A footbath can be prepared for the mother-to-be with herbs and oils. While one of the sistahs gives the mother a footbath, the others can write words of inspiration in a journal for her.

- Write down on pieces of paper fears concerning birth and motherhood. Burn the fears away in a fireproof incense burner or holder; use charcoal and sage. The paper can be smudged with frankincense and myrrh.

- The ritual should be followed with a celebratory meal.

23

BECAUSE THEY MATTER

Tashee Meadows

Her feathers are skeletal and dirty. The skin under them is visible and raw from rubbing against the wire. There is purple skin stretched thin over round cysts shutting the hen's eyes and causing incredible pain to her feet. The placement is not random. She has to balance her full weight on slanted wires twenty-four hours a day, causing her joints distress. The wire allows urine and feces to fall through and pile up beneath her, giving off enough ammonia to sting and infect her eyes. She is in a cage with nine other hens. Each has a space about the size of a piece of paper and must climb over the others to reach the food and water at the front of the cage. Some have their necks wrapped around the wire and others hang by wings also caught in the wire. Immobilized and unable to get to food or water, they die of starvation in the cage. The living stand alongside the dying, dead, and decomposing. The cages are stacked from the floor nearly to the ceiling in a warehouse and extend back until they disappear into the darkness. This is a battery-cage system where the chickens never see the light of day, their feet never touch earth, and they can never spread their wings.

I became vegan because I don't want to support captivity, torture, physical mutilation, and killing. I first picked up a pamphlet about veganism and animal rights at an Earth Day celebration in Washington, D.C., my home of sixteen years before moving to Alabama. I saw pictures of the hens I've described and was shocked. The chickens didn't look at all like the white, fluffy, feathered birds of my mind's eye.

I became vegetarian on my next birthday, as a gift to others and myself; but I had to learn more. I chose chickens as a topic for a school paper. I quickly realized that it was hard to find any information on chickens as animals because they have been declassified as animals and reclassified as objects; as "food." I had to do searches, instead, for poultry. I read *Fast*

Food Nation by Eric Schlosser, *The Dreaded Comparison* by Marjorie Spiegel, and *Animal Liberation* by Peter Singer, and many articles. I visited websites and was particularly impressed with Compassion Over Killing (www.cok.net) and Farm Sanctuary (www.farmsanctuary.org). The more I learned, the more the animals' suffering resonated with me. Somehow, I felt that eating *suffering* and calling it *nourishment* could only produce more suffering. I thought of my ancestry as a Black woman: the rapes, unwanted pregnancies, captivity, stolen babies, grieving mothers, horrific transports, and the physical, mental, and spiritual pain of chattel slavery. I'm convinced that animals of other species, many of whom are more protective of their young than humans, grieve when their babies are taken away. I thought of how much I missed my mother, brother, and sister when I was in foster care. I made the emotional connection that other beings must feel this pain, too, when they are separated from their mothers and other family members. When I saw the battery cages, I thought of the more than two million Americans who know cages firsthand in the prison-industrial complex. I thought of the economically oppressed workers at killing plants and wondered if people who kill and cut all day could still make love at night. I had to learn more, so I went to work for The Fund for Animals.

With access to, and influence from, The Fund for Animals and Compassion Over Killing, my eyes were opened with a reality check. I learned that baby chickens are hatched thousands at a time. At an egg-laying farm where they use the battery-cage system I described, the male chicks are thrown away—alive—into what looks like a thirty-gallon garbage can. Packed against each other's bodies, they eventually suffocate. The female baby chickens have their beaks seared off with a hot iron, without anesthetic. This sometimes cuts off part of their tongue and often burns their eyes and nostrils. This is done to keep them from pecking themselves or each other while confined so closely. Their front toes are amputated at the outer joint without anesthetic for the same reason. Once grown, the hens are routinely denied food for at least ten days, which induces molting and shocks their systems into laying eggs. The integrity of these sensitive beings is totally violated. They do not control their bodies, their reproduction, their social structure, or their food.

Pigs suffer, too. The piglet is held by his rear with his head dangling toward the concrete floor. The worker cuts off his tail without anesthetic. He then cuts into his scrotum and pulls out his testicles. The piglet wiggles and screams. The female piglet is chosen as a breeder.

She, too, has her tail cut off. She then spends her life in a continuous cycle of insemination, pregnancy, birth, and nursing. While pregnant, she is restricted in what is called a gestation crate, a cage of metal piping the size of the pig, allowing her only to stand or lie down. She has no room to turn around and certainly no room to walk in any direction. Once she has given birth, she's transferred to a farrowing crate and confined to lying on the industrial grated flooring by metal bars or straps. Here, she nurses her babies. One advertiser of such contraptions boasts cast iron as their first flooring option. When the mother pig's birthing rate slows, she is packed into a crowded truck with other pigs and unloaded at a killing plant. There, she is hoisted into the air by a chain on her hind leg. While she is writhing around trying to break free, a worker cuts her throat. She is replaced by another pig who will reproduce more quickly.

Like pigs and chickens, cows also know captivity and have their reproductive systems hijacked by their captors. Cows and bulls do not choose their mates. They are bred instead to increase desired traits like heavier weights, higher volumes of milk, or to be polled (born without horns). Cows, like humans, carry their young for nine months. Most cows raised for their flesh give birth in the spring. They graze together through the summer and then the baby calves are stolen from their mothers in the fall. They are taken to a feedlot where they are crowded into pens on dirt outdoors or confined to solitary cages inside a facility. They are fed a mixture engineered to make them grow as quickly as possible. As a result, they reach slaughter weight within a year, even though they have not fully matured. Cows that are held captive for their milk suffer one pregnancy after another, allowing them to produce milk for ten months after each birth. If a cow produces a high volume of milk, her female calf may be chosen to replace older cows, who are killed when their production slows. The majority of calves born to cows who produce milk are killed within weeks of being born, and are sold as veal.

Cows and bulls also suffer mutilation in their youth and at the killing plants. Within weeks of being born, their horns are cut out of their heads to adapt them to confinement. Male calves who will not be used for breeding are held down while someone cuts their testicles from their bodies. Then to mark ownership, their sensitive skin is burned with a red-hot branding iron. All of this is done without anesthesia. For many, the physical brutality escalates to the unthinkable at the killing plant. By law, cows and bulls do not have to be dead prior to being butchered. They are, however, supposed to be struck unconscious, usually by a single bolt shot into the head. Unfortunately, unlike car parts on an assembly line, these "products" are living beings that move, often causing the shooter to miss his mark. They are dismembered while still alive and conscious.

They resist. At the stockyard, bewildered calves try to turn around and run away, only to be beaten and prodded in their face, anus, and anywhere in between. The pigs who don't get off the truck are dragged or thrown off. Those who resist being confined to small metal cages are hit in the head with pieces of wood, metal piping, electric prods, and anything else that the workers can get their hands on. Chickens fight for their lives as they are shackled in the killing plant before having their throats cut. These beings resist at every point of their captivity and torture. They surrender only to the force used against them.

We, too, should resist. We should resist the notion that cows "give" their milk and flesh because we know that, like their babies, they are taken. We should resist being fooled by images of happy cows, pigs, and chickens that smile at us from advertisements, because we know there is no happiness in captivity, torture, and death. As Black people, we can resist being insulted by historic comparisons to animals that are intended to hurt us and embrace our fellow beings with respect, awe, and wonder. We should resist arguments about the natural food chain because, for one, we've killed the part of it that would *naturally* eat us, and two, there's nothing natural about breeding for genetic modification, captivity, and systematic mutilation. We should resist in solidarity with souls who long for freedom they've never known.

It has never been easier to take a stand for the billions of individuals created and destroyed for human consumption—by going vegan. It's been fourteen years since I stopped consuming dead animals; five years since I gave up dairy and eggs. For the first two years, I was the lone vegetarian among my friends and family, trying to live off bean burritos. I must say this is not the way to go, and if I had to do it over, I'd do two things differently. First, I'd join a vegetarian society like the Black Vegetarians of Georgia or the Vegetarian Society of D.C. These and other vegetarian groups, which are all over the country, are a great place to meet other vegans, exchange recipes, sample home-cooked foods, and try out restaurants. Secondly, I'd learn five vegan recipes for foods I love. Keep in mind you have the whole world to choose from. Try Indian *palak daal*, African peanut stews, Thai coconut curries, Ethiopian lentils and split peas, and Chinese bean curd. When we broaden the horizons of our dietary choices, it's easy to find recipes that are authentically vegan and require no substitutions.

It is important to remember that our dietary choices can have negative or positive consequences. If we are what we eat, we can choose to be fear and terror or bright green sprigs of broccoli. We can choose to be orphans and prisoners or strong, leafy collards. We can choose to be pain and death or vibrant mangoes. Each time we sit down at the table, we can choose to consume violence and dine on terror or choose a vegan lifestyle that nourishes our bodies, gives us peace of mind and provides sustenance for our souls. I easily choose vegan. Peace begins on our plates.

24

JOURNEY TOWARD COMPASSIONATE CHOICE
INTEGRATING VEGAN AND SISTAH EXPERIENCE

Tara Sophia Bahna-James

LIFE OUTSIDE THE BOX

Growing up, I built an identity on straddling extremes. Black and white, divorced and functional, extravagant and financially struggling, intuitive and intellectual. I took pride in my family's ability to defy preconceptions. Even as an individual, I have been a woman of color in a white family, a thin woman in an overweight family, a Christian wife with a Jewish husband, a Catholic woman at a pro-choice rally, and (in a cliché's most literal incarnation) the hyphenated kid whose name wouldn't fit on the Scantron sheet. Finding myself "outside the box" has always been a fact of my life. The up side of this, or perhaps of living this existence in New York City, where uniqueness is a virtue, is that I have always embraced that individuality and quite early was able to learn the power of flouting expectations through self-labeling.

In college, for instance, when friends would ask me about my Catholicism in light of my more Buddhist-humanist philosophy and political convictions, I would say, "My religion doesn't only describe my beliefs: it describes the stories I was told, the rituals I was taught, and the community I was born into. It describes the vehicle through which I first learned to understand my own spirituality and connection to God." To me, Catholic was more of a language I spoke than a statement I had made. "Then why not convert?" many friends would say. But to my mind, the notion that I could alter my identity based on my beliefs, or even that I would want to, seemed ludicrous. To me, labels spoke not of where we are (which is open to repositioning with every choice we make) but of where we have come from. And I *loved* where I came from, regardless of where I might be going.

155

Refusing to relabel (or insisting upon adding to my hyphens instead of dropping them) gave me a unique position from which to express my changing views to my own community: "The church *needs* pro-choice and pro-gay Catholics," I would insist. "I owe it to others like me to stand up and declare that I exist." Every one of us marginalized by our own community—whether intentionally or not—is a living example of diversity within that community. In this case, my mission was to be a living example for those who identify as Roman Catholic. I wanted to show them that my religion could and does include people who want to protect a woman's right to choose. To those who would argue with that, I needed simply to say, "But I am one of them!" My very existence proved them wrong.

Journey Toward Vegetarianism

Like most vegans, I did not come from a family of vegans or even vegetarians. But unlike many of them, I had a conversion experience characterized more by a gradual process of awakening than by a single event. When I was a child, my mother, the product of Depression-era working-class parents who took pride in putting meat on the table, fed me pork and lamb chops, chicken cutlets, and meatloaf. My grandfather was a cook by profession and whipped up *crème fraîche* and blueberries for me when I came home from school.

But the presence of animals in our home was not confined to the dinner table. We lived with our share of companion animals—most of them four-legged and furry—and as an intuitive lot, we had comfortably acknowledged a spiritual connection to our animal companions for generations. Though it would take time for me to appreciate the incongruity of the way I ate, it was not difficult for me to listen to arguments about the plight of animals because (along with friends and relatives who were overweight, female, Black, or not American-born) they were among the family members of mine whom I understood to be misunderstood and oppressed within the American society at large. From as far back as I can remember, I chose to give half of my allowance every month to Greenpeace because I once saw an after-school special about the plight of the whales. By the end of high school, my meager sum would be split between Greenpeace, the Humane Society, and any number of human- and animal-advocacy groups that had a Christmas mailing list.

I was first exposed to vegetarianism at the age of six, thanks to a young playmate, D, who was famous in our elementary school for refusing (on ethical grounds) to eat meat or eggs.

If I remember correctly, D was also lactose-intolerant and, given the limited state of vegan cuisine in the mid- to late-1970s, could be seen eating only peanut butter and jelly on matzoh for the entire holiday of Passover.

Needless to say, D was teased considerably in our little elementary school. The cruelest boys and girls would ask her why she didn't eat meat, just to laugh at her offbeat and seemingly precocious arguments on the sanctity of life. But somehow, although it would take days for me to defend her outright and years for me to join her cause, I never wanted to tease her. Even to my six-year-old brain, all of her arguments seemed entirely sympathetic to me. They just "made sense." At first, it was an intellectual realization: there was a contradiction between what I knew to be true (namely that nonhuman animals were also sentient beings worthy of love and respect) and what I ate. There was something ethically puzzling to me in how I could pat my beloved bunny rabbit each day after school and still condone my mother's serving up hot dogs for dinner. Meat still tasted good to me, but eating it just did not make sense. And at first, that was enough.

So finally, for my New Year's resolution, at the age of twelve I stopped eating red meat and poultry. However, I would keep fish in my diet, as I liked seafood too much and was afraid to have a reason to cheat (something I had learned from my mother's dieting: if you're too hard on yourself from the onset, you're more likely to throw in the towel).

My pescetarianism remained relatively strong for the next six years, until college. Up to then, my transgressions included a single hot dog eaten at Coney Island for nostalgic reasons on a date in junior high. I had grief and guilt for several months after that incident, and I was devastated on a foreign exchange trip to France when I couldn't get a bilingual priest in Paris to absolve me for my deed on the grounds that "that isn't a sin." I tried very patiently to explain to my confessor that *for me* hot-dog eating *was* sinful because I believed it was wrong and I had made a commitment to myself not to do it, but he was unimpressed. Though outraged at the time, I now think this was one step in a progression toward realizing I couldn't always count on someone being there to absolve me. In life, eventually I would need to discover a way to absolve myself.

When I started college (not surprisingly during a time I was physically separated from my companion animals), my commitment to my lifestyle subsided and the impulse toward more frequent transgressions rose. For the first year, I remained vegetarian-identified, but after that, partially out of curiosity's sake and partially out of not wanting to be denied anything campus life had to offer, I began to reintroduce poultry into my diet on rare occasions, first a little guiltily, then almost absentmindedly.

I met my husband working for an Internet company in 1997. Me being a mainly fish, grains, and veggies "-ivore" with rare dalliances into eating chicken or turkey afforded us the possibility of eating at the most ridiculously decadent New York restaurants on our ridiculously decadent late-'90s techie-bubble salaries. And though I noticed I felt healthier when I avoided poultry and fish, I associated no guilt with the indulgent impulse itself. In this pre–September 11th world, following a New York childhood at once sheltered from real tragedy and exposed to infinite forms of diversity, any guilt was theoretical. On the contrary, as the youngest and a well-educated member of a not particularly well-to-do family, I felt almost a responsibility to indulge and enjoy my life to the fullest.

It's not that I'd forgotten D's heroism entirely. By now, I was so used to not eating beef and pork that I'd lost my interest in them entirely. They smelled foul to me. But the connection to fish and fowl was easier to ignore. It remained an intellectual argument about the sanctity of life, one I agreed with but not one that was personal. My diet—in fact, my entire attitude toward animal activism—became as knee-jerk as its predecessor. I stopped *seeing* the animals in what I was eating and became instead "the decider." I simply said, "This is a behavior I've decided is taboo" (eating beef, pork); "this is a behavior I've decided is not taboo" (eating fish); "this is a behavior I've decided is not preferable but will be forgiven" (eating chicken). It *is* possible to practice most ethical behaviors without feeling *real* compassion.

During this time, the Humane Society and their lesser-known cohorts in direct mailing would continue to inundate my mailbox with T-shirts, umbrellas, and endless photos of emaciated foxes caught in traps and puppies left malnourished and tied to junkyard chains. For a long time, I remained bound and restricted by my sentimentality and helplessness in the face of this "awareness." I would fret over each piece of junk mail I threw out. When I felt I was too poor to lend my dime (most of the time), I'd stare for precious minutes at each photo as though it were the sad animal itself. In these moments, quietly and insidiously, my false two-dimensional understanding of these flesh-and-blood creatures was reinforced, their body and bones reduced to lightweight, ink-stained cardboard, like a tasteless church wafer between my undeceived finger pads. My grateful ego then reinterpreted my misdeed to this lesser present moment, transferring any guilt meant for all of my *truly* culpable moments (in which I'd supported the poultry market with my purchase or did *not* actively get out of my car to lead the stranded or abandoned creature I had passed to safety) to this infinitely less egregious moment in which I threw out some junk mail instead of sending in my dollar. This was the passive state of my activism until January 2004, when a trip to India radically transformed my way of looking at the world and the way I thought about activism and human and animal rights.

Forgiving Ourselves for Where We Are

It started with the dogs. We'd always had pets in the family I grew up in, but for my husband it was his appreciation for our adopted dogs that first caused him to consider giving up meat. By 2004, we'd been sharing our home for three and a half years with a lovable, feisty, emotive, proud, cuddly, and vivacious canine whose free will could not be denied. We were used to seeing her laugh, cry, try, succeed, demand, share, and give. But, above all, we were used to seeing her smile. The first thing I noticed upon arriving in Mumbai was that the dogs didn't smile. I also noticed that they looked hungry and tired. Then I saw there were thousands of them, everywhere I looked. So many starving animals crossed my path that I finally understood something differently. I realized that the type of "pity" I'd succumbed to previously in the United States was actually a way of distancing myself from the real face of suffering.

At home, I had been a person who donated what little amount my student lifestyle would afford to this or that charity, letting my face drop and my heart bleed for whatever painful or gruesome picture graced the cover of the latest PETA mailing. I would look longingly at Internet listings of abandoned mutts I wished I could bring home to my apartment, already overflowing with dog hair, feeling somehow my own little mini-catharsis over the fact that I at least had taken the time to look and diminish my own carefree attitude in the process. This feeling, which I had not yet recognized as pity, was what made me naively think that my behavior was humane.

But in India, beset with far too many people and animals to feel for, I realized the ridiculousness of the exchange. Each glimpse of suffering, I realized, was a way of paying my dues, allowing myself to feel human for a moment, before continuing on with my day. This kind of pity was not compassion, for it was useless and coma-inducing whereas compassion is active and equalizing. It may be possible to practice ethical behaviors without real compassion, but it is not possible to *really* feel compassion and not act ethically. Compassion writes laws and provides shelter and builds houses. Pity is a masturbatory exercise for the privileged. It is self-conscious, self-reflective, and limited. It considers weeping and then moves on.

Although I didn't think of it in these terms at the time, it is no wonder to me now that this came to me in a moment when I felt limited culpability. These were not my country's dogs nor my country's people. I was powerless to improve their conditions on my brief visit (or at least temporarily ignorant of the way to do so). Even more so, I had been and was planning to be eating vegetarian for the entire duration of our trip anyway—barely a sacrifice in India, where the cuisines of whole regions were meatless and delicious. What I didn't understand then was that India provided the ideal conditions for the conversion experience I needed—a harsh view of my need for change and a safe space that suspended my own complicity and showed me an easy road to adjusting my lifestyle (in this case, to a truly vegetarian one). At once, it woke me up *and* it softened the bitterness of my awakening.

Weeks later, I returned home to New York as a first-time aspiring vegan, with a renewed commitment to animal rights in particular. The first book I read upon my return was *The Dreaded Comparison* by Marjorie Spiegel. I'd bought a copy online a couple of years before, almost entirely due to Alice Walker's foreword, but didn't end up reading it until that moment. That work changed my life irrevocably. I was not shocked by the existence of oppression but rather by the complexity of my complicity.

The Dreaded Comparison's primary task is the examination of the similarities between the social and economic conditions that made human slavery and allowed it to continue in the U.S. for as long as it did. It is a striking parallel that shows how American factory farming is allowed to continue today. As often cited in similarly controversial comparisons made to the Nazi Holocaust, among these conditions were: 1) the separating out of animals (and Blacks and Jews, respectively) in public discourse as "other" and essentially "less than human"; 2) the transportation of animals (and people) in squalid and tightly confined spaces; 3) the economic complicity of the public at large; and 4) the actual separation of the population in question and the removal of the scene of their torture to a location behind closed doors and out of mainstream public display (such as ghettos, internment and work camps, slaughter-houses, and so on).

As I read points one and two, it seemed not only obviously inhumane but also somehow beyond my control in any immediate way. But then I realized that points three and four were not only more subtle and insidious, but were also somehow related. It is because the grossest examples of cruelty take place behind closed doors that the public can stand to be economically complicit. And in fact, the public's participation in institutionalized systems of oppression (whether it be through the purchasing of factory-farmed meat, the purchase of cotton from slave labor, the turning a blind eye to domestic violence, or the verbal and financial support of the war in Iraq) is contingent upon their willingness to be kept in a state of denial about the details. People tell themselves the incidents of cruelty are somehow nonexistent, inconsequential, or, worse yet, justified, and in doing so they are allowed to continue their lifestyles unaltered.

The following year, I was reminded of this realization when I heard the renowned psychologist and feminist Carol Gilligan speak at Omega Institute's Women and Power conference, in upstate New York. Gilligan mentioned the "point of initiation" girls typically encounter when they first receive cues to discard and discount their own experience in order to enter into society and uphold the hierarchy of authority. Just as silently, was I once stripped of my own ability to judge my eating habits. We are dragged into this contract from such an early age that, by the time we are cognizant of actual cruelty being done in our name, we are so deeply complicit that to be illuminated would be to initiate a process of guilt and grieving so painful that most are afraid to ever look behind the curtain in the first place. And so continues the nefarious unspoken social contract, "Don't ask, don't tell." We are encouraged to participate further, then deny further, then participate again, circling in on ourselves, betraying ourselves at every turn on and on into infinity.

Here was the kernel that has helped to shape my understanding of animal-rights activism ever since. If this cycle is ever going to end, two things must happen: people need to be awakened to the reality they have denied, *and* people must be made to believe in the possibility of forgiveness; they must not be made to feel shame at the process of their awakening. Everyone who has ever been in therapy knows the difficultly of acknowledging one's pain, and every AA member knows the difficulty of acknowledging one has a problem. Often, when we truly move on in our attitudes, it is because we are first able to forgive ourselves for where we are.

Sistah Nonvegans

By the spring of 2005, after attending and volunteering at my first animal-rights conference, I found myself for the first time with vegan friends and an awareness of a larger, multi-dimensional vegan community. Yet, as my enthusiasm for this new lifestyle, philosophy, and community grew, I could not help but realize that the most vocal skepticism I encountered came from my other female, Black-identified friends.

One friend made the connection that often veganism meant having the luxury of enough time and money to go out of one's way and engage in specific, harder-to-find consumer choices; a prerequisite that makes assumptions about class and privilege that are largely at odds with the more mainstream Black American experience. Another, more financially successful Black friend had been put off by hearing vegans make ethical arguments that analogized animal agriculture to slavery. Still another friend, whom I watched go from childhood in the projects to a law school degree by the sweat of her own brow, couldn't help but interpret what I said as though someone was asking her to sacrifice after all she'd been through. And though I'm committed to veganism, I don't necessarily disagree with their arguments. I still feel I can see where these friends are coming from, simply because I know where they've been.

Outside the Vegan Box

As I talked to these women I realized that my feelings for them didn't amount to having forgiveness while I waited patiently for them to change their minds; rather it amounted to having respect for the fact that they were in the middle of a process of integrating their own experience, just as I was in the process of integrating mine. I was not uncommitted to my cause, but I didn't need for them in particular to change their minds. Nor did I fear that the different, honest conclusions they had come to (about what was right for them) would alter mine or sway me from my own. Diversity, the different needs and opinions of an infinite number of individuals, was for me a fact of life. If there were an underlying truth, it would have to be big enough to encompass *all* of our experiences, natures, and inalienable rights:

mine, theirs, *and* the animals'. And my faith that such a truth does exist is what kept me from desperately wanting to impose my particular piece of the puzzle on those on honest quests to discern their own.

It wasn't until I started to deconstruct my lifelong relationships with these women and to understand that my acceptance of their nonvegan choices was born out of appreciation for their own divinity, and their journey toward embracing that divinity, that I came to understand my strangeness in the context of what I felt had been outlined for me as the larger vegan movement.

This strangeness wouldn't come up often, but it would always rear its head when, in an attempt to explain how one tolerates living in a nonvegan world, someone would say something like, "If I could just force all the people in the world to stop eating meat right now I would, but I can't." This always stopped me in my tracks to pose the question mentally to myself: "If I could *force* everyone to stop eating meat, would I?" And the answer came back, invariably, "No."

I've never been fond of hypothetical questions. I think they are a big distraction created by debate-minded folk to take the heat off of what people can actually do in the world. We think we know how we feel or what we would do in seemingly cut-and-dried situations, but we really have no way of knowing. Still, this one question haunts me because of its far-reaching implications. If the question came to me as "If you could *encourage* or *influence* everyone in the world to stop eating meat, would you?" I believe I'd be able to say, "Yes." But in the more common phrasing of the question lurks a condition I cannot abide. Forcing sentient beings to behave in a particular way—especially with regard to their own bodies—is always wrong; and although as a vegan I can see the connection between my nonvegan friend's purchase and the financial support of an unspeakably cruel institution, I do not have the right to usurp her decision-making in this regard, *nor would I want to*. Any prayer or dream for mind control and world domination, even a benevolent, hypothetical one, only perpetuates the cycle of domination and oppression the vegan lifestyle seeks to end.

To my mind, the cause ought not to be to end slaughter, but to end the cycle that causes people to choose it. Fight ignorance, fight deception, fight self-loathing, fight fear of the other, be a witness to the truth as you have experienced it—reject the inevitability of that unspoken social contract—and in doing such, empower people to make compassionate choices for themselves.

It breaks my heart to come to the realization that veganism is not the bottom line for me, especially because it's still a lifestyle I continue to engage in and support, primarily for ethical reasons. More and more, I learn the bottom line has to be truth. For me, the only truth that has withstood the test of time is that we're all inherently unique individuals and yet part of a single divine life-force; each of us is completely responsible for our own actions and, quite justly, unable to truly control anyone else's. It's this underlying reality that calls me to veganism, because it is the vantage point from which I consider life sacred; but it is ultimately the same underlying reality that forces me to consider sacred the power of choice.

This may seem like an argument from an antivegan consumer-advocacy group. But when I look back, what outraged me most on reading *The Dreaded Comparison* was learning all the ways in which choices were being made for me and acts committed in my name simply by virtue of the fact that I was an American consumer. We are forced to raise our voices to opt *out* of having our shampoos sprayed in rabbits' eyes, *out* of pus-laden bovine hormone being sprayed into our coffee cups, *out* of feeding our children jellybeans bursting with horse byproducts, *out* of eating party snacks laced with the feces of downed cows. Never *in*. When was the assumption made that I was among the masses who were fine with this? When was it determined that the *masses* are fine with it? When did my government, my senators, and my representatives first ask me if they could condone slaughter and torture in my name? The answer of course is, "Never." And I wanted out. Why don't folks who want products inhumanely raised and tested on animals have to go out of their way to the specialty market?

I can't say my outrage came from a particularly Black woman part of my soul, because that part of my soul is inseparable. But I can say that mine was an outrage (that decisions had been made for me, that norms didn't apply to me, that choice was unavailable to me) that Blacks and women have been dealing with for generations.

The Desperation of the Converted

It is not that I think the larger vegan community is impervious to these arguments. But I do think the radical conversion experience more common to vegans who have woken up one day to find themselves deeply embedded, and privileged even, within the culture of "the oppressor," is often less conducive to really accepting what those on other parts of the journey, or on the same journey for different reasons perhaps, are saying. And this is one of the most important ways in which falsely race- and gender-neutral, mainstream vegan culture has failed to address the Black community.

It is true that the vast majority of ethical vegans have eaten meat at some point in their lives. But when waking comes suddenly and a person realizes precious lives are at stake and there is blood on his own hands, he is tempted to distance his awakened self from his former meat-eating self *and* from all whose actions remind him of his former ones. In this distancing, ethical vegans are in danger of forgetting where they have come from.

This is why some of the most adamant fanaticism comes from those who have spent time identifying with the oppressor—the conversion is full and self-righteous. That is *not* to say it is selfish. On the contrary, when we come to understand suffering, it is natural that we want to hasten its end (both for those who suffer at the hands of others and for those who we believe will suffer in coming to know their complicity). But when our own conversion eclipses our appreciation for others and their own narratives (even narratives we have come to associate with the behavior of an oppressor), it is desperate. And there is a reason desperation is suspicious. It is always too personal.

Compassion and Cruelty

It is perhaps unfair to bandy around terms too much without articulating their definitions. Over time, I have come to believe that to *appreciate* someone, human or nonhuman, is not to value them as good, nor even to judge them as good or bad, but rather to accurately perceive their own *free will*: you may call it their truth, their divinity, or their capacity for change. It is this quality of free will that ultimately gives us the power to reject others' labels for us. This quality makes us all unpredictable and boxless if we are willing to embrace it. And as surely as we have all at some moment in our lives been cruel, it is this chameleon-like power that liberates us from our history and makes us capable of choosing from a compassionate place today.

I define *compassionate* actions as those that are born out of appreciating the object/other; that is, seeing the divinity or the capacity for change or the reality of the truth in this being and thereby identifying with him/her and his/her divinity. For me, divinity is defined as actions born out of recognizing and identifying with God in someone—actions born of love. Similarly, I take *cruelty* to be actions that are born out of illusions about the nature of the object/other: specifically, the illusion that he or she is or can be made nondivine, permanent, unchanging, and/or nonchoosing (that is, actions that are born of the unnecessary fear of our falsely perceived permanence, or born of false longing for the permanence of our illusory self).

The difficulty is that before we can learn to choose compassion, we must learn we have a choice. Sometimes we learn this through realizing we no longer have to oppress another out of habit, sometimes through realizing we no longer have to let ourselves be oppressed out of habit. You can never know which history an individual person is working to overcome in any moment.

If we are ever to truly act with compassion, we must be willing to see people, animals, and especially ourselves for what we truly are: ever-changing and capable of growth, decay, transcendence, destruction; witnesses to our own inalienable experiences; ultimately, living testaments of the choices we have made, the acts of compassion or cruelty we have witnessed, and the lives we have known. Each life lived is foremost and always an honest testament to its own truth, never to a truth someone else supposes to have been or once tried to impose.

Women and people of color in America have learned the hard way to stand up to individuals trying to tell them what's best for them. They have learned how to say, "You do not speak for me," "I am not you," and, "You cannot tell me what I need or where I've been." They've learned to say this to their husbands, their employers, their hairdressers, their songwriters, their advertisers, their teachers, and their politicians. And in this dawning day, they aren't willing to sacrifice the hard-won virtues of self-love (and embrace their ability to choose) for the acquisition of a virtue that has been largely presented to them as love of "the other" (the cow, the chicken, the turkey). Nor should they be.

This is why so many Black individuals cringe at the argument that compares animal husbandry to slavery. And this is why many Black vegans emphasize the health benefits of veganism along with the arguments for compassion. For a lifetime, falsely race- (and gender-) neutral mainstream American culture has taught us to view ourselves as the other whose self-determination and will needs liberating. Any undermining of that fundamental right to choose what one needs in a given moment—whether it takes the form of passing judgment on a poor family in the Bronx who has to do their shopping at the local Coca-Cola bodega rather than the expensive organic market at the end of a hard workday; or passing judgment on a wealthy Black lawyer who chooses to make it big on Wall Street rather than returning home to make small change in his poor community—any judgment of your neighbor's choice is a return to an oppressive model.

On Loving the Body

The importance of the body in this equation cannot be overlooked. The body shows me decay (or growth) where I most fear it. Ultimately, my body is simply a map of where I've come from. Quite literally, it is the trail of my electrons coursing, racing, and whirling through space—what my eyes see is the trace of where they've been. I ran ten miles; I ate wheat; I skinned my knees, and experienced pleasure, pain, love, and birth. My body remembers all of these things, even when I am not reflecting on them. The body remembers experiences once endured and actions once taken, things I am capable of because I have once done them.

This is why recognizing ourselves as beautiful is in some ways more powerful than recognizing that we can be "good." To love my body is to reconcile with where I have been and thus what I am capable of. By appreciating myself, and what I am capable of, and hence knowing the roads I didn't take in spite of that capability, only then does my current action become a choice. Only then may it be called good or bad. Without choice, judgment has no value. It is meaningless to call something "good" or "bad" that simply is. Only that which is chosen can be said to be chosen out of compassion or cruelty.

Thus, recognizing that our bodies are beautiful becomes a powerfully political act, a celebration of compassion directed toward the self. And this is what is behind the Black woman's love of her body, which is so present in the ethos of contemporary Black culture. It is imperative that we love our own bodies *and* that we love others' bodies in their diversity. Ultimately, loving people for who they are should never be about disregarding the body—but about embracing it.

Toward Compassionate-veganism

I think it's so important that Black women be included in the vegan dialogue, not only because we are so frequently left out of it, and not only because falling victim to blind consumerism can be considered another form of allowing ourselves to remain oppressed and suppressed, but also because the vegan cause will not be wholly effective until it addresses the diverse spectrum of circumstances and psychologies that contribute to the practices it is trying to overcome.

As lack of diversity compromises any species, so does it impoverish and compromise any progressive movement. If the vegan movement is going to broaden its outreach, if it is going to make any headway in preaching to the unconverted, it must extend its arms of compassion not only to the animals it seeks to save, but to the animal-loving carnivores whose attitudes it hopes to change. We must leave behind our desperation and seek to truly love (that is, respect their divine right to govern their own bodies as they choose) *all* those who cross our path. For me, this is the crux of my veganism.

Personally, I don't see this as a reason to give up my vegan title. Self-labeling is still a powerful tool. And it is still important to me to stand up and say "But I am one of them!" But someday I may opt for another hyphen. I have heard the phrase "ethical-vegan" used to describe those who choose veganism not for health reasons but for animal-rights reasons. But for my part, I will aspire to be worthy of the title "compassionate-vegan," that is, one who chooses veganism out of compassion for my body, for the bodies of the animals who love life no less than I, and for the bodies of my sisters, who are each of them beautiful.

25

VEGANISM AND MISCONCEPTIONS OF THINNESS AS "NORMAL" AND "HEALTHY"

Sistah Vegans Break It Down in Cyberspace

Compiled by A. Breeze Harper

In the year 2006, I initiated a discussion about body image on the Sistah Vegan Yahoo list-serv. The sistah vegans had an honest dialogue about how we felt about our bodies. As women of the African diaspora practicing veganism, we expressed our experiences with struggling to fit the "normal" model of how our bodies "should look." Some of us spoke of being ridiculed for being "too big" to be a vegan. Others spoke of how we were ridiculed for not having "enough curves" or a "booty" like a "real Black woman." Below is the first message I sent to the listserv.

From: Breeze Harper

Dear Ladies,

A few months ago we had an interesting dialogue about body-types and the challenges to debunking the myth that "being vegan" doesn't mean that EVERYONE will be thin. Furthermore, "thin" does NOT equal "healthy" for everybody.

Last night I just finished reading a chapter out of the book *Recovering the Black Female Body* [edited by Michael Bennett and Vanessa D. Dickerson]. It's called "On Being a Fat Black Girl in a Fat-Hating Culture" by Margaret K. Bass. It was REALLY good and it got me thinking about the conversations we have had.

There is a quote from Margaret's essay in which she talks about how one is NOT allowed to be outwardly racist or sexist in American society because it's not politically correct in the

U.S. anymore. However, people who are "fat" (she uses this word because she doesn't feel that using a politically correct word for it is productive) are constantly receiving prejudiced remarks and comments that sound like it could be from the same mentality as "racism" and "sexism." She quotes from [Susan] Bordo, who talks about how U.S. society views people who are fat:

> The obese embody resistance to cultural norms…the obese—particularly those who claim to be happy although overweight—are perceived as not playing by the rules at all. If the rest of us are struggling to be acceptable and "normal," we cannot allow them to get away with it; they must be put in their place, be humiliated and defeated.[1]

Margaret continues by commenting on Bordo:

> I am defeated. I am humiliated and put in my place, and as I write I marvel at how closely related this language is to the language of racism. MY racial self would never allow this, but my fat self concedes, gives up. I don't think any middle-class person, woman, in this country can be fat and happy. Despite the worthy efforts of fat acceptance crusaders, I don't believe they've made a dent in this culture's prejudice against fat people. Oh, you can love your life, have a great job and great friends, a wonderful marriage or partnership, but fat and happy? Not likely. Ask Jenny Craig, The Diet Center, Weight Watchers, Overeaters Anonymous. Consider the hundreds of women who would rather expose themselves to the risks of dangerous drugs than to be fat. Middle-class America, Black and white, won't let you be fat and happy, and I resent it. I resent the ways in which I feel compelled to capitulate to someone else's standard of health and beauty. There are actually studies that suggest one can be fat and healthy.[2]

This was an amazing chapter to read. Margaret brought up a lot of much needed reflections to talk about. I'm very curious about how I often see veganism/vegetarianism advocacy centered on "a great way to lose weight." It's actually always bothered me and I wonder why it has been "normalized" that thinness is normal for everyone and that "being skinny" is a "good health" reason for engaging in veganism. Honestly, how is "healthy" defined? Who defines it? We all know that there are many cultures outside of white middle-class America that do not perceive a thin body as "healthy" or "beautiful." I am very concerned about how veganism is advocated if it still is founded upon white Eurocentric middle-class standards of morality, health, and beauty.

I'm just thinking out loud here, as Margaret's article really touched me. I practice very hard not to be judgmental of body-types; I, too, often have to check myself and make sure I'm not falling into the land of "isms" when I talk about the vegan lifestyle and my perceptions of health with everyone. I always tell people, "Well, everyone is unique and whole-foods veganism has worked for me." However, I have seen many vegan and vegetarian people become judgmental toward female vegans and vegetarians who are not thin. They can be harsh and prejudice in a way that actually parallels "racism." This really bothers me. After all, there are plenty of thin veg*n ladies who are extremely unhealthy.

Anyway ladies, I just wanted to share this with you and see what your take is on this. Remember, we can all have a friendly dialogue about this. You do not have to agree with me. I just hope we all understand that on this Yahoo group we can all "agree to disagree."

Hugs,

Breezie

From: nappilocs

RE: Veganism and Misconceptions of Thinness as "Normal" and "Healthy"
Breeze,

It's funny you would bring up this subject. I recently had a conversation about this subject that brought me to tears of frustration. I am a size 12–14. This petite sister butted into a conversation I was having with another sister about vegetarianism/veganism. She said, "Being a vegetarian is NOT healthy because all you can eat is carbs and they make you gain weight." Of course, she said this while looking me up and down. Then she started giving me advice about how she eats cottage cheese, string cheese for snacks, chicken breast, etc. Then she said, in a condescending tone, "This is why I look the way I look. I weigh 122 pounds and I am in my 40s." (Whooptie doo, good for you!) I said to her, "For my body-type your weight would be unrealistic and probably unhealthy so, instead of focusing on my weight, I am focusing on health, and veganism works for me." We went back and forth with a few indirect catty insults to each other. She was calling me fat in a roundabout way. I glorified the Afrikan in my hourglass figure. She tried to say that men don't like "all of that." I said that brothers don't like flat asses and no curves.

I hate the fact that I had to resort to petty insults especially with another sistah in order to defend my size and my lifestyle. But it seems as if I run into that type of B.S. often and quite frankly, I'm sick of it! If the subject comes up that I am a vegan, I notice the first thing that some people do is look me up and down.... I see the doubt in their eyes and their tone of voices. If one more person says some comment like, "I tried to be a vegetarian but I GAINED weight" or "I heard that this can make you gain weight" I am going to scream!!!!!!! I know I shouldn't take it personally, but sometimes I feel as if they are directing those comments to me. A family member once asked me why I am not eating meat, I said, "To be healthier," and he cut me off and said, "You are far from the perfect picture of health." That hurt. It's hard not to take it personally when people are constantly undermining you, trying to make a mockery out of you based on some blanket perception of health. Correct me if I am wrong, but I don't believe that smaller vegan sistahs have to engage in these types of conversations. Anyway, I will stop my ranting now, I don't want to turn this into a "woe is me" conversation. But I am in total agreement with the author.... While I have a much healthier body image than I used to, it is not always that easy to feel good about yourself in this society, even when you are doing the right thing.

Jameelah

FROM: JOLYNN

RE: [sistahvegan] Veganism and Misconceptions of Thinness as "Normal" and "Healthy"
OK, Jameelah,

Peace and Love. But whoa now, who said that being a family member is grounds for allowing rude people to speak to us in less than loving ways? Who says that being scrupulous about what you take into your body/spirit is anyone's concern other than those we designate to fulfill the role of familiar intimate?

Look-a-here, sweetie-pie.... The next time someone steps to you, crosses your plane of intimacy, and dares to engage you in intimate terms about your diet, your practice, your butt, etc., simply say, "Sister, I don't know you nor do I choose to engage you further in conversation," and with that turn your big vegan behind and switch it away. OK?

FROM: JOLYNN

Re: Veganism and Misconceptions of Thinness as "Normal" and "Healthy"

Dear Breezie,

Good health should always mean not just some mythically agreed upon benchmark that some invisible being hands down like Moses's commandments. We should always be guided by how we feel. Sisters, listen to your bodies. Get quiet enough to listen to what your bodies say.

Respond with rest, baths, vacations, spas, fasts, cleanses, whatever we need, our response should be quick and immediate. Eat energizing foods. Surround yourselves with brilliant conversationalists. Eat beautifully prepared food that is colorful and lively like yourselves.

Speak positive words. Lead contemplative lives. Find time to be still. Stop talking so much. Have at least two hours for yourself each day. Do something special for yourself daily. Treat yourself as if you were a personal garden and create place of beauty and awe.

FROM: FITNESSBABY

Re: Veganism and Misconceptions of Thinness as "Normal" and "Healthy"

This is SO CRAZY because, last night, I was searching the Internet for a "vegan weight loss plan." I will tell you that I lost weight once I switched to vegetarianism. I lost 20 pounds in three months EASILY. Then I got stuck. Now, even though I teach yoga three times a week, pilates three times a week, hip-hop aerobics twice a week, and weight train when I can, I'm stuck.

My waist is about a 6 but my butt is a 10. :) I work in a highly stereotypical field that is full of young, thin white girls and it did, at one time, create mental havoc as I didn't feel like I was good enough. When I was a size 22, I was miserable as hell even though I was "smart" because all people ever saw was "fat."

People are so easy to try and discredit what you do anyway. Yesterday, I was mentioning to a coworker that I could make her some callaloo with chicken broth instead of coconut milk. Two other coworkers went to whooping and hollering because I said the word "chicken." My response was, "If I told you it was 'fake chicken broth' would you have turned your nose up?" I wasn't making it for me anyway but I feel like I had to "defend" my veganism just like I had to "defend" being fat. I have a big ole glob of mass hanging out in front :) but it's not like it used to be and now I have the energy to run with it instead of laying on the couch crying about it.

That's my rant... Now back to your regularly scheduled programs!! :)

Tasha

FROM: DONTAE980

Re: Veganism and Misconceptions of Thinness as "Normal" and "Healthy"

I agree totally with you, Breezie! I can relate to this completely, ladies. I am a size 16 and I'm not going to say my weight. :-) I don't look what I weigh, I'll say that. LOL. I truly have a larger frame and I'm big boned. I have this body structure from both my parents' sides, so it is hereditary. I have always had meat on my bones and that's just how I've been shaped. I have struggled with weight all my life and I was subject to a mother who thought I was pretty much fat. I was home-schooled and therefore I didn't participate in any outside activities that "normal" kids get to participate in. I didn't exercise as much so the weight stayed on me more. When I was 12 years old I looked like I was a damn college student. I've always looked older than what I was and the weight probably had a lot to do with it. I get so sick and tired of the dirty and nasty looks that I sometimes get whenever people find out I'm a vegetarian AND HAVE BEEN ONE ALL MY LIFE! I have a beloved brother that teased me and my sister with NO mercy about our weight. He called my sister a "refrigerator bandit" and "eat 'em up." He told me that he wondered how I could eat no meat and look the way that I do, in other words still be larger framed or "big" and not eat any meat. Y'all better believe I went OFF on his ass MANY times about that. He said some really mean things having to do with weight about me and my sis (my sis is larger framed also but differently shaped than me). I'm 5 feet 7 inches and my weight is proportionate to my height I think. According to those damn medical standards, I'm OBESE! I admit that sometimes I have piled on the junk food more than I needed to and stress has also contributed to my latest round of weight gain. But I am not stupid enough to let myself get out of control where I blow up to an unbelievable huge size.

Yes, people are very, very comfortable in criticizing you about your weight (especially if you are a female). I always try to be sensitive to others who are larger framed because just because you are larger framed doesn't mean you are unhealthy. Everyone wasn't meant to be thin.

S.S.

FROM: BREEZE HARPER

Re: Veganism and Misconceptions of Thinness as "Normal" and "Healthy"

I wanted to let ladies know that I'm in no way saying that thinness is or isn't healthy. I just want to clarify that I am not attacking thin women on this group but just wanted to bring this subject to attention.

It is so important for me (and probably important for many of you ladies, regardless of whether you are "thin" or "full"—sorry if I'm not using the "right" words) to explore this because I am very fearful of how science/medicine/health specialists create health standards. As women of the African diaspora we KNOW how many parts of Western science have been used to construct white middle-class BODIES and lifestyles as "normal" while directly positing it AGAINST the Black FEMALE BODY/lifestyle as "abnormal" and "deviant." Though it's not as DIRECT today as it was 100 or even 50 years ago, it still happens ALL the time in an often very covert way.

I guess what I'd like to do is just for us to continue talking about the aesthetics of the BODY and how "healthy" has been constructed through the times (well, since European and American colonialism). Let's start talking about how we have found the meaning of "health" on our own terms, regardless of what science in the West has "proven."

Jameelah, don't apologize for talking about your experiences. Please keep on talking about them. SHARE SHARE SHARE. Don't feel you have to be silenced. The silencing of "taboo" issues is NOT cool. Be heard, girl. I would love (but I can't force this, of course) for all of us here to be supportive of us ladies. It is challenging enough to live in a society that is racist, sexist, and elitist AS WELL AS unapologetically phobic and hateful toward "full" female bodies (especially Black female "full" bodies) who embrace their appetites.

Tasha, don't apologize for wanting to go through "weight loss" needs. This doesn't mean you're doing something wrong or right. We're all simply trying to find ourselves in the many facets of our lives in terms of: dietary philosophy, ethnic/race consciousness, spiritual practice, etc. Please feel you can share your feelings on this site. Other ladies, please feel comfortable with opening up. Let's not let us feel that we are the ONLY ones who feel the way we do. Let's not complacently advocate SILENCE by not speaking up for each other.

Shawntaye, you're not the only one whose family members have hurt them with such horrible words. Whether it be weight issues, color-tone (you know, "My daughter was born light so I'm glad" type of crap), to intellectual capability, we've all had to experience this from people who say they love us. I'm just hoping that we can all help support you and help you if you need some interesting, assertive responses to your siblings. Maybe some of us on here can tell you how we manage these situations or have gotten to the point to tell our families to STOP BOTHERING us in a language that they finally understand.

Hugs,

Breezie

FROM: NIAYAA

Re: Veganism and Misconceptions of Thinness as "Normal" and "Healthy"

I just have to jump in because I am thin. Actually I have been the same size since high school, about 20 years. I have four children and have not been able to keep any weight on me at all. As a result, I have been called "little girl," "string bean," "pencil," and told I look too young for my children to be mine. This was cute for a while, but I have been trying to gain weight for the last 10 years so I can look close to my age.

I just want folk to know that it goes both ways, whether thin or thick some will be happy and some not. Life is just funny that way I guess.

Much love and blessings ya'll.

FROM: PLUMPDN

RE: Veganism and Misconceptions of Thinness as "Normal" and "Healthy"

As much as I completely agree with everything that has been said, I must honestly talk about the feelings I have been dealing with in regards to larger Black women. Larger, in this sense, means obese, NOT a size 12–14 (since when is this big anyway? Aren't we Black? When I was a 12, I weighed maybe 165 pounds…twenty-five pounds more than I do now…not close to obese). I have been feeling very ashamed and embarrassed and condescending toward these women when I see them in the street or talking to a group of white people because I feel like I know what the white people are thinking…something about Mammie and fat, happy darkies (and they are OFTEN smiling when in this situation—like playing a role). I have been trying to analyze my feelings for a few weeks now. I think it is also related to my past eating disorder and my concern with public health, and the fact the white people are driving me crazy on this campus. Beyond that, there is nothing wrong with having meat on one's bones (though I wish I could get me some meat on my bones). If it makes anyone feel better, people say the same thing about going vegetarian making them gain weight, even though I am quite thin. They say it because it is true. When most people become vegetarians, they eat bread and cheese, either in the form of pizza or cheese sandwiches, etc. My response is that there is more to being a vegetarian/vegan than removing the burger from between the white roll, cheese, ketchup, and wilted-ass iceburg lettuce. I explain the concept of whole foods, then add that eating this way should not make you gain weight (though it might maintain your weight).

Another culprit that we often forget is lack of breastfeeding. I was breastfed for only three months or so before my mother had to go back to work and breast pumps were not in existence in 1976/77, so I took my Similac like a good lactose-intolerant baby with severe colic (because they were giving me cow's milk). Formula-fed babies are larger than breastfed babies and can develop larger fat cells that stay large forever (I am a skinny woman with large fat cells…and I have been heavier at two times in my life…preteens…and freshwoman in college). These things make it difficult for people to lose weight, just because your body finds its equilibrium at a higher weight. The important thing, as has been said, is to eat to be healthy, not to be skinny.

Adria

FROM: DONTAE980

Re: Veganism and Misconceptions of Thinness as "Normal" and "Healthy"

Ya know, I used to be ashamed of how I looked. I HATED the fact that I had hips and thighs and an ass. I absolutely hated it. I always had wished I could be thinner. Thinner was better, my problems would go away, people would like me better if I were thinner!

I guess when you are a certain size, be it small or larger, you really have to tune out what other people say or think about you. That's one very hard lesson to learn. Yes, I'm sure that some white people will look at a Black female who is obese in their eyes and liken her to the "mammy" stereotype. Of course too, being that there are more of them who are overweight than there are us in this country, I think they have a lot of nerve in even going there.

S.S.

FROM: RAQUEL

Re: Veganism and Misconceptions of Thinness as "Normal" and "Healthy"
Hello Ladies,

What a loaded, difficult issue. Loaded for all of us, difficult for most. I know when I read someone :) describing their size 6 stomach as a "big ole glob of mess" I have to fight back searing pain at my own self-judgment...and remember that it's not about me.

First...commendations to all for using gentle words.

You all have heard my mess already ;) but every medical professional (Western and non-Western) has confirmed: "Raquel, your body SIZE has NOTHING to do with your intake. NOTHING." Sure, people are skeptical at that (I was, which is a part of what led me down the dark road of anorexia and compulsive exercising)...but it is so true. Which means it sucks. I didn't lose that weight when I became vegan at age 11. I didn't lose weight when I transitioned to more raw foods. I grew up severely malnourished and with other complications, major weight and body issues. I feel like I'm a testament to all those of us who may feel like "freaks of nature"! I'm approximately 5'2"/5'3" but look much taller based on how I carry myself. It's been determined that I have a medium to small frame, but you wouldn't guess that. However, you also wouldn't call me "big boned."

My family was and is extremely toxic. My mother sold me into childhood prostitution at the age of two for her own drug habit; another pair of relatives had me on ephedrine and forced diets and exercise by four; and in beauty pageants and child modeling (for money, again) by six. My lowest weight was around 85 lbs at 5'2" but that was during a month where somehow, magically, my hormones had been balanced more than not.

No amount of herbs, meditation, yoga, powders, creams/gels/pills/therapy/exercise/raw foodism/water/etc., has ever fixed this problem. I could rant more, however—in this I'm just trying to say:

- I'm 100% vegan, without scarfing pasta and chips and potatoes and CRAP
- I exercise and weight train
- I do yoga/meditation/holistic health . . .

. . . and this is still who and what I am. I won't lie. I cry a lot. I get very, very, very depressed about it. I have to cling for dear life at times as I see the tiny little girls lift their little two-pound weights while I'm pressing 150 and barely breaking a sweat. I have insane endurance and crazy strength. That much is a blessing.

So the next time anyone dares to make an assumption about someone's size (whether perceived to be small or medium or large or, as Missy Elliott would say: "double X-L you can all just tell") . . . you don't know DIDDLY about where they're coming from. I think I'm preaching to the choir here ;) , but so many of us have been quite literally doo-dooed on by family, society, etc. The best we can do is empower ourselves. Try to see the beauty in ourselves. TRY to be gentle on ourselves.

Size 22 may be big for one, but maybe it's "normal" for someone else (lawd knows—at one store I'm an 8, next store I'm asking for a 14 or 16 because I have major body dysmorphia, but in general . . . I'm about a 10—which would surprise some, others not—and despite the size of my ladies!!! I wear a medium shirt size, small in men's, often worn by much thinner girls); whereas a size 2 on some folks would be unhealthy. S'all relative. Keep that heart healthy, keep that system clean, build those muscles strong; especially the one between your ears.

Love and blessings,
raquel evita

FROM: FITNESSBABY

Hey, Raquel…(and other Sistahs),

I didn't want you to think I was being "vain" by my comment. If I had a size 6 stomach, then I wouldn't be complaining. :) (Although I don't believe that is true because it seems like when we reach our goals, we always want more…ESPECIALLY when it comes to body image.) And the reason I mentioned my size at all is because I have to remind MYSELF of where I have been in terms of weight and investigate the reasoning behind the deep-seated body issues I have.

My mother always told my sister and me how she didn't want "fat teenagers." I danced my entire high school career and had a PERFECT shape. I was built just like a Coca-Cola bottle. However, on my dance team, I was STILL the big girl. I never thought about what I ate or how much of it I ate because I was dancing on most days (by my senior year) five hours a day. I went off to college, started eating bad, quit the dance team, got married, had a baby, lost a baby, got pregnant again, and here comes 232 pounds. My husband had an affair with a thin, white girl and it almost killed me—the affair AND the fact that I felt like he was disgusted with my weight. I went to see a childhood friend right after I had my son and I wrote him a letter after I got back saying how good it was to see him, blah, blah, blah. He sent the note back, let his girlfriend curse me out, and then said, "Why would I want to be with you? You're FAT. . . ." UUUUGGGGHHHH!!! This is a boy that I shared my first kiss with, my friend since I had been 11, and it hurt the hell out of me. It still does.

When I teach my classes, I try to wear long shirts and control-top panties to keep my size 100 stomach from falling out of my pants. It has happened on a few occasions and I was sick with embarrassment. I feel like I should be a "role model" and a Pilates teacher with a fat stomach, in my eyes, is not motivating. Then again, perhaps if I saw someone who "looked" like me then I would be more apt to stay with it saying, "Hey…they're doing it and I can too."

Raquel (and other ladies)—I feel you, baby girl. As painful as it is, I'm glad we are having this discussion.

Love and Peace,
Tasha

Re: Veganism and Misconceptions of Thinness as "Normal" and "Healthy"

Ditto ditto ditto on what has already been expressed. Thanx for broaching this topic, Breeze. I bought the Bennett and Dickerson book about five years ago, but only skimmed this article. I read it just now and am quite moved.... This is such a complex issue....

When I was a grad student at Michigan, I recall that one of my sister colleagues was pissed off with a white, female former professor because this woman spoke of body image and obesity without dealing with race, ethnicity, and culture. No joke. This "respected" scholar was equating fat discrimination WITH racial discrimination, rather than considering the intersection of body-type, size, race, culture, class, AND gender. You can't—how can you separate them? She argued that the experiences of obese white people are the SAME as those of people of color. Never mind that a heavy, working-class sistah in a metropolitan area might experience life differently from a heavy and wealthy white woman, or even a heavy middle-class sistah in the deep South.

Two nights ago, a sistafriend and I were talking about class, culture, body-type, and food. She laughed at how she bugged out during a visit to Africa when they prepared to discard the remainder of the chicken. She grew up, as did I, with the mindset that you DO NOT throw away good food! Additionally, she, as do many of us, had difficulty shaking the idea that most Africans are starving and can't afford to throw away food—even though some of us know better....

This led to a discussion of how we've both had and witnessed arguments about food with or between loved ones. She admitted tearing into her partner about butter. I recall laying into my sister for throwing out leftovers once. I've also continued eating after I felt full, on occasion, because I felt that I was supposed to clean my plate. And good Lord, I remember my mom telling my sister and I (when we were little), "Gimme that drumstick! Y'all don't know how to eat chicken. Look at all that meat left on that bone!" Well, my mom grew up poor, so that factored into some of her ideas about food.

Regarding my own body, I was a heavy child. My mom wouldn't allow family or friends to tease me or comment on my weight. On a number of occasions, I recall her intervening on my behalf. I took comfort in "knowing" that it was "baby fat" and that I was just "big-boned." And like the author of that chapter Breeze referred us to, I had high racial self-esteem. Never wanted to be light-skinned, have thinner lips, or a thinner nose, although I didn't learn to appreciate my kinky hair until I was in my early 20s. I lost the weight during my sixth-grade year. However, after a classmate informed me (in the fifth or sixth grade) that I had a flat booty, I learned to feel self-conscious about another part of my body. Don't you just love how screwed up life is?

Anyway, I was a size 7 and loved it (although my big boobs and small booty make clothes shopping nightmarish and elicited inappropriate comments from men/boys that often made me cringe) until I went into the military. Forced to eat three meals a day, which were high in simple carbohydrates and animal-based protein, I gained weight, a lot of it muscle. However, when my activity level slowed, some of the muscle converted to fat. It didn't really bother me 'cause many of the women I grew up around were sized 12 or larger. Single-digit sizes were perceived as skinny. So, I accepted my size-12 self and thought I was cute.

Over the last 12 years, my weight has fluctuated depending on my stress level and my increasing education about nutrition. In terms of hurtful things that family sometimes says, I endured the jesting of my brother who, whenever I visited home, referred to me as "the fattest vegetarian he had ever seen." This usually evoked laughter, because the running joke was that I was sneaking off and eating pork on the down low. Of course! How else could I be that "large"? Also, did I mention that too much education has caused me to develop strange ideas and habits about food and religion? Too much of that caused me to reject pork. However, my continued education at a white institution really made me crazy and caused me to reject meat, etc., altogether. According to some people, either I'm a "crazy Muslim" or I have become "white-identified."

What I have since discovered is that although I had eliminated meat, dairy, etc., I wasn't a healthy vegetarian. I recall, some years ago, thinking it seemed odd that I could be vegetarian or even vegan and not eat many fruits and vegetables. I was also ignorant about whole grains, EFAs [essential fatty acids], raw foods, etc. Essentially, most of us, unless we're among the fortunate few who have parents who are food conscious (in a healthy way), have to learn how to live healthy.

I mentioned this a few months ago, but for me I actually began losing weight when I starting eating healthier. Unexpectedly, I surpassed any weight-loss goal that I had (I recall that I ran out and got an HIV test just to check). I just wanted to get back into my clothes, not get cramps when I crossed my legs, and not pant like crazy after climbing stairs. And as much as I hate to admit it, I would be lying if I said that as a heterosexual sistah, it bothered me that brothas didn't find me as attractive when I hit nearly 180 pounds. If I could've carried 50 pounds of it in my butt, I thought, I would've been happy, but NO! My disproportionate self resembled a "lampshade" as I recently heard some unfunny Black male comedian say as he callously described women who are all breasts and no behind.

Although I was never on the skinny side, I was active growing up, and prided myself on being one of the best dancers in my community/school, being able to lift heavy objects (not being a fragile or "weak" girl), running, etc. So, when I couldn't do the things I used to do and couldn't wear my clothes (I was around size 14, and physically, just didn't feel good), I made some changes.

It's funny how the memory of who you used to be sticks with you mentally. When people describe me as "small" or "little"—mind you, only Black people have called me skinny—I still look around to see who they're talking about. In my mind, I'm still larger. In fact, it only dawned on me about a year ago that my bras were ill-fitting because my BAND size had decreased. I was so focused on my cup size—thinking that I went from a DD to D—that I was buying the wrong size bras! As my girlfriend says, that's just bananas! I was so stuck on a size 38 that it never occurred to me that that number had decreased, 'cause in my mind, I was still a size 12. It turns out that I'm a 32 or 34 F—depending on the brand.

Anyway, that's my long-long-winded two-quarters worth on the subject. As I move into my late 30s, I've grown more accepting of my body-type. However, it has been a process.

peace,

angie

FROM: BEATTYA

Re: Veganism and Misconceptions of Thinness as "Normal" and "Healthy"

Just checking myself on language. As big as I am on the significance/meaning of language, I nevertheless stated that I was "panting like crazy" when I was at my heaviest weight. Dogs pant, people breathe. I guess as progressive as I think I am, living in this jacked-up society has socialized me to internalize various stereotypes. It bothers me when I hear people refer to over-weight women and girls as cows.... Generally, I avoid using language that compares people to animals. However, this one slipped through. It reminds me that we never stop learning, and that it is arrogant to assume that one has completely escaped or risen above particular "isms."

Although I have moved closer to the more progressive end of various continuums, I feel the need to constantly check myself—especially if I do not currently or have never held membership in a particular group.

later,

angie

FROM: PROLIFICPROSE

Re: Veganism and Misconceptions of Thinness as "Normal" and "Healthy"
Hello Amie Breeze,

I've been out of the loop for a while (finishing up school and vacationing after graduation) but I am really happy to have returned to this circle of openness and honesty about the various myths that need to be debunked surrounding this lifestyle.

Personally, I'm new to veganism and actually still in the transitional phase. I guess it is safe to say I'm vegetarian at this point. I've learned a wealth of knowledge as a member of this group and continue to learn every day. To be quite honest, this is my sole support for my health-conscious decision to purge unhealthy foods and byproducts from my body, mind, and spirit as where I live is highly carnivorous and unhealthy. I'm sure the transition would be much smoother if I were home in South Florida as there are many resources and places in which I could patronize while discovering what's best for me. However, out here in the Midwest, people tend to frown upon it or give into the myths or false beliefs about it.

That passage you shared was extremely powerful and I do know many people who've considered a vegan lifestyle because they believe they will immediately become thin. However, that is not my reason for making the conscious decision to change. My family in the islands for the most part is largely vegetarian and I grew up in that environment until my parents split and we returned to the United States. But I am straying from the topic at hand.

I am short (5'2"), and I don't think any amount of dedicated veganism would ever make me thin. I have what they call a medium frame, which basically means I'm not meant to be thin. I have met some vegans who are extremely thin and, in all honesty, lacking certain nutrients. While I understand fruits and veggies provide us with significant nourishment, I think some people tend to overcompensate in some areas while neglecting other important areas. I think health is a combination of proper nutrition, and mental, physical, and emotional balance as well. I don't think one should enter into any situation, be it life-changing or otherwise, with preconceived notions because usually it sets us up for disappointment.

Collier

FROM: FITNESSBABY

Re: Veganism and Misconceptions of Thinness as "Normal" and "Healthy"

Again, thank you for this discussion.

Raquel, thank you so much for your previously listed compliment. I am so hard on myself because of what I have basically been brain-washed to believe. I had a photo shoot last night (of course, on my casual pictures I was sporting my Sistah Vegan tank!). The photographer was a friend and he kept reminding me to "show my muscles" that I had worked so hard for (in his words, "So other sistahs can be inspired") and how I should be thankful that I am so brown and how my short haircut (that I am still trying to get used to) was "banging" and how our men don't really care about our stretch marks the way we do and how they like our butts and we shouldn't be ashamed of them, etc. I believed him until I looked at the pictures.

All I could think about was how my nose was too big and my fat rolls were hanging on the side and how my hair makes me look retarded, etc. There is even a pic where I didn't wear a belt and my booty was solid in my jeans but my waist is smaller and it makes this "gap" in the back of your pants. He was laughing like, "Yeah, that's a real sistah picture right there. It shows who you are." All I did was think about how "imperfect" I was. On top of that, we have a mutual friend who is also a dancer and all I could see in her pictures was how slim she was and how her legs kicked higher than mine and how pretty and long her hair was. I couldn't believe that, at 31 years old, I was still going through this.

Last night was an "eye-opening" experience about how I perceive beauty and strength. This morning, even after I got off the scale and it didn't say what I wanted it to say, I looked at my stretch marks and my hair and my nose, turned the light off, and started my day. I am still me; whole, perfect, and complete, and there is no stereotype or lack of self-esteem or false misconceptions that can do away with that.

Have a great day!
Tasha

LIBERATION AS CONNECTION AND
THE DECOLONIZATION OF DESIRE

pattrice jones

A lot of us have been wishing for this book for a long time. Now that it's here, I can hardly contain myself. Literally. Again and again, as I tried to write this afterword, my thoughts overflowed their boundaries, spilling off of the page and into each other until finally I had to accept that my hyper-excited inability to keep ideas in their places was not a temporary technical writing problem but rather a natural reaction to an anthology that is all about crossing categories to make vital connections.

Editor Breeze Harper started with simple questions about perceptions of veganism and animal liberation among Black American females. The answers she got from Black-identified vegan women led her to more complex questions about veganism as "health activism that resists institutionalized racism and neocolonialism." Collectively, she and the contributors to this anthology set out to explore those questions while producing an antidote to the erasure of Black vegans implicit in the dismissal of veganism as "a white thing." Since many of the contributors themselves came to veganism through books such as Queen Afua's *Sacred Woman* and Dick Gregory's writings, I'm sure that they hoped to produce a similarly transformative book.

They've done it. In amplifying the voices of Black vegan women, many of whom condemn injustices against nonhuman animals and almost all of whom see diet as a political choice inescapably linked to questions of social and environmental justice, this book kicks over all kinds of stereotypes about vegans, animal advocates, and Black women. But it doesn't stop there. By presenting veganism as a Black feminist and antiracist practice, this book illuminates inconvenient connections that the feminist, antiracist, animal liberation, and environmental movements have too long ignored. In the dialogues that go on across the pages, we get a glimpse of what the necessary conversations about those connections might sound like.

And it doesn't stop there! By highlighting the holistic thinking that informs the every-day choices of Black vegan women, this book puts forward a theory and practice of liberation as connection. By asking and answering uncomfortable questions about chicken wings and factory farming, this anthology demonstrates the necessity of decolonizing desire, not only among formerly colonized peoples but among all of us whose socially constructed appetites are eating up the world. In short, this collection of stories, essays, and poems by what might seem like a too sharply circumscribed demographic of contributors brings us all closer to the theory and practice we need to liberate everybody in this subdivided and subjugated biosphere.

And not a moment too soon. *Sistah Vegan* arrives at a particularly perilous moment in human history and, indeed, in the life cycle of our planet. Never has there been a more urgent need for us to act from within an integrated awareness not only of the intersections among race, sex, and class oppression but also of the ways that these and other disparities among people influence and are influenced by the ways that people exploit animals and ecosystems. Climate change, fueled more by meat consumption than by transportation, charges forward faster than predicted. In the context of continued racial and economic inequality, this ensures that more unnatural disasters like hurricane Katrina are on the horizon. Meantime, a worldwide surge in meat consumption further depletes and poisons world water resources while bringing the diet-based diseases that already kill so many people of African descent in North America and the global South.

Confronting these emergencies are animal, environmental, and social justice organiza-tions that are too often compromised by internal inconsistencies and lack of solidarity with other movements. All movements seem to start out with a relatively narrow focus, which then widens in response to the recognition of the interconnectedness of oppression. All movements struggle with the tendency for societal imbalances in power and privilege to reproduce them-selves within groups. The relatively young animal-advocacy movement has only just begun to wrestle with the often agonizing conflicts that always arise when social change movements broaden their analyses while addressing internal power disparities. Neither as affluent nor all white as it is stereotyped to be, nor as diverse as it ought to be, the movement is in the midst of an active process of internal change initiated by the many animal advocates who, like some of the contributors to this volume, came to animal rights as a result of commitment to social justice or environmental causes. Together, we are working toward a comprehensive analysis and activist practice that includes speciesism along with racism, sexism, and other forms of intraspecies oppression. As is often the case when movements begin to shift, this is more evident at the grassroots level than within the high-profile national organizations, where there is greater resistance to change.

Unfortunately, there has yet to be an answering engagement from environmental and social justice activists. Even though going vegan is the most effective way for people to sharply reduce their own water consumption and greenhouse gas emissions, environmental organizations rarely mention this as an option, much less an obligation. Even though the action plan of the 2002 NGO Forum for Food Sovereignty included a call for people in affluent countries to "reduce or eliminate" meat consumption, that agenda has not been taken up by any of the major nonprofit organizations working in the realms of hunger, agriculture, or trade globalization. Feminist activists tend to ignore scholarly work demonstrating the historic and ongoing linkage between speciesism and sexism. Efforts to talk about veganism in progressive circles are often dismissed with the phrase, "That's a white thing."

Besides bringing the good word about veganism into Black communities, this book encourages activists of all stripes to look at the things they haven't wanted to see. Best of all, it does so in a manner more likely to provoke change than to inflame defensive stubbornness. I think that's because so many of the contributors talk us through their own process of change. In sharing their real lives—missteps, backslides, and changed minds not excluded—they suggest how we too might realize a concept of liberation rooted in connection rather than separation. This is ecowomanism as Layli Phillips defines it: "Social change as healing rather than protest, integration rather than disruption."

Before I go further, I ought to explain who I am. Breeze Harper asked me to reflect on this anthology from the perspective of the interconnectedness of *all* oppressions that informs my book, *Aftershock*. That perspective is an organic product of my life. I'm a white lesbian from a working-class background who now has, by virtue of advanced education, many more options than others who grew up on my block in Baltimore. I came out and quit eating meat as a teenager in the 1970s. Doing gay rights work within a multiracial organization in that

Black-majority city, I began to think naively about the intersections of race, gender, and sexual orientation while I was still in my teens, but it wasn't until I was well into my twenties that an offhand remark by an African-American friend provoked me to realize how profoundly I had failed to see my own white privilege or think deeply about the impact of racism in the lives of my friends and lovers of color. What a sickening and rightfully destabilizing realization that was! My subsequent efforts to educate myself about race led me to the writings of many feminists of color, whose insights have informed my work ever since. I am especially grateful to Gloria Yamato's "Something about the subject makes it hard to name" for teaching me that it is possible to be a trustworthy white ally in the struggle against racism. My integration of a race analysis into my teaching and my AIDS activism led me to be invited to work with a center for antiracist education. I've also been involved in struggles against welfare reform, for tenants rights, against rape, for disability rights, and against trade globalization (to name a few). I used to teach speech at a historically Black university and run a chicken sanctuary in a rural region dominated and despoiled by the poultry industry, so I know firsthand the injuries that factory farming inflicts not only on the animals who are its primary victims but also on farmers, workers, and waterways.

When Breeze asked me to write this afterword, I felt uneasy. As a white woman, I felt—and still feel—uncomfortable having the literal last word in an anthology of writing by Black women. On the other hand, I was—and am—excited and honored to have the opportunity to participate in a project I support so wholeheartedly. So, please take this in the spirit it's intended, not as an exegesis by somebody who thinks she's some kind of expert on Black people who practice veganism but rather as the very excited utterances of a fellow reader who is very, very enthused about this book we've both read. That said, here are my thoughts about two of the themes that I see in this anthology and, more important, what I think we all owe its contributors.

LIBERATION AS CONNECTION

Integrity may be the central problem of our time. We live in a social world defined by divisive lies that isolate us from the biosphere and then sort us into constructed categories. Bands of armed men compete across the boundaries of those categories, doing the same damage whether they call themselves gangs or governments. Wielding other weapons, scientists and industrialists split atoms and chop off mountaintops. Ultraviolet radiation streams in through the hole in the ozone layer as polar ice cracks under the stress of accumulated climate change.

We're born into this world with pollutants already in our bloodstreams, our bodies corrupted by atmospheric poisons all the way down to our DNA. Our relationships, both within and across the categories to which we've been assigned, are strained and often break under the weight of the lies we've been told about ourselves and each other. We're estranged from other animals and the rest of the natural world, which we can only vaguely perceive through the haze of the stories we've been told all of our lives.

Sometimes we can't even feel our own bodies! We don't know when we're thirsty or when to stop eating. We can't distinguish our own wishes from the desires implanted by the barrage of advertising and other coercive messages that batters our brains every day. How can we be true to ourselves or others in such a disconnected state? And, if we can't be true, how can we hope to do the things that we need to do to make things right?

In "Terror," contributor Tara Sophia Bahna-James turns a familiar image upside down, suggesting that the assurance we see in the eyes of dogs is not trust in us but rather self-trust. It's not that they don't know that "someday we may casually break their hearts," but rather that they know "they will never break ours." The terror of the title is the fear of hurting others that we all must carry as long as we are so dangerously fractured.

Like most poems of substance, "Terror" takes some thinking about before the breadth of its implications emerge. And, of course, the implications of images differ from person to person. To me, this brief meditation on trustworthiness or the lack thereof goes to the pulsing heart of the problem addressed by so many of the contributors to this anthology: How to gain and maintain bodily and ethical integrity within the context of a world where violence is not only embedded in everyday life but also inscribed on our bodies?

Writing from their lived experience as women of the African diaspora living in North America, the contributors to this anthology are uniquely positioned to see and help their readers to see the often painful interplay between privilege and lack thereof. They know race, sex, and class oppression from the inside—often literally, as their bodies have struggled with health problems such as allergies from wading in a polluted stream and pregnancies made more difficult by misguided medical advice. Upon learning that the diseases afflicting them and their loved ones were related to diet, some were stunned to realize that among the guilty foods were those most prized by their families and communities. Legacies of slavery that had become markers of Black identity were inscribing racist oppression on Black bodies all over again. In coming to desire dead bodies for dinner, they had unwittingly become complicit in the destruction of their own bodies.

And the bodies of others. Animals. Other people. Other *Black* people.

For anyone who is or has been oppressed, the question of complicity with one's own or—worse—somebody else's oppression can be profoundly unsettling. Tara Sophia Bahna-James writes that, after reading *The Dreaded Comparison,* "I was not shocked by the existence of oppression, but rather by the complexity of my complicity." In one of the most vivid moments in the anthology, Michelle R. Loyd-Paige, a "socially aware college professor who challenges her students to think about how...their privilege allows them to be unconcerned about issues they do not think pertains to them," shares with us the moment at which she realized that in "unconsciously participating in patterns of indifference and oppression, *I was guilty of the offense with which I indicted my students!* And here was truth in a Styrofoam box, which held six whole chicken wings covered in hot barbeque sauce with a side of ranch dressing."

Writing about sugar, coffee, and other destructive commodities as well as the environmental costs of animal agriculture, Breeze Harper notes that "racially...oppressed minorities in America...are collectively complicit—and usually unknowingly—in being oppressors to our brothas and sistahs." Well aware of her mixed position on the matrix of oppression, Melissa Santosa writes of the "privileges we take for granted as humans living in the global North and the responsibility we have for the ecological, animal, and human costs of our way of life."

Whether their emphasis is on animals, environment, or other people, the contributors to this anthology are united in their answer to complicity: integrity. Like Santosa, all of the contributors to this anthology seem to have "serious problems with dissonance." The striving for integrity, for actions that are consistent with beliefs, is implicit on every page. Over and over again, we read of discordance leading to discomfort leading to change.

None of the contributors was raised vegan. Many made the shift after realizing that their diets were inconsistent with their commitment to good health for themselves, their families, and their communities. Often a health crisis of some kind supplied the necessary spark as when Nia Yaa and her mother decided to become vegetarian after her grandfather died of colon cancer. Other contributors learned about factory-farming practices that were inconsistent with their ethical or spiritual beliefs. Joi Maria Probus visited some websites suggested by the new (vegan) girlfriend of a friend and found herself shaken in her belief that "I already stood for and against everything worthy of my convictions." She went vegan that day. Tashee Meadows picked up a pamphlet at an Earth Day celebration and found herself thinking about the parallels between the exploitation of animals and the subjugation of people. That launched a process of self-instruction that culminated in her going to work for an animal-rights organization.

While the stories in this volume differ significantly in their details, just as the contributors sometimes disagree significantly about the meaning of veganism, the themes of honesty, wholeness, and holistic thinking appear consistently. These are the antitheses of the divisive violations at the root of our shared sorrows.

Virtually all of the contributors approach veganism from multiple, integrated angles. Race. Sex. Class. Health. Sexual orientation. Environment. Decolonization. Animal liberation. Try to talk about any one of these in the context of this anthology and you soon find yourself talking about one or more of the others. For example, most of the contributors discuss health but none treat the meat–disease link as an isolated problem. Most contributors approach health from a perspective that is holistic not only in the sense that "holistic health care" differs from allopathic medicine but also in the understanding that personal health is a political problem. Many approach health from an Afrocentric perspective that integrates political and spiritual commitments.

Holistic thinking extends from the personal into the political. Worries about poisons in our bloodstreams lead to worries about industrial pollutants in our waterways. Questions about the wholesomeness of animal products lead to questions about the treatment of animals exploited for food. Investigation of factory farming here at home leads to investigation into slave labor abroad.

Michelle Loyd-Paige writes that, "All social inequities are linked. Comprehensive systemic change will happen only if we are aware of these connections and work to bring an end to all inequalities—not just our favorites or the ones that most directly affect our part of the universe." Delicia Dunham asserts that "When we as a people learn that 'isms' are interrelated and that oppression of any being of any kind is tied to our own oppression, then we can begin to overcome those oppressions for the benefit of all."

For many contributors to this volume, "all" includes nonhuman animals. For Nia Yaa, the Caribbean concept of living *Ital* "helped me to understand the animal-rights aspect of being a vegetarian."

Many of the contributors are animal-rights activists or support that struggle even if they are not active within it. Breeze Harper argues that "we must extend our antiracist and anti-poverty beliefs to all people, nonhuman animals, and Mother Gaia."

Some contributors disagree. Ma'at Sincere Earth says that she "doesn't understand" animal rights, feeling that time spent pursuing that goal would be better spent in the pursuit of human rights. But she, too, comes from a perspective of connection rather than lack of compassion, arguing that animal abuse is rooted in social inequality and agreeing that "they should pass laws regulating and limiting the unethical treatment of animals." Like many animal advocates, she identifies the consumption of animals as the most urgent problem facing them.

But we ought not glide too quickly over the disagreement between Sincere Earth, who dares animal activists to "scream at a brother in the 'hood wearing a fur" and Delicia Dunham, who explicitly challenges the idea that her Black identity means that she "must be ever-rocking the chinchilla coats" and "dissing, if not totally ignoring, anyone who dares to call me out about my choices." No, most brothers in the 'hood probably don't care what people they've never met think about their clothing choices. Why would they? Antifur tirades of distant animal-rights activists probably seem as irrelevant to them as the antigay tirades of Christian fundamentalists seem to me. That's why conversations about the ethics of chinchilla coats and dog fighting have to go on *within* Black communities rather than across the (real or perceived) racial divide between organized animal activism and communities of color. One of the greatest strengths of this anthology is that its contributors don't always agree. That's how such urgently needed conversations begin.

This book began when Breeze Harper "listened in" on a virtual conversation about one of the most contentious questions of all: Whether and how to compare injustices perpetrated against animals to historic and ongoing injustices perpetrated against people of African descent in the Americas. Given the media coverage of angry denunciations of such comparisons, readers may be surprised by how frequently contributors to this volume describe themselves making that link. While exploring the concept of *Ital*, Nia Yaa "remembered seeing animals packed on farms and in trucks. They were being treated just like our enslaved ancestors." Tashee Meadows researched factory farming and found herself thinking "of my ancestry as a Black woman: the rapes, unwanted pregnancies, captivity, stolen babies, grieving mothers, horrific transports, and the physical, mental, and spiritual pain." Looking at images of caged animals, she "thought of the more than two million Americans who know cages firsthand in the prison industrial complex."

Some of the contributors themselves may have been surprised to find their thoughts trending in that direction. Michelle Loyd-Paige writes that "seeing a connection between the treatment of feed animals, laying chickens, and people of color is a rather recent phenomenon for me. Two years ago, I wouldn't have believed there was such a connection." In her description of her chicken-wing epiphany and in other contributions, we can hear the thudding emotional reverberations of suddenly thinking something you never thought you would think.

Scholars can talk about how the idea of race grew out of the idea of breed as understood by the inheritors of patriarchal and pastoral cultures whose ideas about daughters and dairy cows evolved in tandem. Activists can and should think deeply about how that helps us to understand the sexualization of race and the "race-ing" of gender as well as the causal and continuing role that speciesism plays in both racism and sexism. But the power of such theorizing pales in comparison to the impact of the reaction—at once visceral and ethical—of a Black woman who, like the young Tashee Meadows, encounters an image of animal exploitation and thinks, "That's what they did to us. It's not okay, no matter who they do it to."

It's that reaction, I think, that PETA tried, however heavy-handedly, to provoke with the controversial exhibit that did in fact provoke the train of thought that led to this anthology. I hope that this anthology teaches animal advocates *not* that they ought to be trying to provoke such reactions but rather that they can trust that people are going to make the connections that are most meaningful to them without special prompting. Tashee Meadows didn't need to be shown pictures of slave transport ships or people in prison to perceive the parallels. And, because nobody was trying to make her think about slavery, she didn't feel like the suffering of her ancestors was being manipulated to make her see somebody else's point of view. When she wrote about her own perceptions of those parallels for this anthology, she started with the plain facts about the treatment of animals and then shared her own reactions to those facts, implicitly insisting that we face the facts but not demanding that we share her associations.

In this and other contributions, we begin to see what Black animal advocacy looks like. All of the contributors who advocate for animal rights do so within an understanding that speciesism is meaningfully linked to social injustice and environmental despoliation. But note: none suggests that speciesism is worth our time only because of those links. I also notice that some of the contributors who are not advocates of animal rights still condemn the cruelties implicit in animal agriculture and sometimes go further than that.

THE DECOLONIZATION OF DESIRE

Milton Mills coined the phrase "dietary racism" for the institutionalized racism implicit in USDA dietary guidelines that recommend daily dairy consumption, despite the fact that the majority of African-Americans are lactose intolerant. A scattering of activists and nongovernmental organizations in the global South, particularly in Asia and the Pacific Islands, have begun to agitate against the "dietary colonialism" or "dietary imperialism" that began when Europeans forcibly replaced subsistence crops with cash crops, an approach that continues with trade globalization policies that make it cheaper for poor people to eat at fast-food restaurants owned by multinational corporations than to buy healthy food from local farmers and vendors. *Sistah Vegan* brings us a new tool to use in the struggle against the insidious process that has brought heart disease and diabetes to people of African, Asian, and indigenous American descent around the world.

Let me say that again, because it might be hard to swallow in one gulp: desire for the steaks and shakes and deep-fried mystery meats that clog the arteries of so many African-Americans might best be seen as a form of literally internalized colonialism. And now come the sistah vegans asking other Black people to recognize their appetites as potential artifacts of white colonial rule. Anyone who has wrestled with the emotional reverberations of realizing that an intimate craving is the result of socialization—or, even worse, some kind of abuse—knows how sickening such revelations can be. And yet that nausea must be gone through in order to purge our bodies of the infectious ideologies that lead us to poison ourselves, each other, and the earth.

It may seem strange to think about going vegan as a way to take back your body, especially if you've ever resented vegetarians telling you what you ought and ought not eat. Even though eating meat is something you do to somebody else's body, it feels like a purely private choice that ought not concern others. That's because the "somebody else" in question has been conveniently erased. Also mostly invisible are the historic and ongoing social processes that have helped to shape your desires. The process of decolonization of desire requires us to give up pleasures that are hurtful to us or others but also allows us to reclaim the natural pleasures that our socialization suppressed.

Breeze Harper was maybe on to something when, at the start of the process that has birthed this anthology, she wondered whether there might be some reason that the lone voice speaking up for animals on BlackPlanet was that of a Black lesbian. And maybe it is not a coincidence that such a question would lead eventually to a theory of veganism as potentially a central component to decolonization. Those of us who come out despite societal pressure to be straight maintain our integrity by reaching for our hearts' desires rather than for the partners we have been taught we ought to take. Those of us who go vegan even though we may still desire animal-based foods maintain our integrity by forgoing desires that were implanted in us. In both instances, we preserve our ethical, emotional, and physical wholeness by resisting the colonization of our most intimate wishes.

Back in the 1970s, those of us who dared to work for gay liberation were, like the animal liberationists of today, often dismissed for the seeming silliness of our concerns. At best, we were frittering away our time on a bourgeois issue of interest only to those too privileged to worry about anything else. At worst, we were stealing energy and resources from much more serious problems. Homosexuality itself, of course, was "a white thing."

Collectively, Black lesbian and gay liberationists (and other queer people of color) raised their voices against such misperceptions and for a struggle against heterosexism that would be linked with, rather than estranged from, struggles against racism, sexism, and other injustices. Often writing in small press anthologies like *Home Girls* and *This Bridge Called My Back*, feminists of color helped us all to think through the many ways that sexism, racism, and heterosexism support, compound, and interact with each other. I expect that this volume will be similarly helpful when it comes to speciesism.

The intersections between speciesism and heterosexism go beyond the superficially similar dismissal of veganism and homosexuality as "white things." Most of the stereotypes by which we excuse the exploitation of animals began as justifications for animal husbandry, the success of which depends entirely on the ability to control reproduction. Homophobia serves the same essential function for patriarchy, policing gender roles so that it will be easier for men to exercise reproductive control over women.

Here in the Americas, both homophobia and factory farming are direct legacies of colonization. Often seeing themselves as superior because they ate more meat, invading Europeans brought animal captives with them. Seen by both Catholic conquistadors and Protestant pilgrims as a sign of godless animality, same-sex pleasure was ruthlessly suppressed throughout the process of the subjugation of the Americas. When the Tairona Indians on the Caribbean coast of what is now Colombia rebelled in defense of their sexual customs, the resulting repression nearly erased eighty communities. As Eduardo Galeano has remarked, it is one of the ironies of history that the Caribbean, where indigenous people literally fought for their right to same-sex pleasure, is now among the most homophobic regions of the world. Just as many African-Americans perceive unhealthy food preferences that are legacies of slavery as valued aspects of Black culture, many Jamaicans claim homophobia as an authentic element of Caribbean culture.

Even thinking about these ironies feels queasy. Speaking of them is even more jeopardizing. Confronting them truly is a process of decolonization, with all of the internal turmoil that always attends such upheavals. Nonetheless, like the contributors to this volume, women around the world are asserting their own appetites against those imposed by governments or multinational corporations. Lesbian activists continue to organize in Thailand and Uganda despite violent government repression in the name of traditional culture. From the highlands of the South American Andes to the lowlands of sub-Saharan Africa, women farmers are returning to traditional vegetable varieties, thereby improving the health of their families, the stability of their ecosystems, and the economies of their communities. And so the decolonization of desire brings us around again to liberation as connection.

Our Turn

Breeze Harper did us all a favor by bringing together the voices of a diverse group of Black-identified vegan women. The contributors shared their stories, reflections, and aspirations, even when it must have been difficult to write honestly about such emotionally complicated and ethically challenging subjects. Now it's our turn to extend the conversation.

Many of the contributors to this anthology write of being turned around by books. I know I have been. Maybe you have been, too. This is one of those books that will be personally meaningful to many readers while also helping to shape the thinking of scholars and activists for years to come. But only if we do our part. Small-press books don't distribute themselves. Independent publishers don't have lots of money for publicity. It's up to those of us who believe in this book to get it into bookstores, libraries, and the hands of other readers.

Share this book with your friends and relatives, veg*n and nonveg*n alike. Make sure that your local public library has a copy. Ask your local independent book and grocery stores to carry it. If you can afford to do so, buy a copy for a local organization working on issues of race, health, or poverty. Make sure your local vegetarian society knows about it. Review it on your blog, in your local independent newspaper, or for the newsletter of an organization to which you belong.

Visit the Sistah Vegan Project website (sistahveganproject.com) to find out what's next for the project. If you consider yourself a sistah vegan or ally, join the project listserv and jump into the conversation. Carry the conversation into your community by seizing every opportunity to write or talk about the ideas and information in the book. Talk with your coworkers or neighbors. Write letters to your local newspaper.

But don't stop with words. The contributors to this anthology all made changes in their lives in response to what they learned about how their dietary decisions were affecting their own lives and the lives of others. We all need to be similarly willing to change in response to new information now and into the future.

But don't stop with your own diet. Find out whether your local health-food store takes food stamps and what your local school district is putting into its free or subsidized meals. Join or initiate efforts to bring a farmers market into a low-income community or get a soy milk option added to your local school milk program. Support and defend community gardens that grow fresh food for local families while offering meaningful activities for local youth. At the national level, contest the use of your tax dollars to subsidize those one dollar cheeseburgers at fast-food restaurants, which cost so little only because of the farm aid doled out to industrial animal agriculture. Find out what the Food Empowerment Project and other national organizations are doing to empower low-income people to make healthy food choices.

Maybe you're already busy with activism in other realms. You can still be sure to integrate the connections explored in this book into your work. (And, of course, you'll have more energy for that work and more years to do it if you're vegan!) If you've not been in the habit of doing so, please do begin to include vegetarian and animal advocacy organizations among your potential coalition partners.

FRUITION

As contributor Layli Phillips writes, "Contrary to what others looking in might perceive, all this actually feels really good." So let's end by remembering the joys of connection and the pleasures that come when we remember to listen to our bodies' true desires.

When we decolonize desire, we are better able to enjoy uncomplicated sensual pleasure. Fruit tastes better to tastebuds that haven't been barraged by high-fructose corn syrup. Giving up those mass-produced animal-tested soaps provokes us to explore the rich lathers and complex scents of handmade locally produced soaps. All of these and other vegan delights bring us into better communion with ourselves.

When we seek our own liberation through connection with others, striving for Melissa Santosa's "authentic life of informed interdependence," we have more and better relationships.

We have more true friends and are better friends to others. We can count on the support of the branches of a much more extensive family tree.

All of this is the icing on the (whole grain, naturally sweetened) vegan cupcake. The contributors to this volume remind us of the basic benefits of veganism: more energy, improved health, and an overall feeling of physical and spiritual well-being. It feels great to get those rewards for doing something that, in the words of Nia Yaa, can "save the world and make a better living space for us all."

Tashee Meadows says, "If we are what we eat, we can choose to be fear and terror or bright green sprigs of broccoli. We can choose to be orphans and prisoners or strong leafy collards. We can choose to be pain and death or vibrant mangos." The sistah vegans are going with the mangos. What about you?

NOTES

INTRODUCTION: THE BIRTH OF THE SISTAH VEGAN PROJECT

1. Speciesism: a belief that different species of animals are significantly different from one another in their capacities to feel pleasure and pain and live an autonomous existence, usually involving the idea that one's own species has the right to rule and use others. From Marjorie Spiegel, *The Dreaded Comparison: Human and Animal Slavery* (New York: Mirror Books, 1996).
2. Spiegel, *The Dreaded Comparison*; Charles Patterson, *Eternal Treblinka: Our Treatment of Animals and the Holocaust* (New York: Lantern Books, 2002).
3. Spiegel, *The Dreaded Comparison,* pp. 27–28, 30.
4. Ethical eating is the manifestation of one's belief of moral justice through a dietary practice that causes the least amount of ecological and social suffering. For example, purchasing equal-exchange coffee instead of regular coffee because it directly supports antipoverty measures among Third World coffee growers is a form of ethical eating. Organic and fair-trade food consumption as well as veganism are types of ethical eating or ethical consumption.
5. Alka Chandna, "Are Animal Rights Activists Racist?" Retrieved December 10, 2008, from www.americanhotmama.com/are_animal_rights_activists_raci.htm [emphasis added].
6. Doris Witt, *Black Hunger: Soul Food and America* (Minneapolis: University of Minnesota Press, 2004), pp. 133–134.
7. M. K. Gandhi, *Non-Violent Resistance (Satyagraha)* (Mineola, N.Y.: Dover, 2001).

THINKING AND EATING AT THE SAME TIME: REFLECTIONS OF A SISTAH VEGAN

1. Retrieved from en.wikipedia.org/wiki/Kairos.
2. National Agricultural Statistical Service, USDA, Washington D.C. Retrieved from www.slate.com/id/2112698.
3. Retrieved from www.spcnetwork.com/mii/2000/000508.htm.
4. Ibid.
5. Marilyn Hughes Gaston and Gayle Porter, *Prime Time: The African American Woman's Guide to Midlife Health and Wellness* (New York: One World Press, 2001), p. 174.
6. Erik Marcus, *Vegan: New Ethics of Eating* (Ithaca, N.Y.: McBooks Press, 2001).
7. Ibid.

8. Genesis 1:26 (Living Bible) reads, "Then God said, 'Let us make a man—someone like ourselves, to be the master of all life upon the earth and in the skies and in the seas.'" Many people interpret this passage of scripture as God's mandate for humans to dominate animals.

9. Andrea Smith, *Conquest: Sexual Violence and American Indian Genocide* (Cambridge, Mass.: South End Press, 2005), p. 117.

10. American Cancer Society, *Cancer Facts and Figures for African Americans 2005–2006* (Atlanta: author, 2005), p. 1.

11. Ibid.

12. Retrieved from www.americanheart.org/presenter.jhtml?identifier=3018809.

13. American Cancer Society, *Cancer Facts and Figures for African Americans 2005–2006*, p. 16.

14. Marcus, *Vegan: New Ethics of Eating*, p. 4.

Veganism and Ecowomanism

1. Pamela A. Smith, "Green Lap, Brown Embrace, Blue Body: The Ecospirituality of Alice Walker," *Cross Currents* 48 (1998/1999), 471–487.

2. Chela Sandoval, *Methodology of the Oppressed* (Minneapolis: University of Minnesota Press, 2000).

3. Mark Achbar and Jennifer Abbott, directors, *The Corporation* [documentary film, 2003].

4. Anita Roddick, *Body and Soul: Profits with Principles* (London: Crown, 1991).

5. Norman Walker, *The Natural Way to Vibrant Health* (Prescott, Ariz.: Norwalk Press, 1972); Norman Walker, *Colon Health: The Key to a Vibrant Life* (Prescott, Ariz.: Norwalk Press, 1995).

6. John R. Lee, Jesse Hanley, and Virginia Hopkins, "How We Got into Xenohormone Hell and How to Get Out," in *What Your Doctor May Not Tell You about Perimenopause* (New York: Warner Wellness, 1999), pp. 76–92.

7. Carol J. Adams, *The Sexual Politics of Meat: A Feminist-Vegetarian Critical Theory* (New York: Continuum, 1990).

8. Jeremy Rifkin, ed., *The Green Lifestyle Handbook: 1001 Ways You Can Heal the Earth* (New York: Henry Holt and Company, 1990).

9. Thich Nhat Hanh, *Anger: Wisdom for Cooling the Flames* (New York: Riverhead Books, 2001); Research Department of the Universal House of Justice, ed., *Health and Healing* (New Delhi, India: Baha'i Publishing Trust, 1996).

10. Edmond Bordeaux Szekely, *The Essene Gospel of Peace: Book 1* (Colorado Springs, Colo.: I.B.S. International, 1981).

11. Layli Phillips, ed., *The Womanist Reader* (New York: Routledge, 2006), p. xx.

12. Ibid.

13. Barbara Smith, ed., *Home Girls: A Black Feminist Anthology* (New York: Kitchen Table/Women of Color Press, 1998); Martin Delveaux, "Transcending Ecofeminism: Alice Walker, Spiritual

Ecowomanism, and Environmental Ethics" (2001), retrieved December 10, 2008, from www.eco-fem.org/journal.

14.   Alice Walker, *Living by the Word: Essays* (San Diego, Calif.: Harvest, 1988); Alice Walker, *Anything We Love Can Be Saved* (New York: Random House, 1997).

15.   Alice Walker and Sharon Salzberg, "The Power of Loving-Kindness," *Shambhala Sun,* January 1997 [interview moderated by Melvin McLeod]. Retrieved December 10, 2008, from www.shambhalasun.com/index.php?option=content&task=view&id=2049.

16.   Chikwenye Okonjo Ogunyemi, *Africa Wo/Man Palava: The Nigerian Novel by Women* (Chicago: University of Chicago Press, 1996).

SOCIAL JUSTICE BELIEFS AND ADDICTION TO UNCOMPASSIONATE CONSUMPTION

1.   Quoted in Witt, *Black Hunger*, pp. 133–134.

2.   Ibid.

3.   Ibid.

4.   Vernellia Randall, *Dying While Black: An In-Depth Look at a Crisis in the American Healthcare System* (Dayton, Ohio: Seven Principles Press, 2006); John Robbins, "Racism, Food, and Health" (2006), retrieved December 10, 2008, from www.healthyat100.org//display.asp?catid=3&pageid=7.

5.   Witt, *Black Hunger,* pp. 133–134.

6.   Psyche A. Williams-Forson, *Building Houses Out of Chicken Legs: Black Women, Food, & Power* (Chapel Hill, N.C.: University of North Carolina Press, 2006); Witt, *Black Hunger*.

7.   Carol Simontacchi, *The Crazy Makers: How the Food Industry Is Destroying Our Brains and Harming Our Children* (New York: Penguin-Putnam, 2000).

8.   William Dufty, *Sugar Blues* (New York: Grand Central Publishing, 1976).

9.   Sydney Mintz, *Sweetness and Power: The Place of Sugar in Modern History* (New York: Penguin, 1985); Dufty, *Sugar Blues*.

10.   Simontacchi, *The Crazy Makers*.

11.   Dani Veracity, "The Politics of Sugar: Why Your Government Lies to You about this Disease-Promoting Ingredient" (2005). Retrieved December 10, 2008, from http://www.newstarget.com/009797.html.

12.   Kymberlie Adams Matthews, "The True Cost of Coffee," *Satya,* March 2007, p. 45.

13.   Dufty, *Sugar Blues*.

14.   Mintz, *Sweetness and Power*; Dufty, *Sugar Blues*.

15.   Derrick Jensen, *Endgame, Volume I: The Problem of Civilization* (New York: Seven Stories Press, 2006), p. 153.

16.   Dufty, *Sugar Blues*.

17. Nancy Appleton, *Lick the Sugar Habit: How to Break Your Sugar Addiction Naturally* (New York: Avery, 1996); Connie Bennett and Stephen Sinatra, *Sugar Shock! How Sweets and Simple Carbs Can Derail Your Life—and How you Can Get Back on Track* (New York: Berkley Publishing Group, 2007).

18. "830 Million are Hungry," *The Ecologist,* March 2001.

19. Michael F. Jacobson, *Six Arguments for a Greener Diet: How a More Plant-Based Diet Could Save Your Health and the Environment* (Washington, D.C.: Center for Science in the Public Interest, 2006).

20. Ibid., p. 93.

21. pattrice jones, *Aftershock: Confronting Trauma in a Violent World: A Guide for Activists and Their Allies* (New York: Lantern Books, 2007), pp. 206–207.

22. Jacobson, *Six Arguments for a Greener Diet.*

23. Ibid.

24. Neal Barnard, *Food for Life: How the New Four Food Groups Can Save Your Life* (New York: Three Rivers Press, 1994).

25. Randall, *Dying While Black*; Robbins, "Racism, Food, and Health."

26. Jacobson, *Six Arguments for a Greener Diet.*

27. Adrienne T. Washington, "Timidity No Answer to Racism in Katrina Debacle," *Washington Times*, September 6, 2005, p. B2.

28. bell hooks and Cornel West, *Breaking Bread: Insurgent Black Intellectual Life* (Boston: South End Press, 1991), p. 98.

29. John Robbins, *Diet for a New America* (Novato, Calif.: H. J. Kramer Press, 1987).

30. Ibid., p. 363.

31. Ibid.

32. Simontacchi, *The Crazy Makers*, p. 20.

33. Robbins, "Racism, Food, and Health."

34. Randall, *Dying While Black.*

35. Mark Engler, "The Sugarglades," *Satya,* March 2007, 26–29.

36. Jon Hunt, "Just for the Taste of It," *Satya,* March 2007, 34–36.

37. Celine Anaya Gautier, "Slaves in Paradise," *Satya,* March 2007, 38–39.

38. Jensen, *Endgame Volume I.*

39. Ibid.

40. Ibid., p. 185.

41. Queen Afua, *Sacred Woman* (New York: Ballantine, 2000).

42. Patterson, *Eternal Treblinka.*

43. Jones, *Aftershock: Confronting Trauma in a Violent World.*

44.   Barnard, *Food for Life*; John Robbins, *The Food Revolution: How Your Diet Can Help Save Your Life and the World* (Berkeley, Calif.: Conari Press, 2001); Kerrie Saunders, *The Vegan Diet as Chronic Disease Prevention: Evidence Supporting the New Four Food Groups* (New York: Lantern Books, 2005).

45.   Ibid.

46.   Liz Appel, "White Supremacy in the Movement against the Prison-Industrial Complex" *Social Justice* 30:2 (2003), 81–88; Arnold Farr, "6 Whiteness Visible," in *What White Looks Like: African-American Philosophers on the Whiteness Question,* George Yancy, ed. (New York: Routledge, 2004), pp. 143–158; Chithra Karunakaran, professor of sociology at CUNY and former co-chair of the National Women's Studies Anti-White Supremacy Task Force, personal interview, November 19, 2006; Narina Nagra, "Whiteness in Seattle: Anti-Globalization Activists Examine Racism within the Movement," *Alternatives Journal,* Winter 2003, 27–28; Saskia Poldervaart, "Utopian Aspects of Social Movements in Postmodern Times: Some Examples of DIY Politics in the Netherlands," *Utopian Studies* 12:2 (2001), 143–164; and Rachel Slocum, "Anti-Racist Practice and the Work of Community Food Organizations," *Antipode* 38:2 (2006), 327–349.

47.   The African Hebrew Israelites of Jerusalem. Retrieved December 10, 2008, from www.kingdomofyah.com/index.html.

48.   Queen Afua Wellness Institute. Retrieved December 10, 2008, from http://www.queenafuaonline.com/hba/pages/home.htm.

49.   Anne Wilson Schaef, *When Society Becomes an Addict* (New York: HarperCollins, 1987), pp. 17–18.

50.   Allison Diamant, Gwendolyn Flynn, Joyce Jones Guinyard, LaVonna Blair Lewis, Lori Miller Nascimento, David C. Sloane, and Antronette K. Yancey, *American Journal of Public Health* 95:4 (2005), 668–674; Robbins, "Racism, Food, and Health."

51.   Vani R. Henderson and Bridget Kelly, "Food Advertising in the Age of Obesity: Content Analysis of Food Advertising on General Market and African American Television," *Journal of Nutrition Education and Behavior* 37 (2005), 191–196.

ON BEING BLACK AND VEGAN

1.   The Vegan Research Panel, "Vegan Statistics." Retrieved December 10, 2008, from www.imaner.net/panel/statistics.htm.

2.   Katherine Turman, "Heeding Hip Hop's Higher Calling." Retrieved December 10, 2008, from www.motherjones.com/arts/qa/2003/09/ma_514_01.html.

3.   To be fair, there are a few rare examples of veganism in the hip hop movement, namely, the songs "Be Healthy" by Dead Prez and "Animal Kingdom" by Prince.

4. "Veganism." Retrieved December 10, 2008, from en.wikipedia.org/wiki/Veganism.

5. The Vegan Society, "Articles of Association." Retrieved December 10, 2008, from www.vegansociety.com/about_us/memorandum.php.

6. Ibid.

7. "Speciesism." Retrieved December 10, 2008, from en.wikipedia.org/wiki/Speciesism.

8. Beyoncé sings these lyrics in her "Ring the Alarm" hit song.

9. "Crazy in Love," lyrics by Beyoncé.

10. Retrieved from www.sfgate.com/cgi-bin/blogs/sfgate/detail?blogid=7&entry_id=2539.

11. Retrieved from www.msnbc.msn.com/id/13370421.

12. Retrieved from en.wikipedia.org/wiki/Saartjie_Baartman.

13. Patricia Hill-Collins, *Black Feminist Thought: Knowledge, Consciousness, and the Politics of Empowerment* (New York: Routledge, 1991), pp. 11, 139.

14. Spiegel, *The Dreaded Comparison*.

15. Retrieved from books.guardian.co.uk/comment/story/0,,1972800,00.html.

16. Retrieved from www.about-tracy-chapman.net/articles_chapmangiggles.htm.

Nutrition Liberation

1. Antonella Dewell, et al., "A Very-Low-Fat Vegan Diet Increases Intake of Protective Dietary Factors and Decreases Intake of Pathogenic Dietary Factors," *Journal of the American Dietetic Association* 108:2 (2008), 347–56; Gwen Foster, et al., "Cardiovascular Disease Risk Factors Are Lower in African-American Vegans Compared to Lacto-Ovo-Vegetarians," *Journal of the American College of Nutrition* 17:5 (1998), 425–34; Reed Mangels, "A Vegetarian Diet Helps to Protect Older African Americans from Hypertension," *Vegetarian Journal* 13:2 (1994), 347–356; M. F. McCarty, "Mortality from Western Cancers Rose Dramatically among African-Americans During the 20th Century: Are Dietary Animal Products to Blame?" *Medical Hypotheses* 57:2 (2001), 169–74.

2. Susus are financial groups that are based largely in Ghana and Nigeria. In Africa, the money collected is held in a susu account and is maintained by a susu collector. In America, the group operating the susu rotates the responsibility of holding the money amongst its members. Deposits are made over a period of time, after which one designated member of the group receives all of the monies collected. The cycle begins again, rotating responsibility and recipient until the susu agreement is dissolved. B. O. Iganiga and A. Asemota, "The Nigerian Unorganized Rural Financial Institutions and Operations: A Framework for Improved Rural Credit Schemes in a Fragile Environment," *Journal of Social Science* 17:1 (2008), 63–71.

3. Retrieved from en.wikipedia.org/wiki/Montgomery_Bus_Boycott#Boycott.

MA'AT DIET

1.   Queen Afua, *Sacred Woman*.
2.   Retrieved from www.setiadd.org/articles_bin/art_sounds.html.
3.   Naomi Doumbia and Adama Doumbia, *The Way of the Elders: West African Spirituality and Tradition* (Saint Paul, Minn.: Llewellyn Publications, 2004).
4.   Retrieved from www.enn.com/today.html?id=8239.
5.   Diane Peters, "Heal Your Home," *Black Woman and Child* (2006), pp. 12–13.
6.   Retrieved from www.drmcdougall.com/newsletter/march_april97.html.
7.   Retrieved from birthpsychology.com/primalhealth/primal10.html.
8.   Sobonfu E. Somé, *Welcoming Spirit Home: Ancient African Teachings to Celebrate Children and Community* (Novato, Calif.: New World Library, 1999).
9.   July Goldsmith, "Traditional Childbirth," *Mothering* (Spring 1989).
10. Retrieved from birthpsychology.com/primalhealth/primal10.html.
11. Brian Lanker, *I Dream a World: Portraits of Black Women Who Changed America* (New York: Stewart, Tabori and Chang, 1999).

VEGANISM AND MISCONCEPTIONS OF THINNESS AS "NORMAL" AND "HEALTHY"

1.   Margaret Bass, "On Being a Fat Black Girl in a Fat-Hating Culture," in *Recovering the Black Female Body: Self-Representations by African American Women*, Michael Bennett and Vanessa D. Dickerson, eds. (Rutgers, N.J.: Rutgers University Press, 2000), pp. 219–230.
2.   Ibid.

CONTRIBUTORS

Tara Sophia Bahna-James is a singer and mystic writer and a co-founder of Majority of One (www.majorityofone.org), which seeks to inspire humane and ethical practices in businesses and individuals through programs in the arts, education, and cross-community exchange. As a bookwriter and lyricist, Tara has co-authored seven musicals and has adapted the text for Robert Rival's *Maya the Bee*, for orchestra and narrator. Her academic writing has appeared in the *Journal of Negro Education* and will be featured in Lisa Kemmerer's upcoming anthology on women in animal advocacy.

Melissa Danielle is a New York–based community wellness advocate, sustainable food communicator, blogger, and photographer. Through her lifestyle company, she works with individuals and community groups to promote a seasonal, local, and whole foods approach to healthy living. For more information, visit www.MelissaDanielle.com.

Ain Drew was bred in Nashville and raised in Detroit and is now yet another Atlanta transplant. She maintains that her talent for writing was originally sparked by hip-hop and nourished by reading authors like Langston Hughes, Kwame Touré, Pearl Cleage, and James Baldwin. She's a poet by night who by day works diligently as a freelance writer and account coordinator for a boutique management and publicity firm. You can purchase her work on Lulu.com, search term: Ain Drew.

Delicia Dunham is an actress and vegan and lives in Chicago, Illinois. She has a B.A. in drama and English, a certificate in film and video studies from Duke University, and a J.D. from Northwestern University School of Law. Delicia has been vegan since January 1, 2005, and is a member of numerous animal-rights organizations.

Ma'at Sincere Earth, born under the zodiac sign of Libra, seeks balance in everything, hence her name symbolizing supreme balance and truth. Head-wrapped before and after badu, she embraces the truth of Clarence X and sees herself as earth. A sky-diving, world-traveling, Baltimore native who grew up believing she would be the next Oprah, Ma'at is currently employed as the next Harriet Tubman, freeing inner city women's souls with

209

education about breast health and cancer. She started the first Black literary magazine at her alma mater, Towson University. Vegan for seven years, vegetarian for eight years, she wants to be a raw foodist when she's much older and more stable. "Like Jay-Z say, I'm like Che Guevara with the bling on, I'm complex."

Tasha Edwards is a personal trainer and teaches yoga, dance, and other fitness classes. She lives in Madison, Alabama, with her husband Tremayne and their two children, Jaizon and Xanyah.

Breeze Harper is currently a Ph.D. student at University of California, Davis, in the department of geography. Her passion is food and health geography as it pertains to females of the African diaspora living in the United States. To name a few, she has been inspired by bell hooks, Frantz Fanon, INCITE! Women of Color Against Violence, James Baldwin, Thich Nhat Hanh, Dick Gregory, Derrick Bell, Arundhati Roy, the Harper family, her husband Oliver Zahn, and the collective consciousness of Black womanists, Black feminists, and the plethora of global South scholars and activists that have come before her. She can be reached at breezeharper@gmail.com and her ongoing research can be found at www.breezeharper.com.

Ajowa Nzinga Ifateyo enjoys sharing her knowledge of health and nutrition gleaned from twenty-five years as a vegetarian, twelve of them as a vegan. Her hobbies include studying all types of spirituality and learning about the lives of different people, especially women, the environment, and the so-called paranormal. She is fascinated by crystals, ancient Egypt, oracles such as the I Ching, and the effects of internalized oppression. She recently earned a dual masters in business administration and community economic development from Southern New Hampshire University and wants to spend the rest of her life building a more just and economic world. Ajowa believes every person has a unique story to tell others so that we can all learn from each other's lives. She is currently writing her memoir, *Outside Child,* about growing up as the child of the "other woman." She lives in Washington, D.C., and can be reached at ajowa.ifateyo@gmail.com.

Janine Jackson, a native of Florida, has created in various aspects for ten years, using acrylic and oil paints, illustration software applications, image-editing programs, and standard pen and pencil to create works that focus on the strength and beauty found in every aspect of life. Her intentions are that viewers will experience abundance, introspection, and vitality while experiencing her work. In addition to working with several independent businesses, her creations served as inspiration for community-based radio station WMNF's identity items. A detail of her piece "Yum" graces the cover of this anthology. For further information, please contact: Janine Jackson, at janinejackson@peacemail.com.

pattrice jones, until recently, operated the Eastern Shore Sanctuary and taught at the University of Maryland Eastern Shore. Her book *Aftershock: Confronting Trauma in a Violent World* is available from Lantern Books. She thanks Mignon Anderson and Alka Chandna for their helpful advice on the preparation of an adequate afterword for this remarkable anthology. Thanks are also due to the participants in the 2007 Inadmissible Comparisons conference sponsored by United Poultry Concerns, at which some ideas that inform this essay evolved in the course of group discussions.

Robin Lee, on a self-imposed exile from biomedical inquiry, is a sister of the African diaspora from the South Bronx, New York (born and raised), and a vegetarian neat freak with a passion for animation and narrative writing. She would label herself a visual griot who chases questions with possible answers.

Michelle R. Loyd-Paige earned her Ph.D. in sociology from Purdue University in 1989. She is professor of sociology and the interim dean for multicultural affairs at Calvin College in Grand Rapids, Michigan. Her most recent course offerings include Sociology of the African Diaspora, Diversity and Inequality in the United States, and A Christian Response to Racism. In addition to teaching, Dr. Loyd-Paige is an Afro-Christian scholar who studies and writes about the social and spiritual lives of African-American clergywomen; the transformational role of Afro-Christian worship; and the religious roadblocks that hinder the elimination of domestic violence. She is the founder of Preach Sistah! Inc., an organization that advocates for the inclusion of women in ministry roles and calls for the ending of domestic violence directed toward women. Dr. Loyd-Paige began eating like a vegan in 2005. She can be contacted by email at lopa@Calvin.edu or by U.S. Post at Preach Sistah! P.O. Box 4909, Muskegon Heights, Michigan, 49444. You can also contact her through her website: www.PreachSista.com.

Adama A. Maweja is minister on behalf of the Cosmic Community for Conscious Cosmic Citizenship, producer and host of The Meeting of the Inner Circle on 89.3 FM radio,

WRFG Atlanta. She works on inspirational lifestyle change as a holistic wellness consultant. She is a creative expressionist of life, light, wisdom, and truth in the media of movement, rhythm, verse, and sound. She can be contacted through her website: www. AdamaSpeaks.com.

Tashee Meadows is simply an artist/activist currently residing in Alabama.

Thea Moore currently works as a pharmacist specializing in mental health. She has interest in alternative healing and, more specifically, herbal remedies. She has been vegan since early 2001. It has been a steady process for her. She originally stopped eating pork and beef in September of 1997 and then stopped eating poultry about six months later and became a complete ovo-lacto vegetarian in 1998. When she started reading more and also recognized that dairy was the cause of some very painful menstruation, she decided to become vegan. At this point, she told her father that she was "giving up dairy, too." He replied, "What are you going to give up next? Air? Are you going to stop breathing?"

Layli Phillips is associate professor of women's studies and associate faculty of African-American studies at Georgia State University, where she teaches courses on womanism, Black feminist thought, women and hip hop, and African-American LGBTQQI activism. She is the editor of *The Womanist Reader* (Routledge, 2006), an anthology documenting the first quarter century of womanist thought "on its own." Her emerging research interests include applied womanism and spiritual activism, as well as natural healing modalities and transpersonal psychology. She has been a vegetarian off and on since high school and has been a vegan since 2004.

Joi Maria Probus has been an ethical vegan since 2002 and resides in Houston, Texas, where she is the director of volunteer services at the Museum of Fine Arts, Houston. In addition to animal welfare, she is actively involved in charity work in support of autism awareness, the arts, and human rights. She currently serves on the executive board of the Friends of Avondale House, a nonprofit agency that provides a school, a day habilitation program, and residential services for children and young adults with autism.

Iya Raet is a mother, birth doula, and the author of the book *Holistic Parenting from the Pan-Afrikan Perspective*. For more information go to www.afrikanparenting.com.

Angelique Shofar is a holistic health practitioner and artiste with a designed role as holistic relationship, love, and sexuality expert and sensual lifestyle coach. She founded the Spirit of Wellness in celebration of the birth of her son and the triumph of her self-healing efforts. With yoga and dance at the heart of her life and spiritual practice, she adds a touch of sensual movement to her style of *Soulfull Yoga*. Her repertoire of healing modalities includes her background and training as a Kripalu yoga teacher, certified massage therapist, energy and movement therapist, and reflexologist. She fuses her passion for astrology and her intuitive healing gifts with cultural therapeutic practices derived from the African, Asian, and Native American traditions. She is a freelance writer, talk show host (formerly of Pacifica Radio), and new media producer. She has been featured in the *New York Times*, ABCNews.com, the *Washington Post*, the *Baltimore Sun*, Voice of America, XM Satellite Radio, *Heart & Soul Magazine*, and other online and international publications and media outlets. She is publisher of *The Cultural Erotic Link!* Visit her blog at sexualgriot.blogspot.com.

Melissa Santosa is a vegan of ten years who shares her life with Sahr, a vegetarian of fourteen years, vegan five of those years. They live in Dover, Delaware, where she and Sahr graduated from Delaware State University. Melissa works as a mediation coordinator at the Center for Community Justice, spends her free time reading to kids at a shelter in her neighborhood, being a big sister to Tre, kickboxing, and going through training to volunteer at a rape crisis hotline. When she isn't wandering through the park with a book or writing letters, she's fattening up her friends and family with vegan food. Her biggest goal is to translate isolated vegan and globally conscious lifestyle into active community building. Any suggestions?

Mary Spears has been a vegan for fifteen years. She has a background in visual arts but started writing poetry as a teenager. She is interested in nutrition, veganism, and animal rights. Mary lives in Washington, D.C., with her daughter and her cat.

Venus Taylor, Ed.M., is a certified family and relationship coach and founder of Paramount Family Coaching (www.paramountfamilycoaching.com). She is a raw-food vegan but still cooks vegan meals for her husband and two homeschooled children, ages twelve and fifteen. They reside in Boston, Massachusetts.

Tishana Joy Trainor is a thirty-four-year-old vegan mother of two teenagers. Currently, she is studying electronic engineering at DeVry University in Atlanta, Georgia. Tishana strives to improve public transportation and recycling techniques.

Psyche Williams-Forson is assistant professor in the department of American studies and an affiliate of the women's studies and African-American studies departments at the University of Maryland, College Park. She is the author of *Building Houses Out of Chicken Legs: Black Women, Food, & Power.*

Olu Butterfly Woods is creative director of BlackOut Studios where she coproduces many events, including Organic Soul Tuesdays, a weekly independent art venue, and is cofounding director of Poetry for the People Baltimore, a community organization of renegade brilliant poet-activists. This award-winning author of *The Revenge of Dandelions* tours the world with the soul jazz world band Fertile Ground, Sankofa Dance Theater, as well as independently. Visit: www.olubutterfly.com.

Nia Yaa-Nebthet is a certified Ra Sekhi Kemetic Reiki Master and for the past eight years has taught throughout the United States. She is a heal-thyself ambassador of wellness, natural healer, priestess, community activist, holistic health consultant, spiritual warrior, sacred woman, educator, mother, tree hugger, nature lover, vegan, and promoter of health, wellness, and natural living. She is currently offering reactivating sessions, services, and workshops. For more info visit www.rasekhi.webs.com.